Michael Jackson and the Quandary of a Black Identity

SUNY series in African American Studies

John R. Howard and Robert C. Smith, editors

Michael Jackson and the Quandary of a Black Identity

SHERROW O. PINDER

Cover image of Michael Jackson from WikiMedia Commons.

Published by State University of New York Press, Albany

© 2021 State University of New York

All rights reserved

Printed in the United States of America

No part of this book may be used or reproduced in any manner whatsoever without written permission. No part of this book may be stored in a retrieval system or transmitted in any form or by any means including electronic, electrostatic, magnetic tape, mechanical, photocopying, recording, or otherwise without the prior permission in writing of the publisher.

For information, contact State University of New York Press, Albany, NY
www.sunypress.edu

Library of Congress Cataloging-in-Publication Data

Name: Pinder, Sherrow O., author.
Title: Michael Jackson and the quandry of a black identity, Sherrow O. Pinder.
Description: Albany : State University of New York Press, [2021] | Series: SUNY series in African American studies | Includes bibliographical references and index.
Identifiers: ISBN 9781438484792 (hardcover : alk. paper) | ISBN 9781438484815 (ebook) | ISBN 9781438484808 (pbk. : alk. paper)
Further information is available at the Library of Congress.

10 9 8 7 6 5 4 3 2 1

In Memory of Remy Landau
1943–2020

Contents

Introduction: The Epigrammatic Layout of the Argument		1
Chapter 1	Conceptual Framework	13
Chapter 2	Blackness and a Black Identity	37
Chapter 3	Michael Jackson and Racial Identification	63
Chapter 4	Michael Jackson's Nonconformity and Its Consequences	91
Epilogue: Reflections		115
Notes		131
References		191
Index		211

Introduction

The Epigrammatic Layout of the Argument

> The Negro is a sort of seventh son, born with a veil and gifted with second-sight in this American world—a world which yields him no true self-consciousness, but only lets him sees himself through the revelation of the other world. It is a peculiar sensation, this double-consciousness, this sense of always looking at one's self through the eyes of others, of measuring one's soul by the tape of a world that looks on in amused contempt and pity.
>
> —W. E. B. Du Bois, *The Souls of Black Folk*

> Ontology—once it is finally admitted as leaving existence by the wayside—does not permit us to understand the being of the black man. For not only must the black man be black; he must be black in relation to the white man. Some critics will take it on themselves to remind us that this proposition has a converse. I say that this is false. The black man has no ontological resistance in the eyes of the white man. Overnight the Negro has been given two frames of reference within which he has had to place himself.
>
> —Frantz Fanon, *Black Skin, White Masks*

How the black body is habituated by race as an identity category is clearly depicted in Jean-Michel Basquiat's 1981 painting, *Irony of Negro Policeman*, in which the artist draws our attention to blackness social determinism.[1] In other words, *Irony* points to the fact that a black person is viewed as an animal and a fungible commodity. In the words of Saidiya Hartman, the [black] body is thus fixed "in terror and dominance."[2] This indicates how blackness presence is "held within a general absence."[3] That is to say, a black identity is always "overdetermined from the outside" and is singularly performed through the body. Being black outside positions blackness as the unassimilable otherness of whiteness and makes it impossible for the black person to transcend their racial identity. As Toni Morrison aptly puts it: "once blackness is accepted as socially, politically, and [physically] defined,"[4] it has a tremendous impact on both blacks and whites, which neither of them can rid themselves of or undo. Unlike the Hobbesian project of "the war of all against all," it is understandable that it is whites against blacks. In this sense, whites position themselves as different from blacks and seek to maintain their white-skin privileges at all costs; blacks, in turn, make do with whiteness preeminence by fashioning another way of being (a being + something else) in a world where whiteness is the norm. For blacks, then, how to live this relationship to whiteness is hard work. The French postcolonial scholar Frantz Fanon writes: "As long as the black man is among his own, he will have no occasion, except in minor internal conflicts, to experience his being through others. There is of course the moment of 'being-for-other' of which Hegel speaks, but every ontology is made unattainable in an [oppressive] and civilized society."[5] So, for Fanon, a black cannot indeed be an "other" for another black; a black can only be an "other" for a white. As such, they represent a threat to the white social body.

Accordingly, it is difficult for a black person to develop a solid sense of self. The self, which eventually *becomes*, in the Beauvoirian sense, finds in whiteness their model of personhood and transforms the consciousness of blacks such as to conform to whiteness as the norm. What can be said is that the "self," which *becomes*, is an inauthentic self in the Sartrean sense. What this means is that it remains untrue to itself. In other words, it is a false self, alienating blacks from a self of their own constitution and propelling them, as Fanon observes, "to run away from [their] own individuality";[6] that is, to be self-conscious of their own presence. This self-consciousness then manifests itself in the form of psychic instability. And while a black identity is marked on the body, racial identification is a deeply ambivalent and fragmented process and confines blacks to a "third space,"[7] a liminal space of ambivalence. It is in this undefined space that I envision Michael Jackson as a racialized subject being discursively confined.

Michel Foucault comments on identification in *The Archeology of Knowledge*: "Do not ask me who I am and do not ask me to remain the same,"[8] exemplifies Michael Jackson's racial stance. The singer resists facile racial identification and refuses to identify himself to any preestablished racial identities, whether black or white, but gravitates toward a form of racial ambiguity that would precisely prevent him to "remain the same."[9] To put it differently, Michael Jackson's racial identity, *not black* (other) and *not white* (the self's other), a way of being "out from," what can be described as the either/or racial binary, to which I will return, is not locked in the symbiotic relationship of subordination (blackness) and domination (whiteness), but positions him as an "other 'other.'" The King of Pop continues thus to be seen through what Fanon calls the "corporeal malediction" of his blackness.[10] To say it differently, even though race is culturally constituted, it does not, or cannot, disavow the materiality of the racialized body—a body that is read and interpreted in racial terms as a *lack*, null, and void of racial transcendence; a body that is constituted, re-constituted, and de-constituted through the fear of the "other"; and a body that seemingly appears to be outside of the either/or racial category, drawing attention to the limits of the power of blacks for self-making. Michael Jackson confirms Fanon's assessment of the black person's situation in the white world: wherever he goes, he remains a black person[11] whose identity is marked on the body, or, as Fanon puts it, is "overdetermined from the outside," which is in fact always under some form of surveillance and repudiation. And this applies whether one is a nameless black person or the King of Pop.

In *Michael Jackson and the Quandary of a Black Identity*, I focus on the queerness of the pop singer's racial identification by drawing from W. E. B. Du Bois's "double consciousness" and Frantz Fanon's concept of the doubling of identity, both functioning as an otherness of the "other," *not black* (other) and *not white* (the self's "other") and representing a form of racial liminality. This alignment of a constructed and constructing self, or the "twoness" as Du Bois calls it,[12] leads to the question: What does it mean to be black in America? In this book, this question is reinterpreted and reformulated through the theoretical lens of Frantz Fanon's *Black Skin, White Masks* so as to acknowledge the fact that like all blacks in America, Michael Jackson had difficulties in developing his sense of "self" within a culture that upholds whiteness as the norm and blackness as the "other." The facticity of blackness as null and void of racial transcendence has created an identity "crisis" for Michael Jackson, which is visible in his attempts to resist classical racial models of identification and free himself from the either/or racial category. Michael Jackson, as Michael Awkward puts it, became "whiter"—"less ebony, more ivory";[13] that is, Michael

Jackson's skin/surface seemingly appears to be "white," "but that don't help" Michael Jackson's case, "cause, [Michael Jackson] can't hide what is in his face," in the words of blues singer Louis Armstrong from his song "Black is Blue." And even though Michael Jackson, in his song "Black or White," can say: "See it is not about races/Just Places/Faces/Where your blood comes from," in the Lavinasian sense, "the face speaks"[14] and gives meaning to the appearance of race.[15]

Michael Jackson's resistance to racial identification provides a negative reading of the King of Pop and, in a less charitable vein, fuels epithets such as "weird" or "freak," each fastened into a relationship with each other notwithstanding the multifaceted psychological, epistemological, and ideological layers that Michael Jackson's self-construction of another possible "self" materialize. Such name-calling (weird/freak) points to the way in which this form of naming (of talk), which, as a form of "nanoracism," to borrow from Achille Mbembe,[16] acts on a person and dissolves him into "abnormality." Furthermore, one does not have to be a psychoanalyst to recognize that Michael Jackson's exposure to this kind of name-calling (weird/freak), makes him indeed susceptible to such name-calling. That is to say, once one is named, the naming is used to denigrate one and is reimposed on one because one takes on the name. In other words, naming Michael Jackson as weird/freak, as a form of "citational practice," produces the effect that it names[17] and Michael Jackson becomes that name. In fact, there is a performative effect of having been called a name such as weird/freak—a name you yourself did not know and have never chosen. Michael Jackson inhabits a weirdness to which all blacks are subjected because a black identity destabilizes the epistemic, political, and social regimes of "the normal" that is defined by whiteness. *Am I that name*,[18] interestingly, continues to be the existential question to which all blacks are confronted.

I am, here, interested in the disciplinary power that whiteness exercises on Michael Jackson as a black subject, and the ways in which such a subject is produced, reproduced, and counterproduced as fixed in his racialized essence and often attacked in his identification. And even though in its protean state, "*Black Is . . . Black Ain't*,"[19] which communicates a sense of richness and abundance among blacks, race as marked on the body is produced through racial discipline and determines a black person's identity. In the end, Michael Jackson's attempt at self-fashioning "a *not black, not white* identity" trumps the either/or race category and positions him outside of the distinguishing norms of race assignment.

This is the very reason why Michael Jackson provokes a threat to the social body and must be disciplined.

The Extent and Organization of the Book

Chapter 1, the conceptual framework, provides a counterhegemonic basis for thinking of blacks' identity formation and its racial implications. It provides the theoretical basis for an in-depth study of the King of Pop Michael Jackson and the quandary of a black identity. It draws on the works of political scientists, social historians, feminist theorists, sociologists, philosophers, and critical race theorists that have informed the discursive and nondiscursive ontological, epistemological, and positioning of blacks in the United States. This chapter conceptualizes what constitutes a black identity and how it is inscribed on the body. I point out that the identity of blacks is "overdetermined from the outside" because the maleficence attached to their race is marked on the body in a way that essentializes blacks.[20] In other words, a black person is, to use Fanon's language, the "slave not of the 'idea' that other have of [them] but of [their] own appearance,[21] acting prophylactically contra racial transcendence.

The construction of a black identity in the United States leads to the idea that blacks are all alike. That is to say, in Claudia Rankine's words, "all black people look the same."[22] This sameness elides racial difference and other differences that stem, for example, from class, gender, transgender, disability, sexuality, age, and speech and language impairment. In other words, race as a social phenomenon is a signifier that is fastened to the signified of the "other." Furthermore, in American society, race has become the supreme signifier of otherness in the face of whiteness. This chapter considers W. E. B. Du Bois's conceptualization of "double consciousness"[23] as an inevitable condition of blacks looking at themselves through the white gaze; it also draws on Fanon's articulation of the "implicit knowledge"[24] that blacks acquire after being thrown into a racist society. It further analyzes the complex ways in which blacks' identification processes depend on how race is fixed on the body or, as Fanon aptly sums it up, is "epidermalized," on the skin/surface. In line with this, I want to show how the reconfiguration of race goes beyond the somatic racialized body and provide a framework to conceptualize race performativity. What is in fact at stake in the United States is not what race is but what race does. Judith Butler reminds us that "performativity is the reiterative and citational practice by which discourse produces the effects that it names."[25] To this should be added that race, in its basic multitudinous act, assumes different meanings in diverse investigations. However, what race is made to be in praxis does not overrule how race is positioned within whiteness and its implications for the lived experience of blacks in America.

What gets highlighted, then, is how this knowledge about blackness is discursively constructed within a racist society out of "thousands of anecdotes and stories"[26] about blacks and who they are. In fact, there is a focus on blackness as fixed, a simple antithetical usefulness, which, within a social, ontological, and epistemological imperative, structures and upholds the presumptive hegemony of white-skin privilege. For blacks, then, one of the most painful repercussions "to be" a being-in-the-world—a world dedicated to white-skin privilege—is an ambivalent self-identification, a denial of the "self." With remarkable insistence, Fanon describes this as a negating experience. Because "the body is surrounded by uncertainty,"[27] it reacts to, and mimics, the pejorative white gaze through which blacks encounter the "other" and can only experience being black in relation to whiteness.[28] The image of the "other" is never concealed and hidden from sight and invites an essential reading, which we can affiliate to the Sartrean *look*; that is, a *look* that reduces blacks to the object of the *look*. To put it differently, when the *look* is directed from whites to blacks, it creates an ontological condition for blacks that frames their way of being in society, a discussion to which I will return. For now, I just want to say that blacks have no ontological resistance in the face of whiteness because blacks, in the Fanonian language, are "overdetermined from the outside." I will call this the fixing of race on the body, the outsideness of blackness, which is a site for savage exteriority recognizable in whites' gaze, gestures, and attitudes toward the "other." Blackness when juxtaposed with whiteness empties blacks of all values that are continuously devalued.

"Blackness and black identity" is the focus of chapter 2. In this chapter, I will show that the attempt to construct the category "black," which imposes itself upon blacks and continues to position them within the distinguishing norms of recognition that is marked on the body, has fundamental implications for racial identification. And if we take seriously Fanon's definition of identification as a pathological condition since one experiences one's "being through others,"[29] in this relational mode, when blackness is measured against whiteness, it is automatically reduced to otherness. Fanon, as a psychiatrist, diagnoses this inescapable condition as a form of neurosis, which for him, even though the lived experience of blacks and whites greatly contrasts, is attributed to both blacks and whites. In his diagnosis, Fanon became increasingly convinced that "the black man enslaved by his inferiority, the white man enslaved by his superiority alike behave in accordance with a neurotic orientation."[30] And since blacks' neuroticism is the ultimate product of whiteness's ignition of power and privilege so painstakingly normalized, blacks cannot experience their own experiences outside of whiteness.[31]

Sartre's contention is that "it is the anti-Semite who made the Jew."[32] In the face of whiteness, Sartre's approach is useful when conceptualizing blackness as always constructed as "other." And, it is therefore very difficult for a black person to develop a solid sense of self. This constructed and constructing black "self" is constantly interrogated, policed, and subverted by the white gaze. Let us consider for a moment Fanon's crucial question: Is it so abhorrent to be black?[33] Posed differently by Du Bois the question becomes: "How does it feel to be a problem?"[34] In fact, as a racialized subject, a black person is confined to a liminal and ambivalent space. It is from this ambivalence that self-identification can sometimes develop into pathological conditions in which the subjectivity of a black person becomes subjugated by a gaze that is directed through the episteme of whiteness. This experience of subjugation leads to an identity "crisis" and a misidentification where the otherness of the "other," which is also othered, is implicated. The subject becomes an unsettled agent. This othering of the "other" is first experienced as corporeal since the body constitutes the material foundation of one's social and subjective formation. The lived experience of Michael Jackson is the perfect illustration of this condition where his identity starts and ends disjointed. What we are dealing with in this disjointedness is that one is forever in conflict with one's own identification in the face of whiteness. And this becomes in itself a source of the disciplinary devise that puts pressure on Michael Jackson to engage in a profound struggle as a liberatory action and interaction to imagine and uncover another possible "self" that must not be intimately connected and impacted by race.

Race is a phantasmagoric creation, a social concept, that organizes a black person's identification process, subjecting them to an identification that is marked on the body, which indeed has racial implications. *Racecraft: The Soul of Inequality in American Life* by Barbara Fields and Karen Fields helps elucidate the distinctive point that in the United States, race cannot be disavowed notwithstanding the triumphalist approbation that there is "the declining significance of race"[35] and an "end to racism."[36] We do not need to look very far to know that race matters are, for example, manifested in the bodiliness of racism; that is, a body positioned within racism, which lends itself to an embodied understanding of race and racism. But behold, the point here is that, in the United States, the phantasm of race, which itself engenders racist attitudes, behavior, and thinking and postulates natural differences "based on real or imagined physical or other differences,"[37] continues to position blackness as a lack, a liability. It is no wonder that blacks, as a way to counteract the devaluation of "blackness,"[38] developed and continue to develop their own form of empowerment in their music, dance, and an ensemble of performances, which are bound up with what Fred Moten would call "a different modality of sociality";[39] that is, another form of "being otherwise," which socially engages the practice of blacks and enhances a sort of freedom (with a small f) away from the normative gaze of whiteness. It is nice when blacks do not always have to be concerned with, and looked at themselves through, the white gaze.

Michael Jackson wanted to break away from the wretched construction of blackness's designation as a bodily mark, the distinguishing feature of a black person's identity. So, he forged an identity that tried to escape (in fact, an inescapable escape) blackness constructivism, the fixity of racial ontology that structures and upholds white supremacy. Indeed, how race is fixed on the body is important for corroborating the ontology of race and the bodiliness of racism that ascertains the "other" as essentially different. This difference is the mark of a black authenticity reduced to anatomy. Unlike sex reassignment involving operations and hormone treatments, race cannot be reassigned or removed.[40] Of course, a black person may pass for white and can, at a social level, successfully assimilate whiteness as an identity. Nonetheless, assimilating whiteness comes at a psychic cost. Not only the "passer" may have to forgo meaningful relationships with other blacks, but they would have to schematically deal with the ontological specificity of whiteness as terrifying for the "other." In a word, blacks cannot live their own relationship to their body except through the intermediation of an interpretive schema that is not of their own choosing.

At the most elementary level, Michael Jackson's attempt to transcend the black/white binary by fashioning a sort of "racial in-betweenness" displays a kind of double self-othering—an othering of oneself that others his always already other self, and leads to a form of racial ambiguity. This could be read as a kind of postmodern racial subjectivity, which is foundational for Michael Jackson's constructed and constructing "possible self" revealed on his body—*not black, not white*—a body that still signals blackness, conceivably a certain flair of blackness, which whites might identify with the pop artist Michael Jackson, but to which whites possibly also find themselves reacting in a way that scripts the very susceptibility of whites' gaze as ideologically and historically intertwined[41] with the "racial epidermal schema," which has replaced the "historico-racial schema" positioned below the "corporeal schema." The latter is the way in which the body's agency is revealed in the historical world as a universal given of human perception, which is, at a foundational level, important for human presence and being-in-the-world with others.[42]

In chapter 3, I will examine how Michael Jackson is positioned on the borderline of race, *not black* (other), *not white* (the self's "other"), which, in effect, transforms him into an "other 'other.'" An "other 'other'" is one who does not quite fit into the rigid boundary definitions of sameness, or, to be more precise, who may be left out of or who skirt the opposite identities: unnatural/natural, black/white, woman/man, mother/father, or gay/straight matrix and the remaking of identities along new lines. In fact, an "other 'other,'" an ambivalent self-identification or, in this case, disidentification of the subject from himself, is the consequence of a conflict between *not black* ("other"), *not white* (the self's "other"), and the "other" binary or opposite identities, creating a "third body," which unsettles the social body. Here, I will draw from Judith Butler's notion of gender performativity to show the materiality of the body and how it is tied to the performativity of gender as "queer performativity" and illustrate in this chapter that the nonnormative construction of Michael Jackson's raced identity can be seen as race performativity—an identity that can be reified and realized through repetitive performance and re-articulations of daily acts.

Furthermore, can we interpret Michael Jackson's racial ambiguity as postmodern in the ways it resists assumptions about racial identity and, as some critics define it, as a Deleuzian "body without organs";[43] that is, a posthuman body that is contra to what is supposed to be the traditional conceptualization of the human that excluded blacks in the United States from indentured servitude to the Jim Crow south from being fully human? Or to forgo how blacks are positioned in society in such a way that constantly dehumanizes them? Let us consider for example the pernicious use of certain body parts in the constitution of the charges of alleged child molestation against the King of Pop and how the police brazenly photographed and displayed Michael Jackson's penis as a part of the evidence. As John Nguyet Erni explains, Michael Jackson's genitals "[stand] for the 'alleged crime' scene unlike hair samples, figure prints or human tissues that can serve to a crime and the crime."[44] And while morality and ethic are transformed into a provocative forum of a familiar black racial aesthetic, this mockery of justice shows that if blacks were actually considered fully human, they would also be able to go beyond the boundary of race, and like whites they would be viewed as raceless. In this chapter, I will show that specific epistemology, ideologies, and practices are in place to systematically sanction and protect the presumptive hegemony of whiteness.

Indeed, whiteness, from the inception of the United States, determined and continues to determine who should be rights-bearing subjects capable of reason; that is, the power of the soul to have acceptable thoughts. When blackness enters the picture, as Achille Mbembe puts it, "reason finds itself ruined and emptied, turning constantly in on itself."[45] As a result, blackness has no ground to stand on and expresses itself as a psychic derangement endemic to the bodiliness of racism, that is: "a site of reality and truth—the truth of appearance."[46] The bodiliness of racism, which is supported by cultural practice, racist ideologies, institutionalized violence, and "the polymorphous techniques of power,"[47] indeed forms the black subject already under negation and provides the actual condition to de-elevate blacks. By writing that race "is that which marks the body prior to its mark,"[48] Judith Butler shows how some modes of appearance for category such as race stand out as visible social signs, "whereas whiteness, which is no less social is nevertheless part of the taken-for-granted visual field, a sign of its presumptive hegemony."[49] And because, in the final analysis, blackness is reduced to an antagonistic otherness, the problem that presents itself in its unbroken continuity is for blackness to be always seen as a threat to the social body. In other words, being black is, without a doubt, inseparable from being different—that is, to be black is to be different from being white, and thus, blacks, as racialized bodies, are "overdetermined from the outside" as a fundamental signal, notwithstanding the multiple ways blacks' lives are lived.[50]

Chapter 4 examines the problematics that self-identification poses for Michael Jackson and how it provides a foil for the negative form of identity that the misrecognition and objectification of the artist takes on. Judging from Michael Jackson's lived experience, he seems unwilling to accept the harsh consequences of being black in a society that normalizes whiteness. The thing that interests me, here, is his attempt to move between racial spaces. And in light of this, in this chapter, I look at the polymorphous uncertainties of Michael Jackson's self-identification process, all operating in complex and different directions, which often explained Michael Jackson away as a "freak" or as a "weirdo." In the context of a highly regulated sphere of visibility, some appearances are considered normative and self-liberating whereas Michael Jackson's "freakiness" or "weirdness"—a euphemism for his ambiguous racial appearance—is subjected to the most excessive forms of derision. Because blackness constructs a body that is already defiant of the social body and the taxonomic "order of things," Michael Jackson's racial defiance is reduced to an otherness that fixes him in the "zone of nonbeing"[51] as not quite human. I will later draw on several paradigmatic examples to illustrate this point.

How, then, does Michael Jackson's "weirdness" or "freakiness" challenge identification as well as misidentification—that is, the doubling of "otherness" that informs his racial and gender self-alienation? Does his "weirdness" or "freakiness," anchored in an identity performance that blurs the boundaries between white and black, male and female, create anxiety because of its subverting potential? Furthermore, is it because Michael Jackson's "weirdness" or "freakiness" challenges identification as well as misidentification that Michael Jackson must be resisted, restricted, or worse, punished, terrorized, humiliated, and disciplined in order for society to safeguard the realm of the rigid either/or race category? To ask these questions is to approach the question I am asking: What does it mean to be black in the United States? And while this and other unasked questions will shape the discussion in chapter 4, I also locate Michael Jackson's "weirdness" or "freakiness" within a larger framework of self-identification and demonstrate that his appearance deconstructs and challenges the corporeal notions of "natural bodies" and fixed identities. Indeed, Michael Jackson must be disciplined and "normalized." In a white world, blackness coupled with "weirdness" or "freakiness" is forever perceived, to take from Michael Jackson's album titles, as *"bad* and *dangerous."*[52] This can be affiliated to what Frantz Fanon, in *Black Skin, White Masks,* describes as a wound to the black psychic, a wound to the head; a condition that is only curable when whiteness is denormalized, rehabilitated, and split open, and a new white subject can be constituted. It is only then that blackness can be reimagined in a positive light in the United States. In my concluding remarks, I try to imagine what blackness will be when whiteness is denormalized.

The aim of this book is thus to offer a different reading of Michael Jackson's lived experience and elicit a new sensibility for us to think in new ways about the analytics of a black identity and its complex histories. When all is said, one has to simply reckon that race is epidermalized[53] and represents a grid for understanding blackness as an identification that is marked on the body. The harrowing inscription of race on the body makes it hard for blacks to develop a solid and secure sense of "self." Consequently, the black body is in inordinate physical and psychological pain; and in order "to be" in this world, it is "put together by another self,"[54] a "possible self" through "a complex labyrinth of discursive strategies, desires and hopes, [and] fears and fortitude."[55] No doubt, the lived experience of Michael Jackson as a case-study-led theoretical methodology is illustrative of this condition.

Chapter 1

Conceptual Framework

In this book, I focus on the complexity of Michael Jackson's racial identity. In a society that normalizes whiteness, a black person's sense of "self" is always in question and is persistently constituted, reconstituted, and deconstituted by the tenacity of the white gaze that sees blackness as null and void of racial transcendence. That said, my undertaking is indexed on the works of political scientists, critical race theorists, social historians, feminist theorists, sociologists, and philosophers. I draw from these works for key concepts, theories, and argumentations that concisely capture the positioning of blacks in the United States and to understand blackness and black identity beyond reductive definitions that crystalize all blacks, including the King of Pop Michael Jackson or, as *Ebony* refers to him, "The World's Greatest Entertainer,"[1] to an alterity. In the Fanonian language, it means that a black person is "overdetermined from the outside." His race is fixed on the body.[2] What I call the outsideness of blackness is, to borrow the words of Sara Jane Cervenak and J. Cameron Carter, the fact "of being black outside."[3] In other words, race is that which *mark* the body before its *mark*, and it is the process "through which the body becomes signifiable."[4]

The outsideness of blackness is "an irrevocable and physical fact, defining and complementing our metaphysical conditions."[5] It produces a form of antiblack subjugation, which Achille Mbembe diagnoses in "The Society of Enmity" and names "nanoracism." For Mbembe, nanoracism is a "narcotic brand of prejudice based on skin colour."[6] Let us remember with professor Gayatri C. Spivak that "to have color is to be visible."[7] To have color is also a prerequisite to suffer from the axiomatic of limitless surveillance and regulation[8] from the white *look* that never fails to reduce blacks to the object of the *look*. It is unquestionable that color brings into play blacks' physicality, which is impelled by what the French postcolonial scholar Frantz Fanon calls the "corporeal malediction" of one's unavoidable blackness. This is what Fanon attributes to "the lived experience of blacks,"[9] which is, among other things, "a constant demand for an ontology of disorder."[10] This disorder is another way to draw blacks into order, or the cultural rules and ways of whiteness.

Consider the sociologist Ruth Frankenberg's three-fold conceptualization of whiteness: "First whiteness is a location of structural advantage, or race privilege. Second, it is a 'standpoint,' a place from which white people look at ourselves, at others, and at society. Third, 'whiteness' refers to a set of cultural practices that are usually unmarked and unnamed."[11] These essentials of whiteness have projected unto whites specific ways of feeling, acting, thinking, and knowing by way of explanation of being white. This can be characterized as whiteness habitus, which is a "socialized subjectivity;" it is unconscious and becomes, as Pierre Bourdieu describes it, a "permanent disposition,"[12] a routine, a second nature. Accordingly, an inquiry into how blacks can resist the intrinsic power of whiteness becomes paramount. Furthermore, how are we to conceptualize blackness relationality to whiteness that discursively and nondiscursively acts, produces, and reduces blacks to a bodily mark? In so much that blackness is a symbol that has a referent to whiteness, it cannot, in the words of Ronald Judy, "enable the representation of meaning"[13] that is outside of whiteness, which is supported, upheld, and serviced by racist structures, institutions and systems, ideology, and epistemology. Indeed, just as much as Jean-Paul Sartre claims that the anti-Semite makes the Jew,[14] one can also proclaim that in the United States the white makes the black. And let us remember that from the start of the United States' formation into a nation, sole white men held power. The feminist philosopher Marilyn Fyre is right to point out that "those who fashion this construct of whiteness, who elaborate on these conceptions are primarily a group of males. It is *their* construct. They construct a concept of their 'us,' their kindred, their nation, their tribe."[15] However, it would be false to argue that white women are positioned outside of whiteness.

In the process of analysis, based on what Michel Foucault characterizes as "the hermeneutics of the technologies of the self,"[16] which, for the most part, is expressed in the form of a "possessive investment in whiteness"[17] to which the very structures and systems that are in place remorselessly subscribe, whiteness overdetermines the embodiment of possibilities and the determinate crux of white-skin privilege that exclude the "other" from privilege. At the same time, this possessiveness asserts itself, in the words of Mbembe, "in seemingly anodyne everyday gesture, often apropos of nothing, apparently unconscious remarks, a little banter, some allusion or insinuation, a slip of the tongue, a joke, an innuendo"[18] directed at blacks. What also must be added is, as Mbembe points out, "consciously spiteful remarks, like a malicious intention, a deliberate dig or jab, a profound desire to stigmatize and, in particular, to inflict violence, to wound and to humiliate, to degrade those not considered to be one of us."[19]

I would place "us" in quotes because "us" is radically unlike "them." And this is precisely a huge part of the nanoracist thought; that is, a dominant registered form of race prejudice according to which whites are superior to blacks. This binary opposition is the crux of the social, psychic, ontological, material, and epistemological underpinnings for the ill treatment of blacks and the negativity that reduces them to their corporeality. As Toni Morrison sums it up, corporeality is "permanently aligned with another seductive concept: the hierarchy of race."[20] How race, as the signifier of black identity, bars blacks, including a figure like Michael Jackson, from any form of racial transcendence is not without significance. Given that "race can be ontological without being biological, metaphysical without being physical, existential without being essential, shaping one's being without being in one's shape,"[21] partly, for this reason, critical thinking on race and the theory of race is now taken up by philosophers working[22] from the margins, "from the outside," within the specific framework of a critical philosophy of race,[23] which, according to Charles Mills, "has been pioneered by blacks."[24] We do not need to investigate deeply into that field. All I want to say, to think critically "comes always from the outside, is directed towards the outside, belongs to the outside, is an absolute relation to the outside."[25] To borrow from Peter Pál Pelbart's title, "the thought of the outside"; that is, the thought from the margins unsettles "the thought of the inside," the center. In this discussion about Michael Jackson and the quandary of a black identity, by drawing on the work of critical race theorists, in Pelbart's words, critical race theorists have "given to the outside its strategic immanence"[26] for us to think "otherwise" about a black identity.

More recently, an ensemble of scholars including Saidiya Hartman, Orlando Patterson, Jared Sexton, Hortense Spillers, and Frank B. Wilderson III have been working within a tradition of black critique: the Afro-pessimism framework.[27] A huge part of their task is to expose the ways historical structures and systems of domination continue to impact what Frantz Fanon describes as "the lived experience of blacks"[28] by which blacks' resistance is inevitably derived.[29] This can only be truly looked into "from the outside." The queerness of Afro-pessimism as another way of knowing, of thinking about blackness, "comes always from the outside," away from the traditional forms of analysis of blackness as a liability. This "other way" of thinking and writing about blackness is a form of resistance, of writing against the taken-for-granted forms of seeing blackness as lack. And since the "outsideness" of thought unsettles the "insideness" of thought, "The Thought of the Outside: The Outside of Thought," the thought from "the outside" in its analysis of blackness is fundamental for a move toward the reframing of blackness—a question I will address in the conclusion of the book. Indeed, Michael Jackson and the quandary of a black identity is propelled by thoughts "from the outside."

Following W. E. B. Du Bois's *The Souls of Black Folk* in conjunction with Frantz Fanon's anticolonialist treatise, *Black Skin, White Masks*, the conceptualization of the place of race and its racialized assemblages on what Du Bois labels the "double consciousness" or the "twoness" that blacks embody—"an American, a Negro; two souls, two thoughts, two unreconciled strivings; two warring ideals in one dark body, whose dogged strength alone keeps it from being torn asunder"[30]—becomes even clearer when thinking about blacks' identification process. It is true that race defines one's social identity and that this thing that we now call race is produced by racism, which, more precisely, Barbara Fields and Karen Fields coined as "Racecraft." Racecraft, as they explain it, demonstrates the illusive nature of race that is produced by racism, "first and foremost a social practice, which means it is an action and a rationale for action, or both at once";[31] that is, "the withholding of equal humanity"[32] that falsely diagnoses blackness as lack.

Michael Jackson knows firsthand the harmfulness, the insurmountable and unspeakable pain that comes with blackness. When he was charged with alleged child molestation, the police went against protocols and took pictures of Michael Jackson's penis, which they consider as a piece of evidence.[33] Every minute, blacks are harassed and dehumanized by the police. What comes to mind is the arrest of Henry Louis Gates Jr., the Alphonse Fletcher University professor and director of the Hutchins Center for African and African American Research at Harvard University in 2009[34] and Bryonn Bain in 2002, a Harvard law student at the time, by the New York Police Department.[35] However annoyed blacks may be about being constantly dehumanized by the police, racial profiling, to borrow from Michael Jackson's song "You are Not Alone," is "here to say." And, in his words, "how could this be"[36] becomes important for any discussion of a black person's ownership of the "self."

If as Fanon writes "what is often called the black [self] is a white man's artifact,"[37] for blacks, then, ownership of the "self" is indeed an endless struggle, especially in a culture that normalizes whiteness and reduces blackness to an alterity that is marked on the body. This point is made clear when we take into consideration Michael Jackson's body in all of its seemingly contradictory binary representations. To borrow from Judith Butler's *Undoing Gender*, Michael Jackson's body "exceeds the norm, reworks the norm,"[38] but remains incapable of "undoing" race as a performative. In its "unnatural" performative, so to speak, Michael Jackson's body, even though it "becomes a site onto which discourses about race, sex, gender, sexuality, age and humanness are projected,"[39] remains a body that signals blackness—a body that remains black.[40]

Although Michael Jackson presents a challenge to "blackness's capacity to signify otherwise,"[41] beyond skin color as seemingly unalterable, in his song "Black or White," Michael Jackson can say "I'm not going to spend my life being a color."[42] What this statement signifies is a disavowal (which certainly contains an avowal in the disavowal) of the reality of what it means to be black in America and to always be under the incessant surveillance of the white gaze, in a manner, as Fanon says, "a chemical solution is fixed with a dye."[43] Certainly, skin color (surface), as we will see with Michael Jackson's skin becoming whiter, giving way to racial peculiarity, announces "a whole range of possibilities for knowing, doing, and existing,"[44] which, however, never fails to signify an otherness of the "other" and functions, in part, as metaphors for the constitution of his identity as an absolute *lack*, a lack that has led the Tabloid to nickname the King of Pop "wacko jacko," "a diminutive title with racist roots."[45] We all know this.

If nothing else, any attempt to release blackness from the register of *lack* would have to take into account how skin, along with other morphologies and physicalities—hair, lips, nose, eyes, and other phenotypic traits—constructed an epidermal schema for fixing race on the body as an absolute mode for the recognition of blackness as "other." An important feature of racist discourse, to borrow from Homi K. Bhabha, "is its dependence on the concept of 'fixity' in the ideological construction of otherness."[46] Blackness, its surfaceness, its visuality, in Saidiya Hartman's rich account of the plantation system, is "a historical, constitutive 'fixing' of the body"[47] by whiteness dominance.

Skin color also establishes blacks' status in a society disfigured by the Cartesian binary logics of racial antagonisms—black and white, inferior and superior, uncivilized and civilized, impure and pure—working to construct "a border" that safeguards the subject from the object, the white "self" from the black "other," and strengthens the boundaries between the "self" and the "other," whose manifestation can only be understood in terms of neurosis, as explained by Fanon. That is, whites enslaved by their superiority and blacks enslaved by their inferiority, which, in no uncertain terms, pervert humanity to such an extent that it downgrades humans' wholesomeness. And while neither blacks nor whites can engage "in the Hegelian ontological dialectics,"[48] I am here interested in blacks' neurosis. Indeed, it is not, as most of us recognized, a path toward self-realization, but above all an effect of white supremacy. Blacks' ontology is always questionable in a society that upholds whiteness as unraced and unmarked.

In Fanon's revelation of blacks' ontology, which places blacks among objects, as the rejectamenta of society, he provides us with the epigraph: "I came into the world imbued with the will to find a meaning in things, my spirit filled with desires to attain to the source of the world, and then I found that I was an object in the midst of other objects,"[49] placed in "a zone of non-being," an *object-in-itself*, and "sealed in this crushing objecthood"[50] with "no ontological resistance."[51] This state of (non)being ("not to be") must be understood in its difference from what Giorgio Agamben calls "bare life,"[52] as an inherently opposite relation to a multifaceted discursive power and the rule of law,[53] but more in tune with what, along with Fred Moten, I call "burdened life."[54] "Burdened life" transforms a black person into "the beast of burden," which is infested with self-doubt: "I am black enough! I am smart enough! I am white enough!" In this regard, for a black person, "consciousness of the body is solely a negating activity."[55] It is a third-person consciousness that is split, broken, and breaks a black person into different modes of being. On the one hand, a black person must exist for themselves, and on the other hand, they must exist differently as they are viewed by the "other world," the white world. It is "the only honorable one." Yet, it bars blacks "from all participation."[56] In this regard, the effects for a black person are quite traumatic. How, then, can one read the trauma that the black body undergoes in the face of normalized whiteness? This is how Fanon explains it: given that "the racial trauma is played out in the open," a black person has "no chance to 'make it unconscious.' "[57] However, one is stripped of everything but "a bodily schema," which does not impose itself on [one]; it is, rather, a definitive structuring of the self and of the world—definitive because it creates a real dialectic between [one's] body and the world."[58]

Since the being of a black man is not about ontology, "ontology does not permit us to understand the being of a black man;"[59] it is about relationality. "For not only must the black man be black; he must be black in relation to the white man."[60] Even in a monastic attempt at any diagnosing of Michael Jackson's position, his unendurable attempts to supplant ascribed blackness with something else, such as an indeterminate self-identification, it is true that we would have to reassign, in the word of Jared Sexton, "its cause and [relocate] its sources"[61] as the inescapability of whiteness. To put a finer point on it: Why should this be? As long as whiteness is the norm, blackness will always be viewed as "other," *bad* and *dangerous*, to take from the titles of two of Michael Jackson's albums, as is clearly depicted in the way the news pointedly presented a mug shot of Michael Jackson taken at his arrest for alleged child molestation charges. In doing so, "it was a particularly harsh image which emphasizes the radical distortions of feature and skin,"[62] and what was even more disparaging is that the image tried to show, according to Seth Clark Silberman, a " 'corroded 45-year-old man' overtaken by deviant desire"[63] to support prima facie the prevailing view of endangerment that blackness presents.

We do remember the Rodney King's case in which the defense attorney for the police claimed that "the policemen were endangered, and that Rodney King was the source of that danger."[64] Michael Jackson and Rodney King never did cross each other's path.[65] But, on the inevitable point par excellence, which is the outsideness of blackness and the danger it presents to the social body, is something that all blacks must undergo. And since the outsideness of blackness positioned blacks as the inessential "other" of whiteness, "a source of danger," how can we understand the alleged influence and constitution of blackness outsideness? How do we rethink blackness to create new possibilities? What can possibly be done? And while some of my remarks will partly focus on reframing blackness, surely, for that purpose, we must start by interrogating whiteness.

First of all, to interrogate the laws, ideology, epistemology, and determinations that have put white privilege in place, making whiteness visible is a task that is now taken up by whiteness studies scholars. At any rate, these days, naming whiteness, a kind of citational practice, has become a major critical industry in the second wave of whiteness studies.[66] Whiteness studies, a term championed by Liz McMillen,[67] is currently a framework within academia that returns to David Roediger's claim of the "wages of whiteness."[68] Whiteness studies now has a growing corpus, focusing on the signification for whites to recognize their privilege and power and to promote a kind of "antiracist whiteness" as an essentiality for making whiteness visible to whites for whom it is invisible. Certainly, it is a start. It allows for whiteness studies scholars to identify with affectivity how whiteness impacts the lives of blacks and other nonwhites and become active in trying to alleviate their sufferings. But it is not enough because these scholars are handicapped by their ways "of knowing, seeing, ontologizing, and evaluating" that are not outside of whiteness.[69] Indeed, scholars such as Michele Fine and her colleagues who originally aimed "to create spaces to speak, intellectually or empirically, about whiteness . . . may have [in fact] reified whiteness as a fixed category of experience;" that they "have allowed it to be treated as a monolith, in the singular, as an 'essential something' "[70] is not without analysis. To be sure, this significant move of naming whiteness as "the problem" is a good starting point to elucidate the effects of whiteness presumptive hegemony.

Fanon's remarkable analysis of the culpability of whiteness as a system as well as an identity concludes with the insightful question: What do blacks want?[71] It is important to bear in mind here the specific way in which the question is posed and the way in which the question becomes posable, since what I seek to highlight is that blacks must grapple with "the double-consciousness"[72]—that is, the affliction of always looking at themselves through the white gaze. This is not unlike what Fanon describes as the "implicit knowledge" of whiteness as the norm, which, for blacks, can sometimes manifest itself in unsettled feelings of powerlessness, doubts, and self-deception. In the end, the posability of the question *what do blacks want* does not suggest its answerability within the term in which it is posed. In truth, on the contrary. Because want—in other words, ontological desire—is not as forthright as it seemingly appears.[73]

A polemical account, then, would not resist to highlight that what blacks claim to want or desire ontologically is not always what blacks actually want or desire. In other words, we do not always act out of desire because our choices are not always preceded by a desire for or even an aversion to one thing or the other. As I have discussed elsewhere, if we do act out of desire, then principles as something separate from the pursuit of desire vanish. Given that "there is a difference of kind between Black desire and White desire," in that "the latter appears as normal desires because they are *a priori* attainable or achievable in the 'thought-world,' "[74] the world of reason, where, when blackness enters, it empties it of all reason,[75] is not without significance. I am convinced at the moment that for blacks the freedom to *will* their own desires, to act as they choose and dream of a better future free from otherness, is foreclosed. Because the *will* might be strong but the flesh (the body) is weakened by race assignment, blacks must practice not to desire, not to want, which is explicitly framed in the language of disavowal. So, if blacks suffer from whiteness envy, it is partly because of whiteness symbolic value as unraced and unmarked, a gargantuan amount of white privilege that accompanies whiteness and, at the same time, makes blacks into this other "thing."

How Michael Jackson's racial in-betweenness, *not black* ("other"), *not white* (the "self's 'other' "), an otherness of the "other," tries to resist the strict dialogical relations between blackness and whiteness, blackness as presumptively assigned to him by working within and through the force of negation embedded in fortifying black positionality,[76] will be expounded in chapter 3. In this chapter, I make use of the concept of "imminent danger"[77] as it is conceptualized by Judith Butler in "Endangered/Endangering: Schematic Racism and White Paranoia," in which the phantasmatic production of "imminent danger" is foundational to the interpretive field surrounding black bodies. In fact, signifiers of "imminent danger" attached to a body[78] that slides "outside and between conventional social categories, and which is itself foundationally embedded in deep social and cultural inequalities"[79] cannot be ignored. The point is that who is dangerous and who is in danger is very much attached to bodily interpretation.

Blacks, by virtue of their blackness, seemingly always present an "imminent danger" and a threat to the social body, what Hannah Arendt calls the "space of appearance": a space in which people are supposed to act together in concert with each other. In this sense, it is a democratic space, but it is still embedded with the mechanisms of power relations.[80] The way in which blackness is visible, and the way in which the black "self" is constituted, reconstituted, and deconstructed, blacks are always watched, policed, and controlled. Underlining the contrast with Arendt's "space of appearance," Michel Foucault found the right formulation for the operation of power in his concept of "a space of surveillance," a space of vertiginal estrangement where identity is constituted through specialized techniques of power, which ruins "the space of appearance." And while the Arendtian space does recognize that collective actions can emerge, for

Foucault, what he calls disciplinary power (and we will see later how this form of power acts to "normalize" Michael Jackson) is what emerges to normalize and discipline the individual who is positioned outside of the social norm defined by whiteness. This helps us to remember that not all "spaces of appearance" are democratic and people are acting in concert. Because spaces are themselves racialized, gendered, classed, and so on, there are the bodies that matter and those that do not as Judith Butler describes them. This is especially true for the black body as the latter. This approach allows us to understand that spaces that are racialized, for example, can and do promote antagonism and stifle difference and even toleration of racial difference. In other words, there are no pretenses to tolerate that which is intolerable. Toleration, in this sense, means putting up with people who make you uncomfortable.

In this regard, who can blame blacks for exhibiting some reactive feeling of ressentiment,[81] in the Nietzschean sense, against the presumptive hegemony of whiteness upheld by laws, institutions and systems, ideology, and epistemologies, which, in a significant way, contributes to blacks' otherness. So, if we tried to apply the observation that, in the words of Slavoj Žižek, "people not only have to 'realize their own (emancipatory, etc.) dreams'; rather they have to reinvent their very mode of dreaming,"[82] we would miss the mark about "the lived experience of blacks" in America, the facticity of blackness, which is another way of stating the facts and conditions of being black. For the racialized subject, ownership of oneself is indeed a continuous struggle, which unrelentingly confines blacks to a bodily state of alterity. In this sense, blacks need to create a space, a place they can call "home" within "the space of appearance," a space where they can continue to strive to make things happen so as to renew their strengths and become essential. The emergence of Black Power and black popular culture are illustrative.[83]

In the end, as we will see with Michael Jackson, blacks' personhood still suffers a defeat, unless, following Fanon's rich labyrinth of awareness, one comes to understand that when blacks are among other blacks, there are no immediate white gazes through which they "will have no occasion, except in minor internal conflicts, to experience [their] being through others."[84] Apparently, this is one reason why Fanon can say, for the "normal" black child, the slightest contact with the white world epistemologically and cognitively damages them and makes them abnormal.[85] You do "Remember the Time"[86] when Michael Jackson was a "cute child dressed in gaudy flower power gear and sporting a huge 'Afro' hairstyle," as Kobena Mercer describes him.[87] It is no wonder then that Michael Jackson can ask: "Have you ever seen my childhood?"[88] In his autobiography *Moonwalk* above else, he says it right off: "I received quite an education as a child."[89] Sadly, this education did not prepare him for the de facto trauma a black person endures in a world where blackness represents otherness and difference; where blackness is seen as a liability; and where the black man can no longer be himself.

He is inserted in an atmosphere which yields him no "true self-consciousness," but only lets him imagine or invent himself through the exposé of whiteness, "the other world."[90] It is a strange experience that robs the subject of "self" and world, of presence and being, of self-consciousness and truth, of affection and reconciliation, and equips him with an "implicit knowledge" of being in "the other world," as Fanon's splendid formulation reveals to us.[91] In a word, he can no longer be himself and is thrusted, to use Fanon's language, between the impossible choice of trying to endlessly assimilate whiteness norms and values and being frustrated at the manner in which blackness is viewed as a pathology.

In sum, Michael Jackson's constant efforts in his adult life to recapture the "cute child" is exemplified in his Neverland ranch, a magical world of "child play," solitude and contemplation, "a world with no pain,"[92] temporarily taking him far away from whiteness, which imprisoned him as much as it imprisons, consciously or unconsciously, all blacks in the United States and other Western populations because white is the norm. And while Foucault, in *Discipline and Punish*, helps us see that a norm—a schema of behavior inculcated by institutions, structures, epistemology, ideologies, and culture—is a concept that is constantly used to evaluate and control people; a norm is never originary. It is a response to the antinormativity, the irregular, the unacceptable and the supposed destruction it has produced. To put it differently, a norm is always an outcome of a naturalizing action of the act of naturalizing. In this scenario, we can see that blackness, in its nonrepresentation, comes before whiteness. So, whiteness must be distinctively manufactured as cultural expectations and bound up with the question of white privilege that demeans anyone who is not white or outside of normativity, the state of being normal, as abnormal. *In fine*, whiteness as a normative category is inevitably exclusionary. It establishes who is excluded, who is left out. So, what it might mean to undo, to unsettle the invasive normativity of whiteness becomes overriding.

Cheryl I. Harris understands very well the dynamics of whiteness in "Whiteness as Property"; she explains the "hypervaluation of whiteness,"[93] and Michele Fine et al. would later, writing in the shadows of whiteness studies scholars, define whiteness as "an essential something,"[94] a kind of property that all whites own, which is not easily transferable and, in some cases, entirely nontransferable. Whiteness must foremost be grounded and contextualized as a diachronic evaluative form of power that on a quotidian basis reduces blacks to this exponentially magnified thingliness or nothingness, "the abject status of the will-less object,"[95] inferior and incomplete with little or no power to move, to be with effect, agency; no homeostatic thought outside of the white gaze. This condition equipped blacks to live, perhaps happily, as best as they can with what Fanon describes as an "implicit knowledge." This is how Fanon puts it:

> I know that if I want to smoke, I shall have to reach out my right arm and take the pack of cigarettes lying at the other end of the table. The matches, however, are in the drawer on the left, and I shall have to lean back slightly. And all these movements are made not out of habit but out of implicit knowledge. A slow composition of my self as a body in the middle of a spatial and temporal world—such seems to be the schema. It does not impose itself on me; it is, rather, a definitive structuring of the self and the world—definitive because it creates a real dialectic between my body and the world.[96]

The basic lesson Fanon brings to the forefront is that to minimally develop and ensure a sense of "self," the phenomenological description of bodily insight demonstrates how the racialized lived body forms its own space precisely by a carefully planned strategy. This is, in part, what Fanon is getting at when he says that blacks have difficulties in developing their bodily schema because they are always forced to view themselves through the white gaze. Indeed, this is nonliberating for blacks even though it is true that "the Negro is not. Any more than the white man," as Fanon reminds us in *Black Skin, White Masks*.[97]

As time went by, Michael Jackson too had to face the reality of being black in a white world where a black identity is singularly performed through the body; a body that is constituted, reconstituted, and deconstituted through a naming and a seeing, "Look a Negro, . . . mama, see the Negro! I'm frightened."[98] When the hip-hop group Public Enemy sings, "The minute they see me, fear me/I'm the epitome, a public enemy,"[99] we understand that the irrational fear of the black person forces him to confirm his own bodily presence. Indeed, the black body is a body to be controlled and excluded from the realm of normality and viewed as a threat to the social body. And since the body is marked by race, blacks encounter the racist world through their bodies. The racialization of the body as a complex interdiscursive process where the language of difference[100] is translated into a praxis of indifference as a criterion for the ill treatment of blacks cannot be disavowed. And even though some try to disavow the ill treatment of blacks, a good illustration is the treatment of Michael Jackson in the alleged child molestation charges, as I mentioned earlier, which is a point to which I will return later in order to show how the "truth" about the economy of sexuality—a site for desires, attractions, pleasures, and anxieties—is another way by which the black body is controlled and stigmatized, which basically positions blacks as unable to control their sexual appetites.

In the British television documentary *Michael Jackson's Boys*, the portrayal of Michael Jackson as obsessed with boys is likened to what has been defined as "object dysphoria"; that is, desire "as the repudiation of the self and notions of imminent (and immanent) danger generally ascribed to bodies in a racialized and homophobic interpretive field. Michael Jackson as the embodiment of not only 'unnatural' desire, but specifically of pedophilic desire is explicitly framed through a language of 'obsession.'"[101] which, in this case, cannot escape its culturally inflected racist discourse and is, of course, riffed with other innuendoes and racist interpellation about the black subject.

Indeed, the same narrative is also embedded in *Michael Jackson and The Boy He Paid Off*,[102] notwithstanding the fact that Michael Jackson sincerely refutes claims of molesting young boys. Given that Michael Jackson's evidentiary is already "on trial," there is no way that his refuting the claim can be interpreted as "not guilty" insofar as phobic judgment against the raced being is always in place and upheld by the eternal myth of blacks as oversexed and unrestrained. In light of this, Michael Jackson's denial of the charges of child sexual abuse reported in the *New York Times* on December 23, 1993, as "totally false"[103] was foremost interpreted as a sequitur for "guilty." And, like the other boys who had a close relationship with Michael Jackson, the well-known child actor Emmanuel Lewis—now an adult—who Michael Jackson once described as "a real inspiration,"[104] when asked about his relationship with Michael Jackson, says, "If you ask me did anything untoward happen, the answer to that question, to your question, is hell no."[105] For those asking the question, Lewis's confession was interpreted as a lie and "the lie becomes the truth," to take from Michael Jackson's "Billie Jean."[106] Furthermore, Lewis's denial of sexual molestation "is effectively recast as (further) evidence" of effectual "truth,"[107] as an overarching guiding principle of the truth that all blacks are oversexed. Thus, we have to be suspicious of a priori knowledge that guides such a "truth" and forecloses other ways of arriving at "truth" and new ways of interpreting "truth." If it is correct that "truth is made, not found," of course, as Nietzsche helps us to see, truth is that which tends to uplift mankind, this conceptualization of truth is a welcoming one.

However, my focus here is not to hint at whether Michael Jackson is innocent or guilty. Insofar as his alleged molestation charges circulate as "truth" and some behave as if these allegations were true, I am very much taken with the crucial question of what counts as evidence and what counts as "truth." And if we recall Rodney King's case, the video shows that Rodney King is violently beaten by the police as irrefutable evidence of the police's guilt. How the jurors reproduced the video in order to "establish police vulnerability"[108] that masquerades as evidence is not surprising. However, if we continue to project "police vulnerability" on the victims of legitimized state violence, the sad state of affair is that police violence perpetrated against "unarmed" blacks will continue.[109]

Needless to say, the media's coverage of Michael Jackson's child molestation charges is notable for having treated the singer's penis as evidence. Certainly, morality and ethics were transformed into a provocative forum for the performance of a familiar black racial drama in which the black penis becomes a fetish. And while Michael Jackson's penis is deliberately made an object of mystery "by his own choreographed crotch-grabbing" that "resists visibility,"[110] when the penis is made to surface, to make visible, as with the photographing of Michael Jackson's penis by the police, it loses its mystery and takes away from the anxiety it presents for the white man.[111] In fact, how the penis "figured so prominently in the history of race relations structured by fantasies of miscegenation and all too real lynchings"[112] of black men for alleged rape charges of white women cannot be disregarded.[113]

More so, if we were to take from Freud's essay "A Child is Beaten"[114] and conceptualize, as Fanon does, "A Negro is Raping Me," to demonstrate the fantasies of a white woman's desire to be raped by a black man would help us get to the heart of the matter. Fanon writes: "It is commonplace for women, during the sexual act, to cry to their partners: 'Hurt me!' They are merely expressing the idea: Hurt me as I would hurt me if I were in your place. The fantasy of rape by a Negro is a variation of this emotion: 'I wish the Negro would rip me open as I would have ripped a woman open.' "[115] And while, on Fanon's account, there is a specific expression of lesbian desire within an apparently heteronormative frame, Fanon nonetheless lets us see that a white woman's fantasy is not about the fear of the black man, which provides us with a counternarrative about the falsification of black men as rapists,[116] but she herself imaging herself as a black man with, in the words of Musser, "carnal desires that she then imagines turning on herself or any other white woman."[117]

Indeed, the stereotype of the size of the black penis is certainly not unrelated to whites' fixation about the black man's sexual capacity and, as Fanon notes, the black man "is the slave of this cultural imposition"[118] because of "the persistent fear of white femininity being violated by black men."[119] So, if we are to see that the "metaphorical substitute for the black man" is the penis,[120] this would not be without signification. As Lewis Gordon further explains, "one is no longer aware of the *nègre* but only of a penis. He is a penis"[121] and he is, as is the case of Michael Jackson, in constant danger by the minute, in the minute, of literal as well as symbolic castration.

In Du Bois's and Fanon's analyses, whiteness is looked on as desirable and operationalizes the terrifying myth, which is recycled and transmitted from one generation to the next, constructing the black male as a rapist, as a good illustration of how a "black man is attacked in his corporeality. It is his tangible personality that is lynched. It is as an actual being that he is a threat."[122] In other words, "black masculinity threatens white vulnerability,"[123] which is grossly depicted in *The Birth of a Nation*. The fear that blackness conjures is not only a huge part of America's history, but the present reality. Too often, the police, trained in militarized methods,[124] would confront a black person and mistreat them, knowing very well that, for the most part, his conduct will remain unchecked is indeed a massive anxiety for blacks. The police photographing Michael Jackson's penis as evidence in his alleged child molestation charge is illustrative. Certainly, how the body is positioned within racism, that the presentation of race operates as a hegemonic and dynamic power, is without disagreement. Accordingly, the authentic lived experience of racism for blacks is positioned within the experiential realm; it is prediscursive and unnamable because it is a feeling buried deep inside the body. On the other hand, for blacks, the lived experience of the bodiliness of racism—that is to say, a body located within racism—is loaded with meanings, and these meanings are not ungrudgingly articulable or easily integrated into the symbolic realm of signification.

When the bodiliness of racism is experienced, there are feelings of racism that cannot be named because the experience goes deeper than mere thoughts. For instance, in returning to Michael Jackson's alleged sexual molestation charges, when his body is objectified, the kind of bodily pain he apparently experiences cannot be explained through language. Indeed, bodily pain, as Elaine Scarry explains in her book *The Body in Pain*, "does not simply resist language but actively destroys it, bringing about an immediate reversion to a state anterior to language to the sounds and cries a human being makes before language is learned."[125] Here are the words of Michael Jackson on the subject as he sings them in "Thriller": "You try to scream but terror takes the sound before you make it. You start to freeze as horror looks you right between the eyes/You're paralyzed." "Speechless" (that is, "lost for words") is also another way of saying it. One "[has] not the words to explain" as Michael Jackson's song "Speechless" blatantly states.[126] Your body's emphatically and crushingly presence is destroyed.[127] It is an assault on the body's capacity to resist. In this sense, when we account for the bodiliness of racism, we cannot take into thinking language and perception only, but more imperative we should take into thinking the black body and its lived experience.

In fact, the prosthetics of identification emerging as an extension of the black body can result in fatal killing of blacks. We do remember that Trayvon Martin's hoodie and Jordan Davis's loud music got them killed. These very modes of representation that provide meaning to blackness and its signifiers, such as loud music and the hoodie, point to the indubitable fact that blacks suffer "in their bodies quite differently"[128] from whites. And given that such bodily pain destroys language, I do not but wonder how the bodily suffering of blacks can be eased. Seemingly, nothing can or does.[129] "My head is spinning like a carousel, so silently I pray/ Helpless and hopeless, that's how I feel inside."[130]

It is true that the perils of being black in the United States is definitely not a part of whites' experience. Obviously, whites are not black. James Baldwin's *The Fire Next Time*, most notably, educates whites about the perils of being black in the United States. Baldwin draws our attention to the death metaphor; that is, "to earn one's death," which, for him, is "to confront with passion the conundrum of life,"[131] a quotidian life, which for blacks is, in the Fanonian pharmakon, "battered down by tom-toms, cannibalism, intellectual deficiency, fetishism, and racial defects."[132] And because, according to Baldwin, "white Americans do not believe in death, and this is why the darkness of my skin so intimidates them."[133] I will conclude on the need to problematize and work contra the materiality of the black body as a lack.

To demonstrate how the black body is tied to a form of race performativity that constructs blacks' identification process as always marked on the body has something to do with the way in which W. E. B. Du Bois, in *The Souls of Black Folk*, contends that a black person "is a sort of seventh son, born with a veil and gifted with second-sight in this American world—a world which yields him no true self-consciousness, but only lets him sees himself through the revelation of the other world."[134] Consequently, a black person is without cover and has no ontological resistance in the face of whiteness. He is produced, reproduced, and de-produced precisely as a stranger to himself, the inessential "other" of the imperative of whiteness. "To be black in 'the white world,'" Sara Ahmed reminds us, "is to turn back towards itself, to become an object, which means not only being extended by the contours of the world, but being diminished as an effort of the bodily extension of the others."[135]

Unfortunately, no individual or group that is situated outside the sphere of whiteness can sustain itself properly even if he is the King of Pop Michael Jackson, who at one time appeared, in the words of Debbie Epstein and Deborah Lynn Steinberg, as "a figure of rapture."[136] "I will come back to one fact," Fanon admits: "Wherever he goes, the Negro remains a Negro."[137] Furthermore, he is always ahead of himself; not in the same way in which Simone de Beauvoir sees it, "as projecting [himself] toward something, toward the future,"[138] but in the sense that he is "always already fixed, complete, given"[139] in its corporeality. The challenge, of course, is for blacks to operate outside such a phenomenon, which we see with Michael Jackson's attempts at self-fashioning, *not black, not white*, and is positioned as an "other 'other,'" an identity that is doubly "othered" but still signals blackness. In short, blackness can never be "in the closet."[140] I will show in chapter 4 how "weirdness" or "freakiness" coupled with blackness disturbs and unsettles the social body.

Fanon's leitmotif, "Look, a Negro!"[141] helps us conceptualize the tabloid racist interpellation, "Look, Michael Jackson!' or 'Look, a black!'[142] and show that blackness begins with racist interpellation, which changes at this staging; that is, it is no longer an illocutionary act because the black is psychically unable to respond to the "hailing." It disrupts the black person's sense of himself and, in its disruption, transforms him into an object among other objects "sealed in this crushing objecthood."[143] I believe this is one of the issues that Fanon's *Black Skin, White Masks* most significantly highlights when Fanon imaginatively describes the little white boy who, in the face of "seeing" race (him), cries out, "Look, a Negro! . . . mama, see the Negro! I'm frightened!"[144]

And while the *look*, when directed at a black person, is always a negating experience that confers their nothingness, it coincides with what W. E. B. Du Bois in *The Souls of Black Folk* presents us as a *presumptive glance* that reduces him to the object of the *glance*. Du Bois writes: "In a wee wooden schoolhouse, something put it into the boys' and girls' heads to buy gorgeous visiting cards—ten cents a package—and exchange. The exchange was merry, till one girl, a tall newcomer, refused my card—refused it peremptorily, with a glance. Then it dawned upon me with a certain suddenness that I was different from the others; or like, mayhap in heart and life and longing, but shut out from their world by a vast veil."[145] In this deconstructive mode, the black body is phenomenological "taken outside" of himself and returned in "bad faith" as inferior, different, ostracized, and made a foil to the white body, which, for a black person, is a "solely negating activity . . . a third person consciousness."[146]

What it means to "see" race, what it means to be black—in this case, to be the "problem" in the United States—and to occupy a space marked by racial indifference cannot be ignored. It is no wonder that Michael Jackson attempts to refuse the constraint of identity in racial terms and declares in a dysphoric manner: "I am tired of this stuff . . . I am not going to spend my life being a color."[147] There again, "to have color is to be visible,"[148] to be the "problem" is inescapable. Accordingly, Michael Jackson, as we will see in chapter 3, attempts to forge another identity, *not black*, *not white*, a racial in-betweenness, positioning himself outside of racial normality and thus creating anxiety among the masses. "Leave me alone"[149] would, indeed, be Michael Jackson's plea because I "Gotta have it my way."[150] However, he cannot have it "his way" because as a black man, he is "the problem," as he then realized.[151] This realization can, in part, account for his *Black or White* video[152] in which he draws on the anger that racism produces for blacks and other nonwhites, in the form of objectifying identities, and tries to "reimage the structure of racial identifications"[153] where, for example, a white man metamorphoses into an Asian woman who is then transformed into a Latino man.

And given that the constituting of a black identity is acknowledged to ensue according to the equation (Black = Problem),[154] certainly, the crucial question, "How does it feel to be a problem?"[155] is asked by whites to blacks, which Du Bois with great lucidly argues against. Indeed, that which remains in the very question posed is something questionable about how whites view blacks as the "problem," and is largely an obligation to debunk the notion of blacks as the "problem." Given that the white power structure's discursive rules, guidelines, and practices construct blacks as the problem, this question has materialized from whites' invention of blacks as racialized, which is in opposition to themselves as normalized. Here, Du Bois's diagnostic thinking is modified by a Fanonian insistence on the fact of the epidermalization of race; that is, literally the inscription of race on the skin, the surface of the body. And while epidermalization is not comparable to other marks of difference such as clothing, headwears, and so on, that can be shed, race as marked on the skin is a grid for racial commonsense. In the end, in Fanon's *Black Skin, White Masks*, the search for blacks to overcome their epidermalization is foreclosed.

As we will see later, the transformation of Michael Jackson's skin/flesh from "black" to "white," in spite of its valid explanations, figures so prominently on the debates about Michael Jackson's race identity. These debates present us with one of the most important insights by Fanon that a black person continues to be seen through the "corporeal malediction" of his unavoidable blackness[156] as a problem for the social body. And while whiteness antithesis is blackness, this inessential "other thing," savage, wanton, hypersexual, evil, barbaric, deviant, and uncivilized, a black person is prohibited from developing his sense of "self" and the *will to power*—that is, not power over others but power over himself so that he can give directions to himself and take care of himself, self-care—and to be recognized not as a threat to the white social body[157] and positioned as unequal to whites. In a reflective mode, if Fanon is correct that "what is often called the black [self] is a white man's artifact,"[158] as I mentioned before, there would be a need for a "self" of one's own constitution before a black person can take care of the "self." In fact, Michael Jackson, in his attempt to construct another "self," another identity, *not black* ("other") and *not white* (the self's "other"), I will show in chapter 3, is positioned as an "other 'other' " as a way to discuss Michael Jackson's artefactual identity.

In fact, in the United States, blacks' otherness is not only a function of the state's repressive policies, mass incarceration, segregated and gated communities, and the institutionalization of police violence, for example. It is more importantly a banal consequence of whites' racialized habitus, a form of unconsciously acquired socialized subjectivity which becomes a "second nature" that is nurtured, nourished, and upheld by what the Marxist theorist Louis Althusser aptly defines as the ideological state apparatuses, such as the educational system, the church, the family, and other systems and institutions[159] that insert the white subject into the symbolic order of normalized whiteness. So, if there is a relationship between racist socialization and "the specificity of dominant subject formation,"[160] are whites capable of transcending their racialized habitus? The question stands because the subjectivity of the dominant group is predicated on institutionalized arrangements, systems, and culture that are paramount in its workings to naturalize what the law professor Cheryl I. Harris describes as "whiteness as property." And while it is impossible to disregard John Howard Griffin's *Black Like Me*, the onus for many whites to disaffiliate themselves from racist socialization, their racialized habitus, which corresponds with whiteness as an intrinsic good, is indeed a gargantuan challenge for whites to be able to say, just as Griffin might have said, "Me, too." In fact, the sociologist Ruth Frankenberg reminds us that most whites are glad when they are able to shout defiantly, "I am not that other!"[161]

So, I want to raise the question of what sort of analytical engagement with whiteness would be crucial for an autocritique of racial difference given that blackness is always already reduced to an "absolute indifference."[162] Is Michael Jackson successful, as some have argued, of transcending race? Another question besides the question: Would this engagement consider a form of denaturalizing or deontologizing race as marked on the body? And even though this question does not conjure up easy answers, it is the kind of question that return us to the presumptive hegemony of whiteness, operating "socio-discursively through subjectivity and knowledge production."[163] In other words, power, "far from preventing knowledge,"[164] produces and shapes how blackness is fixed on the body and underlines its overdetermined outsideness that permits and controls the appearance and knowability of race. Then, the readily posed question in its apparently aseptic, benign form as "How does it feel to be a problem?"[165] becomes overriding. This is why I am here concerned not only with the working of power to exclude and marginalize blacks, but how blacks in their marginalized status seek empowerment based on individual and communal self-determination in face of their connection to and disconnection from each other, even though sometimes it is difficult, if not impossible, for blacks to articulate their desires because of their interaction with existing institutions and social practices in which values, beliefs, bodies of knowledges, biases, ideology, and discourse are imposed on them. Effort to upheld whiteness as the norm is illustrative.

I have already hinted to the facticity of whiteness working on the black body. The conclusive remark is that blacks come across various problems in the development of their "bodily schema,"[166] as "a slow composition of myself as a body in the middle of a spatial and temporal world."[167] I find worthwhile, here, in Michel Foucault's *Power/Knowledge: Selected Writings and Interviews*, how "a whole series of multiple and indefinite power relations"[168] can regulate and sanction the racialized body, a conception that uncovers a comparable illustration in Judith Butler's *The Psychic Life of Power: Theories in Subjection* where she explicates that power must be understood "as forming the subject as well as providing the very condition of its existence and the trajectory of its desire."[169] Indeed, how the subject is positioned structurally, on which, in a Foucauldian corpus, the focus is clearly discourse. And even though "discourse is more than 'just language' or 'just text' [and is] also always in practice, which indeed [is] multiple and contestatory,"[170] taking from Judith Butler's *Bodies That Matter*, we can see how racialized discourse is an effect and a source of daily race performativity, reiterations, and daily acts. In other words, race is not a fact. It is materialized out of its continual racialized performance in Judith Butler's sense to make its meaning real.

First and foremost, the harrowing inscription of race on the body makes it difficult for blacks to construct a solid and secure sense of "self." Because of how the body is positioned within racism—that is to say, the bodiliness of racism—the development of a sense of "self," then, for the black subject is never physiological; it is always cultural because a black person's identity is culturally carved on his body. Michael Jackson's skin (surface) becoming "whiter," to a large degree, constructs and determines his race identification process, as some put it, as Michael Jackson not wanting to be black. Furthermore, because racialized "identity and what marks it is defined by the differences that remain," to use Foucault's analysis,[171] we can hear the heartfelt confession of Michael Jackson: "I'm a black American. . . . I'm proud to be a black American. I'm proud of my race."[172]

While I will later examine a black identification process by drawing on the lived experience of Michael Jackson, which serves as a starting point for discussion around the complexities of identification, I want to show how and why a black identity is constrained by race visibility, a truth that is marked on the body, which, in Denise Da Silva words, "the tools of raciality are deployed to protect."[173] And, as we will see with Michael Jackson, even though the black body is continually negotiable and also under construction, how blacks, in the face of whiteness, confront their identity as racialized beings needs to be analyzed.

It is worthwhile, then, to think of how whiteness, in its double valence of subordinating and producing blacks, imposes itself on blacks. My claim is that through cultural practices, epistemologies, visual representations, and the matrices of power and discourse, blacks, for the most part, have internalized cognitive and evaluative schema that replicate whiteness, and it is not easy for any black person who does not uphold an austere regime of self-censorship of whiteness. And since this postulation about whiteness normativity is correct, those who deviate from the cultural norms of whiteness face some opposition from members of their ascribed groups.

How Michael Jackson and all blacks in the United States have difficulties in developing their sense of "self" in a culture that normalizes whiteness as an ontological neutral category that upholds the subject as raceless and unmarked, in which the rights to dominance,[174] is thereby not so far stretched and unusual.[175] The question that interests me, then, is how blacks are imprisoned by the overall aggregate apparatuses (power) and schemes (epistemology) of the tenacity of whiteness, manifesting itself in two opposite directions, in some cases, either to outdo or undo whiteness as in the case of black music, Black Power as is depicted in the dress and the hairstyle, and black literature, which has a long history as a form of resistance to whiteness. That may be what the poststructuralist Michel Foucault means when he acknowledges that "there are no relations of power without resistance."[176] Indeed, as Slavoj Žižek explains, "the power edifice itself is split from within; that is, to reproduce itself and contain its Other, it has to rely on an inherent excess which grounds it."[177] Nonetheless, how blacks are eliminated from America's history, from its civilization, and reduced to culture is something for us to think about.

Michael Jackson and his quandary of identity, as an effect of "erasure, repetition, and resurrection,"[178] besides signifying a body that is not conforming to the social norms, a body that surpasses the maxima of "acceptable bodily performance,"[179] in the discourse of the spectacle and the graphic, it is a body that is still signified as black, which becomes, through no fault of its own, the site of uncontrollable anxiety and abjection. Indeed, the anxieties the black body stirs up will provide a useful starting point for thinking about a black identity as a bodily mark. This is something I take up in details in chapter 2 as I try to carve out the constituting, reconstituting, and deconstituting of a black identity as fixed on the body, which, in a white world, is not ontological but relational. This is an inevitable weight for blacks who are forced to see themselves through whiteness and are forged into "a zone of nonbeing,"[180] lacking any form of racial transcendence.

Furthermore, for blacks, the hermeneutic of whiteness, a priori, has certain implications as visible, "the mysterious, the strange and the terrible,"[181] on par with what Homi K. Bhabha, in "The White Stuff," brands as the "tyranny of the transparent"[182] as a way of structuring, in part, blacks' identity formation. Michael Jackson and his quandary of identity, besides demonstrating the problematics of self-identification for blacks in the United States, provides a useful starting point to analyze the preeminence of whiteness and the specific ways blacks experience their being through normalized whiteness, which inadvertently takes on an unusual form of racial identification. In what follows, I will try to concretize the perception of blackness and a black identity and what this means for blacks in the United States.

Chapter 2

Blackness and a Black Identity

Identity is fundamental to one's self as a "knowing, feeling, and acting subject."[1] It is predicated on norms of identification,[2] including race, gender, class, sexuality, age, and disability—questionably designated as identity categories. Indeed, race identity, for example, has long been assimilated to a mode of existence that operated as a visual marker on the body—with the exceptions of these individuals who managed to "pass" for whites.[3] This reminds me of the court case *Rhinelander v. Rhinelander*, from the 1920s, in which Leonard K. Rhinelander, a white man, discovered that his wife Alice B. Rhinelander was black and wanted a divorce. Her lawyer's defense was that Mr. Rhinelander had to know that his wife was black when they were intimate even before the wedding. Certainly, whites have the luxury of dismissing racial identity when it shores up their interests.

The work of Angela Onwuachi-Willig provides us with "a formative lesson" on race and identity[4] and on the one-drop rule.[5] In order to show that Ms. Rhinelander was black, she "was asked by her lawyer and the judge to bare her breasts to the jury."[6] And while "similar experiences of the body repeat in the lives of blacks,"[7] for black women, her breast is the timely reminder that she *becomes* a woman. I think Walter Benn Michaels provides one way of thinking about passing by asking the right questions: "How then is passing possible?" "How is it possible to pass for something without becoming what it is you pass for?" "How is it possible to pass at all?"[8] These questions, which help us think about a black identity, as Michaels goes on to say, "in a racial system where racial identity is a function of physical appearance—where it is the color of your skin,"[9] show that race is not the sort of identity that can be hidden. Race is real and is lived in its corporeality. This is a fact that cannot be denied. As we will see later, Michael Jackson's racial self-fashioning, seemingly, *not black, not white*, creates a quandary for a black identity undertook as a bodily mark.

Certainly, the corporeality of race is the criterion by which blacks are judged "irrespective of their social or educational attainments."[10] I can see, then, why Howard Winant would put forward that "race is not a matter of color alone. . . . It is more like a way of life, a way of being."[11] This way of being is very similar to Frantz Fanon's notion of race as epidermalized. Indeed, epidermalization reduces the body "to skin,"[12] "to flesh."[13] It becomes a category of the visual, the seen, and it readily and impeccably denotes the body socially. This manifestation is a pressing concern for blacks' identification process, which for blacks is the hallmark of their lived experiences. In this sense, we would disagree with Paul Gilroy's *Against Race: Imaging Political Culture Beyond the Color Line* in which he asserts that "the idea of epidermalization points toward one intermediate stage in a critical theory of body scales in the making of race. Today skin is no longer privileged as the threshold of even identity or particularity."[14] In other words, Gilroy suggests that we give up the idea of race altogether because race, in his words, "can have no ethically defensible place."[15] Gilroy believes that race is a representation and not a presentation that is always already there to be read as a detriment to the social body when black.

This is why we cannot dismiss Fanon's exemplary reasoning that race is evidently fixed on the body. To use the idiom "skin deep," that always already positioned blacks as the "other," these other things, inferior and lacking any kind of racial transcendence, is paramount. Notwithstanding such an eye-opener, race as a bodily mark does not stop the discourse on colorblindness in its newly founded manifesto to reject the meaning of race in regulating social outcomes and to retreat from the original usage of colorblindness in the 1896 landmark case *Plessy v. Ferguson*. In *Plessy*, Justice John Marshall Harlan emphasized that the Constitution is colorblind and to rob one of one's rights because of race was indeed unconstitutional. In the age of multiculturalism and the politics of recognition, the colorblind discourse, going against Harlan's signature conceptualization of colorblindness, is currently making its most noteworthy mark in the political crucible of America's race relations to disavow race. Precisely for this reason, Cornel West, in his cartography of race matters in the United States, is right to remind us that "race matters" because "race is the most explosive issue in American life."[16] And if Fanon's conceptualization that race is epidermalized is correct, in the end, "no one can completely 'pass' because there will always be some sign, some trace of one's true identity.

Moreover, when you are discovered as black, whites bitterly complain about blacks in disgust, "Don't forget. Don't think that you are above race, that you're one of us."[17] After all, you are just a black; you are raced; not like us white folk who are, in Ruth Frankenberg's words, "just human."[18] And it is from this position that whites are able to declare with an air of certainty: "I am not that other."[19]

For blacks, the abiding truth is that, in the words of Charles Mills, "race is so enduringly constitutive of their identity and so enduringly central to white racial consciousness"[20] that race is the signifier, which, even though it is relational and not essential, has a fixed meaning of corporeality and subjects blacks to ill treatment. In other words, blacks cannot sidestep the exclusionary practice of corporeal identity formation; race is the signifier that is pegged to the other signifiers, such as gender, sexuality, disability, and class. The latter, for example, even though it can be hidden behind conduct, language, dress, and, these days, upward racial mobility, the veneer of black success, are viewed as "honorary whites." Nonetheless, one must admit that "honorary whites" is an exceedingly racially charged term,[21] signifying racial difference precisely through its very discursive practice; for example, its claim to be colorblind; that is, not to see race. However, because America's class system is distinctively racialized, blacks are still assumed to be lower class. So it definitely was for American media mogul Oprah Winfrey while traveling in Switzerland. As attests her notorious altercation with a heedless store attendant in a posh Swiss boutique who refused to show her an expensive handbag (38,000 US$) assuming [how wrongly!] that it "was too expensive."[22] So, what can we say about race as a signifier? Race is inescapable. It is like eating to stay alive.

The common signifier of race as "overdetermined from the outside"—that is, a view of race from the "outside"—has certain implications for a compliant racial identification and social subordination. This, when opened to numerous varieties of self-knowledge, attempts to destroy a black person's capacity for self-knowing or, according to the ancient Greek maxim, "know thyself." However, blacks cannot know themselves because what is often called a black "self" is constructed from whiteness. In this sense, one can see why a black person can have difficulties in developing their sense of "self" and to hold on to one's truth, to one's self. Further, because race is never left to its own devices, always surrounded by an atmosphere of antagonism, and is normally dishonored, for blacks, one of the repercussions is an ambivalent self-identification, a denial of the "self."

With significant insistence, Michael Jackson expresses this very idea in his song "I Can't help it" in which he says, "I look in my mirror and it took me by surprise. . . . I can't help it if I wanted to."²³ The ambivalent image of himself that he catches in the mirror exemplifies the complex nature of a black identity reduced to its corporeality. In fact, as we will see later, all the derogative discourses about Michael Jackson are rooted in his corporeality. Indeed, Michael Jackson's corporeal traces become increasingly more problematic to locate since, as he sings, it is *not black, not white*.²⁴ His racial positioning still signals blackness, as will be clearer in chapter 3, and conforms to the racial norms of blackness as a bodily mark. Blackness as a "device can purify the impure, . . . straying brothers and sisters," as Stuart Hall puts it.²⁵

The fixation on blackness as a form of racial indifference where blackness gets in the way of human wholesomeness poses a constraint on blacks' lived experiences. And while we see that a black identity is fixed on the body, there is a contentious relationship of blackness to its outsideness, which can account for antiblack subjugation as a social fact. In any case, once a black identity is fixed on the outside, we treat it as if it were genetics and, as such, it is constantly policed and fashioned against whiteness as the norm.²⁶ Indeed, the aura of an authentic blackness, while set up to mask identity markers such as gender, class, and sexuality differences among blacks and which allows the illusion of sameness, feeds a special kind of comfort in America. It guarantees the status of whiteness as unraced and unmarked.²⁷

Notwithstanding some common cultural particularities that are supposed to make blacks "authentically" blacks (e.g., there is an identifiable "black way" of singing and dancing),²⁸ there is, as Anthony Appiah points out, "this putative authenticity [that] screams out for recognition,"²⁹ and to which multiculturalism and its politics of cultural recognition subscribe. What is undesirable is the facticity of race that subjects blacks to an identity that is marked on the body.³⁰ It is precisely for this reason that these fretful responses to blackness construct are not surprising for Cornel West. Such a construct, he remarks, "rest[s] on a homogenizing impulse that assumed that all black people are really alike—hence obliterating differences (class, gender, sexual orientation) between black people."³¹ Like West, bell hooks puts us on the right track when she famously states that there is "the assumption that there is a black essence shaping all African American experience."³² In other words, the uniqueness that belongs to the individual is buried deep within their blackness and operates at the level of an essentialized blackness, which determines how a black identity is perceived.

While blackness is wrought by the preeminence of whiteness and is constantly shaped and reshaped by a dominant white identity, blacks are trapped between performing and resisting whiteness. Consequently, racial self-identification develops into a pathological condition in which blacks' subjectivity becomes subjugated by a prosecutorial gaze that is directed through the episteme of whiteness. This experience of subjugation leads to an identity "crisis" and a misidentification where the "self" and "other" that provide an anchor for the social construction of whiteness and blackness respectively have become implicated. And even though Michael Jackson, for one, moves between identities *not black, not white*, where his body seemingly appears as a site of profound refusal that permits and controls the appearance and knowability of racial identity, his body, like all racialized bodies, is surrounded by an atmosphere of antagonism that comes with an "implicit knowledge" about the black body as damaged and fragmented, which has a nonliberating effect on his self-expression. This negative image of the black body has been constructed since the start of indentured servitude in America, which allowed for it to be degraded and mutilated. This, in different ways, is still imposed under the upholding and perpetuation of institutionalized violence on the black body.

Much as the inescapable blackness points to the fact that blacks suffer "in their bodies quite differently"[33] from whites, such grief attests to the performative power of whiteness. Whiteness not only functions as the norm but also it is part of a highly regulatory practice that constructs the black subject, in the words of Judith Butler, "as 'less' human, the inhuman, the humanly unthinkable."[34] However, there is something else. Fanon lets us see this; this is how he puts it: "When the Negro makes contact with the white world, a certain sensitizing action takes place";[35] that is, the body is always ready for action. It is useful here to recall the example in chapter one of his book where Fanon describes, in great details, what he would have to physically do if he wanted to smoke. This is a good example of blacks being oriented toward an object, "a description of a 'body-at-home.'" As Sara Ahmed observes, it "is one that can inhabit whiteness"[36] and it feels a certain kind of "comfort" that "suggests well-being and satisfaction."[37] Indeed, as the idiom has it, "there is no place like home," a "body-at-home," "brought home," it seems to me, is not an accomplishment for the black subject, always dependent on the display of a particular "self."

Early in life, blacks are taught to stay in their "place." They are taught, in the name of racial order, not to go beyond certain limits. This is a practice somewhat hard to uphold because it does not come from autonomy or reflexivity. At first, the practice is matter of fact, distinct, and organized, and then it becomes customized and embodied in institutions, systems, laws, and policies that can be traced back to indentured servitude.[38] It is a practice that comes to us from a carefully crafted value system, promoting racial inequality.[39] It forces upon blacks the need to be always active even when we are asleep. In a word, our dreams are, for the most part, active. For me, one of the most interesting things is in the way a black person's dream is always active, or, in Fanon's words, "always of muscular dreams, dreams of aggressive vitality. I dream I am jumping, swimming, running, and climbing; I dream that I burst out laughing, I am leaping across a river and chased by a pack of cars that never catches up with me."[40] And while there is no subject position behind the "I" but an "object" position that attaches itself to the "them," shaping blacks' existentiality, blackness has an ontological vigor of its own, which makes us, and even drives our actions. This is to say, being in the public sphere with others, making one's presence known through words, conducts, and acting in concert with each other, or, to put it differently, to be acknowledged and recognized by each other. Because we are all the same—"that is, human"[41]—plurality is a condition of human action, of being-in-the-world.[42]

In fact, in many instances, blacks have to seek out what Saidiya Hartman, in *Scenes of Subjection*, calls "a space for action,"[43] which is not usually available and accessible and is already compromised because there is never a "space" for blackness where whiteness is the norm. This "seeking out" can become reactional, which weakens a black person's "psychic structure" and, as a result, the ego/self collapses. When this happens, Fanon observes that "the black man stops behaving as an actional person. The goal of his behavior will be The Other (in the guise of the white man), for The Other alone can give him worth. That is, at the ethical level, self-esteem."[44] For blacks, then, one of the repercussions is an ambivalent self-identification, a denial of the self. First of all, "one ceases to experience one's identity from a locus of self-definition and begins to experience one's identity from a locus of externally imposed meaning."[45] That is to say, one is persistently in conflict with one's own persona[46] as the essential "other" of whiteness, fittingly corresponding to Jean-Paul Sartre's idea that it is the anti-Semite that fashion the Jew or Simone de Beauvoir's concept of white women as the indispensable "other" of white men. In a way, this is what is referred to as "the order of otherness," to use Homi Bhabha's key phrase,[47] or, in Michel Foucault words, "the establishment of an order,"[48] which, in terms of a racial order, does not allow for blacks to be positioned outside of such an order.

In the end, because blacks are constructed as black, it is through this construction that blacks come to know themselves. Indeed, "no one knows yet who [blacks] are."[49] If a black person were to be asked for a definition of self, in Fanon's words, "I would say that I am one who waits,"[50] "lying in wait" for the post-black subject, "as a visionary term delineating an ethical or ideal vision of humanity for all people."[51] The post-black subject would embrace a posthuman discourse in spite of it generating, to borrow from the feminist Rosi Braidotti's *The Posthuman*, "its own form of inhumanity"[52] in the face of whiteness. Waiting, then, not only suggests hope for a post-black subject to be reimagined, but the expectation or anticipation of "the end of the world," the death of "the Black" and "the White." As it is, there can be no Hegelian reciprocal recognition among blacks and whites because of the nonexistence of the "absolute reciprocity" between two independent self-consciousnesses that for Fanon exist "at the foundation of the Hegelian dialectic."[53] In the meanwhile, blacks "investigate [their] surroundings, [they] interpret everything in terms of what [they] discover, [they] become sensitive"[54] to "all this whiteness that burns [them]."[55]

There remains the problem: whiteness as seemingly self-contained, when, in fact, whiteness relies on blackness for its preeminence. In fact, whiteness can exist only as the immanent possibility of blackness as its assumed opposite (inferior, primitive, unnatural, and impure). In these regards, whiteness is not self-sustaining in that it depends on blackness to give it shape and meaning. In so doing, "whiteness alone," as Toni Morrison cautions, "is mute, meaningless, unfathomable, pointless, frozen, veiled, curtained, dreaded, senseless, and implacable."[56] Nonetheless, notwithstanding whiteness parasitic relations to blackness, in its image of self-assemblage, the latter is held imprisoned by the coercive power of the former, in its manifesting itself in two opposite directions; blacks are either outdoing or trying to undo blackness that is performatively acted out. And while there is no genuine blackness beneath the performance, blacks must be black in relation to whites. [57]

The opposite does not hold true; whites can be white exclusive of any relation to blacks[58] because, as Diane Fuss observes, "the sign 'white' exempts itself from a dialectical logic of negativity."[59] To put it differently, "white" is always freed from any dependency on the sign "black" for its symbolic constitution. The opposite holds true for the sign "black" because black functions within a racist discourse, "always diacritically, as a negative term in the Hegelian dialectic continuously incorporated and negated."[60] This phenomenon is what can be labeled "the Negro in comparison," to borrow from Fanon.[61] Michael Jackson and his quandary of identity, as we will see, besides aptly demonstrating the problematics of self-identification for blacks in America, provides a useful starting point to think about the preeminence of whiteness and how it has constructed blackness as the antinormative. In these regards, one cannot help following the works of the two black scholars W. E. B. Du Bois and Frantz Fanon on how race, even though it is not a "fact" or a foundational artifact of nature that predates and regulates lives, is, however, viewed as if it were a property of the body organizing blacks' identification process. In this sense, race depends on an assemblage of practices whose immediate and undeviating focus is the body.

In this chapter, I will show that the attempt to construct the category "black" has fundamental implications for racial identification. When blackness is measured against whiteness, it is automatically reduced to otherness. It is, therefore, difficult for a black person to develop a solid sense of "self." And because the black "self" is always constructed as "other," it is constantly interrogated, policed, and subverted by the white gaze. Viewed in this way, racial identification becomes a deeply ambivalent process, leading to the Du Boisian double consciousness, the disintegration of identity into plural identities, which nonetheless is dissolved to a bodily mark, "to skin" where, in the end, blacks are unable to encounter their true "self." And since identity formation, in this sense, is not self-determined and works autonomously from the racial ordering of society in which blacks are "overdetermined from the outside," this manifestation confines them to a liminal and ambivalent space of alterity. It is from this ambivalence that self-identification develops into a condition in which the subjectivity of a black person is always subjugated by a gaze that is directed through the episteme of whiteness. Accordingly, blacks cannot experience their own experiences outside of whiteness.

The Construction of Blackness and Its Implication for a Black Identity

While it is true that gender operates as a visible identity, in Simone de Beauvoir's *The Second Sex*, "one is not born, but rather becomes a woman,"[62] the now accepted fact that gender is socially constructed can be applied to race also as a social concept. This seemingly straightforward conceptualization of how a gender or a race identity is constituted does not mean that gender or race does not exist. In fact, gender or race gives us a better conceptualization of not what gender or race is, but of what it does in terms of its ontology, its epistemology, and its distinctive modalities of visual performance. In the case of race, for example, it is immediately transcribed into a social phenomenon, and the outcome is the bodiliness of racism or, better said, a body that is located within racism. This is precisely what Fanon repeatedly calls the "lived experience of blacks." It is an experience that blacks know firsthand living in a blackphobic society. In the 1995 documentary, *Frantz Fanon: Black Skin, White Mask*, Fanon shares his own disturbing story of being denied the full status of a psychiatrist when a white woman refused to see him as a doctor because of his race. This is just one straightforward example of how the body is positioned within racism. Other examples include racial discrimination during job interviews in a blackphobic society; "white flights" from white neighborhoods when blacks move in;[63] blacks being predisposed to racial profiling; and blacks being singled out as criminals. It is through the bodiliness of racism that the appearance of race functions as a hegemonic and forceful power.

In any event, Michael Jackson's video *Black or White* tackles issues of racism and shows how race imprisons blacks' lives. His video attempts to provide an alternative way *to be* (being), to "reimagine the structure of racial identifications" that have dominated race relations in the history of the United States. His words might appear naïve to some when he sings that "[i]t's not about races, just places."[64] However, the real anger expressed in the video is against a form of racism that fixes blacks as the "other thing," a racism that allows grown black men to be addressed as "boy" by devotional racists, as Michael Jackson is called when, on a "thriller killer"[65] night, he takes a white girl (his baby) "on a Saturday bang." "Boy" is meant to humiliate and to irritate. This kind of naming (boy) as a citational practice reduces blacks to second-class citizenry and silences them. Adrienne Rich, in her work, clearly captured the way silence functions "in a world where language and naming are power" by concluding that silence is "oppression and [psychological] violence."[66] After listening, searching for the words, with great courage Michael Jackson states: "I had to tell them I ain't second to none." His "telling" is not heard because the words of a black person are never heard.[67] In other words, the dominant social positioning of the white listener prevents the possibility of listening to materialize and, more so, the dominant way of "knowing" everything there is to know about blacks informs a certain kind of epistemology that operates as the tyrant of truth.

In fact, because of the charged stereotype of the violent, lawless, primitive, and oversexed black man, black men are basically not to be trusted around white women. This simple fact puts all black men at risk of being literally and symbolically castrated. In the meanwhile, the assumption of whiteness as desire flaunted in the parks; on television; in films, books, magazines, newspapers; on university campuses; in the board rooms of corporations; in the laws, institutions, and systems; in everyday discourse and language; on the streets; at the banks, homeownerships, and courthouses; in hiring and promotions; in attitudes and behaviors; in the doctor's office; on the tram; in neighborhoods; and in the schools and day cares is certainly inescapable and retains the phantasmatic view of itself. In fact, at one time in the United States, a black man couldn't under any circumstances even look at a white woman, much less date her or take her "on a Saturday bang."[68] We all remember the horrifying story of Emmett Till, a black fourteen-year-old boy from Chicago who was murdered by two white men, Roy Bryant and J. W. Milam, in Delta Mississippi on August 28, 1955, for supposedly whistling at a white woman, Carolyn Bryant, in a grocery store.[69] Henry Champly, in *White Women, Coloured Men*, is convinced that black men "have discovered the white woman as an idol worthy of being desired above all else."[70] On this note, Champly begs white women to reject the allure of sexual promiscuity and miscegenation and return to what he calls "erotic humility."[71]

And while white women are positioned as the gender norm, black women are outside of the norm. At the end of the day, it seems to me that it would be an oddity to deny that for black women, gender and race are not mutually exclusive, which brings us to the concept of intersectionality,[72] a term that has been lately introduced into the hermeneutics and analysis of black women's experience of oppression and attempts to explain how sexism, racism, classism, and other forms of oppressive systems intersect to unequally position black women as the "other." And if there is "an end of racism" as is suggested by some, can we say, then, that an end to racism would automatically change how black women would experience sexism, or how black gays, lesbians, or transpeople would experience discrimination, for example? In any case, it is unquestionable that the visibility of race trumps gender positioning since gender identity is not seen in its entirety. It always shows race as asking to be seen. And since there is no end to how blacks are positioned as raced beings, how race serves the particular purpose of naming the social phenomenon of the bodiliness racism and its broader cultural dynamics to entrap blacks in the realm of corporeality, which attaches social meanings to the racialized body, is not without significance.[73]

Fanon illustrates this in *Black Skin, White Masks* by pointing to the case of a little white boy who, in the face of "seeing" race, cries out, "Look, a Negro! . . . mama, see the Negro! I'm frightened!" Why is the child afraid of a black person? The child must already know that the black person is fearful. And while the child's outburst exemplifies the ways in which the visuality of race is readily transferred to its social meaning, the black body is returned to themself in bad faith as inferior, different, ostracized, and a foil to the white body. Significantly, one might say, then, that this form of black characterologicalism locates its comeback when Fanon writes, with great precision, the following:

> My body was given back to me sprawled out, distorted, recolored, clad in mourning in that white winter day. The Negro is an animal, the Negro is bad, the Negro is mean, the Negro is ugly; look, a nigger, it's cold, the Negro is shivering because he is cold, the little boy is trembling because he is afraid of the nigger, the nigger is shivering with cold, that cold that goes through your bones, the handsome boy is trembling because he thinks that the nigger is quivering with rage, the little white boy throws himself in his mother's arms: Mama the nigger's going to eat me up.[74]

While in this event Fanon draws on "difference embodied"—that is, the body as the material ground for blacks' social existence—he further points out that the black body is returned to them as inferior, as a weight and an annoyance, which rob them of subjectivity and a sense of "self"; that is, of who they actually are. As a result, to "become a self," a black person is forced to take on another "self," which is not a "self" of one's own choosing. However, in Michael Jackson's case, in his attempts at self-fashioning, he chooses another "self," *not black, not white*. Of course, this is not allowed; and, as we will see later, Michael Jackson has to undergo "racial discipline," a form of castigation that both produces and regulates the raced bodies.[75]

This is the reason why any critique of this form of "becoming-self" forced upon black will remain incomplete. We can clearly see that the self that *becomes*, in the Beauvoirian sense, is a false self in the Sartrean sense; a false self, detaching blacks from a self of their own creation and impelling them, in Fanon's words, "to run away from [their] own individuality"—that is, to be uncomfortable by their own presence,[76] to be inauthentic.[77] While this uncomfortableness denotes an absence, a lack, and a stress on the body, "the phenomenological return of the black body"[78] is a "solely negating activity . . . a third person consciousness."[79] In this Fanonian formulation, we get a good idea of how the reciprocal hermeneutic relationship between the physical and social constructs of race as impurity, as the seemingly unnatural state from which the black identity is constituted, and as a social, moral, and aesthetic debasement[80] are made possible. Even more concisely, race is a not just a social construct; it is physical as well. It threatens and obscures black self-identity. As such, it is not I who construct an identity for myself, but it is the identity that was already there, preexisting, awaiting my existence.[81]

We see this clearly with the case of Michael Jackson going against the ascribed black identity as a bodily mark and trying to construct another possible identity, *not black, not white*. Michael Jackson, for one, moving between identities *not black, not white*, where his body seemingly appears as a site of profound refusal that permits and controls the appearance and knowability of race, by its very existence, unsettles the artificial social fact constituting blacks as an authentic group, which, of course, fuels a habitual anxiety for the social body. Like all blacks in the United States, Michael Jackson, as a racialized "other," is "perceived on the level of the body image, absolutely not-self—that is, the unidentifiable, the unassimilable,"[82] in which one's identification is in opposition to whiteness as the norm.[83] And this is where Sara Ahmed's work helps us see how and why the dominant structures, systems, ideology, and epistemology enable whiteness sustainability and functionality. As a matter of fact, "whiteness," Ahmed notes, "is what [society] is oriented 'around,' so that even bodies that might not appear white still have to inhabit whiteness, if they are to get 'in,'"⁸⁴ the "space" that is marked White, with a capital W. When blacks appear in "white space," they are viewed as "out of place," "out of space." To put it differently, black bodies stand out when they are "out of place." After all, such "standing out" unsettles and resettles the whiteness of the space.⁸⁵

From the constitutive and hegemonic positioning of whiteness, seemingly, we cannot move beyond the dichotomization of the white self from the black "other." As it happens, it is this very insidious dichotomy that maintains the ultimate conditions of blacks as the antithesis of whites, in categorical terms, as inferior and uncivilized, and shapes and reinforces other cultural images of alterity and stereotypes that determine blacks' identification process. Blackness produces and fashions the milieu for all kinds of ill treatment, including social exclusions and injustice. These experiences are, for the most part, anticipated by the receivers. Yet the anticipation does not erase the pain and humiliation they experience when such occurrences materialize in their daily lives.

Furthermore, the meaning of blackness and its signifiers, such as loud music and hoodies, are formed and produced in such a way that they appeal to racial commonsense, as a technique of the legitimization of power. For instance, Jordan David's loud music and Trayvon Martin's hoodie got them killed by Michael Davis Dunn and George Zimmerman, respectively, leaving no room for a nostalgic return to a class analysis because in the United States class is racialized. Yet, the racialization of class is overlooked so as to make it easier to categorize poor blacks as lacking in *will* and to view them literally as the "underclass," an essential pronouncement which is devoid of any critical analysis as a racist term. To put it in a different way, even when blacks strive for middle- and upper-class status, they always occupy a lobbying and disquieting position. Blacks are always presumed to be lower class, or, what they have been made into, "the underclass." *Am I that name?*, interestingly, continues to be the existential question for all blacks. In other words, while poor blacks are seemingly made to own the signifier "underclass," all blacks are subjected and hailed as the "underclass." And since the fate of the black middle and upper classes remain tied to poor blacks because of the racial dynamic entrenched in the economy, culture, and body politics, an entire citizenry is impacted.

The white self is signified as disparate from the black "other." It is in this instant of demarcation that the privileged matrix for the technique of dominance, in the form of the presumptive hegemony of whiteness—the interlocking alignment of knowledge, power, spatial position, and history—is fashioned and disseminated. And since whiteness defines blacks not in themselves but as relative to whiteness, in that—whiteness is the "subject," the absolute, and blackness is the "other," the incomplete—blacks are thus led to make an object of their whole selves, to set up themselves as the "other," or, as Fanon explains and describes it, for not only must blacks be black; blacks must be black in relation to whites.[86] This is to say, "on the level of the body image," as "a certain existence which is more than that which the idealist calls representation, but less than which the realist calls a thing—an existence placed half way between the 'thing' and the representation,"[87] the black person is subordinated to the white person as the "other." Here, I am reminded of Fanon's famous observation: "The real Other for the white [person] is and will continue to be the black [person]."[88]

Also, a black person's "contact with white society has opened new vistas, new ideals in his[/her/their] imagination."[89] Hence, they want to appallingly "behave" like whites, since, to use Sara Ahmed's phase, "to be black in a white world is to turn back towards itself."[90] To sum it up, blacks are the "other" for whites, and for itself a fixed object sealed into a "crushing objecthood"[91] without "ontological resistance"[92] to the white gaze, which reduces blacks to the object of the look where there is *no exist*. The racist interpellation, "Look, a Negro!" or, "Dirty Nigger!" stops a black person in their track.[93] To be stopped "is not just stressful: it makes the 'body' itself the 'site' of social stress."[94] Worse still, to be stopped is to experience negation, to feel "out of place." One finds oneself "becoming neither an 'I' nor a 'not-I' "[95] but basically "an object in the midst of other objects."[96] In a black person's experience, as Fanon reveals, "the movements, the attitudes, the glances of the other fixed me there, in the sense in which a chemical solution is fixed with a dye."[97] But, what is more, when blacks are viewed as a threat to the social body, as is expressed in the white child's outburst, "Mama, see the Negro! I'm frightened,"[98] the very body of a black person stresses, fragments, and finally bursts apart. That is, the body is without protection. So, the question is, in its simple rhetorical form, what else could it be for the black person but "an amputation, an excision, a hemorrhage" that covered the whole black body with black blood?[99] Is it a blood "which never dries"? The most immediate reaction for the black person is to take oneself off from one's own presence and make oneself "an object."[100] At this point, one is convinced that a black person "is forever in combat with his own image,"[101] which starts and finishes fiercely fragmented.

But there is something else manifesting itself in blacks' struggle for self-determination, which is of great signification. Given that blacks have access to whiteness as terrorizing, hostile, and aggressive, blacks are equipped with a gift to conceive how things are arranged and seen. They are endowed with the great power of discernment, or what W. E. B. Du Bois in *The Souls of Black Folk* calls "a second sight," a second way of seeing that "resees"; that is, that sees again otherwise; in this particular case, they see whiteness in an evaluative mode.[102] bell hooks, in her chapter "Representing Whiteness in the Black Imagination," in a less optimistic and unsurprising mode, explains her students' discomfort to learn that blacks critically evaluate whites. For hooks, her students' amazement that the gaze of blacks is directed toward whites does not stop there. What can be derived from the discomfort is about whites who get it wrong, who think too highly of themselves, and, in the process, as hooks rightfully assesses, this discomfort "is an expression of racism,"[103] which is not just systematic but is expressed in what can be called "racism in talk." It is "in talk" that hooks's white students make known the mere conceitedness of whiteness. Crucial to this position of hooks's students, by the way, is the existence of "racism in talk" expressed as a form of psychic projection where the dominant group (the "I") projects and the subordinated "other" (the "them") is projected upon.[104] I take it, then, that such a form of racism equips all whites with "talk" that suggests a false sense of ontological superiority over blacks,[105] which, nonetheless, implies a certain kind of confidence and comfort in its expression.[106]

Following from this, of course, is to see that while the black experience "is not a whole," in that there is not merely one black, there are blacks,[107] there is nonetheless an ontological specificity of blackness, given that blackness is constructed against the concept of race as "overdetermined from the outside." How, then, does blackness construct and uphold a black identity that is associated with the norms of racial identification? And what are the implications for the lived experience of blacks in the United States? These are the questions that are inevitably brought to light, suggesting that one way to come to terms with the "lived experience of blacks" is, as I have hinted before, to take into consideration a complicated articulation that a black person through blackness constructivism becomes black but can never be black. To think of this differently, from the beginning in the United States, the construction of blackness and of those who fashioned, elaborated, and upheld it was and continues to primarily be a group of white men.[108] Marilyn Frye's *The Politics of Reality* makes an influential contribution to help us see the syncretizing power of maleness and whiteness. Blackness, then, in Frye's important intervention, to borrow from her, "is *their* construct."[109]

Sadly, what is often overlooked is that blacks' untainted beings are not yet known to the white world. Fanon responds to this with enthusiasm and certainty. In *Black Skin, White Masks*, Fanon lets us see that "no one knows yet who [the black] is, but he knows that fear will fill the world when the world finds out. And when the world knows the world always expects something of the Negro. He is afraid lest the world knows, he is afraid of the fear that the world would feel if the world knew."[110] For now, any attempt of blacks to show to the world that they are bestowed with honorable and exulted capacities—that is, "to write themselves into being,"[111] (*to be*) contra nonbeing (*not to be*)—is what Fanon defines as "existence," the quotidian production of blacks' lives consolidated by antiblack racism, a multidimensional schema of conditions, facts, undertakings, and practices in excess, expressed, for example, in police violence directed at blacks. Other forms of antiblack racism can be seen in the growing poverty in black communities, as the number of black ghettos and superghettos increases, and a large prison population is black and on death row.

Meanwhile, blacks' existence is, of course, an artifact of the white world. It is an acceptance of blackness as acceptable truths about the racialized body. Here are some of the effects, according to Charles Mills's "An Illuminating Blackness": "Blackness really indicates not a particular brand of wavelengths but a particular social position, and not any subordinated nonwhite position but a particular location within the nexus of multiple oppressions created by white supremacy,"[112] insofar as it leaves whiteness normalized. At the same time, normalization makes it possible to individualize, to measure gaps to differentiate according to the norm whose function, while constraining all deviations by its standard measures, makes differences intelligible. However, when blackness enters the terrain, intelligibility falls through the cracks, like an addict waiting for a fix or a person straddled on a desert with no food or water. So, what we can say about normalization is that it "keeps watch over the excessive and the exceptional, delimiting the outcast who threatens the order of normalcy"[113] that is construed from the perspective of whiteness: one, whiteness, claiming for itself the grand position of transcendental signifier, allows for whites to draw their ideological power from being unraced and unmarked; two, whiteness continuously elevates itself over the category of blackness; and three, whiteness asserts itself as "an essential something"[114] and as a form of property that only whites own. Certainly, the ownership of a property, a "possessive investment," is not simply transportable and, in some cases, is nonnegotiable.

In fact, whites do not need to be members of white-supremacist groups to hold on to their "possessive investment" in their whiteness. White privilege perceived as expected and accepted is constantly embraced and affirmed by both whites and blacks. This is a good illustration of how the social and epistemological facts of whiteness have projected unto society particular ways of acting, feeling, thinking, and knowing; in other words, of what it means to be white. Needless to say, while blacks have accepted whiteness normality, whites have been confined and conditioned by whiteness habitus, which, as I have already mentioned, can connect habits to what is unconscious and unchanging, or what becomes a "second nature," is to suggest that whiteness is what bodies do or can do. And while the performativity of whiteness is preserved and enhanced in accordance with the norms of whiteness, it worsens when it is assumed to be incognito; that is, when it goes unrecognized.[115] Whiteness, as invisible to whites, held sway until the recent rise of whiteness studies as a framework for analyzing and conceptualizing the importance for whites, in Cheryl I. Harris's sense, to recognize and acknowledge their "property rights in whiteness."[116]

On the other hand, black is so black that it is now "blue"; that is, blue as in the blues where the blues singer Louis Armstrong, in his song "Black and Blue," lets us know, "my only sin is my skin."[117] The problem before us, in this regard, is that skin is a social and corporeal attribute ascribed to blackness as distinct from whiteness as the norm.[118] In a word, blackness is "like itself," in Sara Ahmed's phrase, "a form of family resemblance."[119] It extends "the family form. Other members of the race are 'like a family,' just as the family is defined in racial terms. The analogy works powerfully to produce a particular version of family, predicted on 'likeness,' where likeness becomes a matter of 'shared attributes,' "[120] skin color. And while "share" is often referred to as having something in common, "likeness is a sign of inheritance; to look like a family is to look alike."[121] The strength of Ahmed's remarks, as I understand them, is that a "good likeness" is not enough. As a result, to say that in this, "all blacks look alike" and other idioms that group all blacks as the "same" is to make blacks feel uncomfortable in their skin, exposed, visible, and different from those who are "being like" whites.[122] And since blacks are reduced to a bodily mark that is visible, important differences among blacks are overlooked.

The visible indication of blackness becomes the ground for the slow production of the "historico-racial schema." That is to say, the deposited personal experience of the bodiliness of racism that obfuscates the development of blacks' "bodily schema," which is culturally fashioned by racist discourse and "is the definitive structuring of self and of the world," creating a "dialectic between [the black body] and the world"[123] in such a way that the formation of a "self" advances through interaction with not only other objects but also with the "thousands of details, anecdotes, stories"[124] out of which blackness has been woven out of whiteness. Blacks therefore exist as a communal subject whose principal misrepresentation is not personal but social. In the meanwhile, the black body "is surrounded by an atmosphere of certain uncertainty."[125] Agreeably, it is from this perspective that antiblackness and its problematics are materialized.

Blackness and Its Problematics

If race is affiliated with blackness as a social category and a social reality, the construction of blackness presents the problem of race and racism as two overlapping but sharply differentiated occurrences. In fact, racism makes sure that blacks have little or no range of personal choice, entitlement, and power. Indeed, racism produces race. Race, then, must be located within the presumptive hegemony of whiteness that gives blackness its othered status. And since, in the United States, the coherence of the outsideness of blackness is upheld, reinforced, and maintained through racist discourse, epistemology, and ideology, it is not without remorse that our attention is drawn to how racism hamstrings blacks and generates benefits for whites even if whites are trying to unlearn their racism and recognize their privileged position. In a word, being white safeguards whites from the distresses that blacks a posteriori encounter living with racism.

Michael Jackson, for one, desires a world beyond racism, as we see in his video *Black or White*, for example. And although Michael Jackson's "Man in the Mirror" is disconnected from the real causes of oppression, desires a world beyond the economy of racism, and suggests that "if you want to make the world a better place take a look at yourself, and then make a change,"[126] it is the philosopher Naomi Zack who persuasively reminds us that blacks "cannot effectively resist racism from within a racialized identity."[127] In such a view, being racially othered reduces a black person to marginalization. When one acts from the margins, one is indeed viewed as tactless. And this affects one at the level of their own subjectivity. And since the "other" is always ascribed a racial identity, in drawing attention to this, it makes sense to ask, what it means, then, to reject a black identity as Michael Jackson does in his song "Black or White": "I'm not going to spend my life being a color,"[128] he confesses. Does this free one from the perniciousness that goes along with one's so-called blackness? Indeed, it is not so easy to escape from the perils of "racial constructivism," which includes, as Charles Mills describes, "an actual agreement of some under conditions where the constraints are not epistemic (getting at the truth) but political (establishing and maintaining [white] privilege)."[129] Along the same line, the ontological question *what is a black?* is hard to answer because of the outsideness of blackness, which is instantaneously recognizable as the inessential "other thing"—violent, immoral, hypersexual, evil, savage, abnormal, and uncivilized in the relations to a whiteness void of racial imperfections and nonthreatening.[130] Clearly, the outsideness of blackness assumes these negative characteristics. It is made clear and it is often reinforced by what Judith Butler, in *Frames of War: When is Life Grievable?*, refers to as "media framing"; that is, the many ways in which the media's rhetoric, language, ideology, and discourse produced an implicit image of blacks as criminals, for example, and how this image corresponds to the political, legal, and social discourses that indoctrinate many whites' views about blacks. It is no wonder that the white child panics on seeing blackness and cries out, "Mama, see the Negro! I'm frightened!"[131]

To be black is always, as the titles of Michael Jackson's albums have it, to be *Bad* and *Dangerous*. Blacks are generally considered as a threat to the white social space. Whites do in fact become very anxious when they are in close proximity to those they see as more or less radically different and assume their inherent inferiority and barbaric ways. We do remember that when whiteness became anxious, the Jim Crow laws were enacted. The General Allotment Act (The Dawes Severalty Act) of 1887 followed, which brought the annihilation of First Nations communities. Other Acts (laws) included the Chinese Exclusion Act of 1882, The Immigration Act of 1924, the Tydings-McDuffe Act of 1934, and the Japanese internment camps. Today, the actions and practices of anxious whiteness are proliferated in state violence, white flights, racial profiling, urban renewal programs, and gated communities.

Given that these gated communities are marked *Whites Only*, blacks who try to enter these spaces are always under surveillance, watched, policed, controlled, and registered as nonmembers. They are literally considered as "out of place" in "this space" like a piece of trash, a piece of dirt that is "out of place" in one's bedroom, kitchen, or living room,[132] which does not belong there and thus must be discarded, removed, and returned to its "proper" place. The act of "registering those who are out of place" actually serves to "create strangers and establish a direction toward them, as those who threaten the place of the 'in place,' as those who generate anxiety"[133] for the white social body. And given that space operates as one of the chief signifiers of racial differences, openness of movement within space turns out to be a white prerogative.[134] Whiteness, in this sense, is viewed as nonthreatening even though it always threatens and terrorizes a body that is "out of place." Indeed, when whiteness views itself as benign, as nonthreatening, dare I say, it endorses a phantasmatic view of itself, which leaves blackness as "a problem," in the Du Boisian sense.[135] To say the least, one can hear whites remarking that blacks make themselves "a problem." "What's wrong with blacks?" But the truth is that blacks a priori are made "a problem" so that whiteness can be constituted unproblematically.

The crucial point here is that blacks are reduced to their black skin and are deprived of alternative identitarian means. When whites see blacks as black, it is to see enough because blackness conjures "false seeing"; that is to say, the inability of whites to "see" the unseen epistemologies, ideologies, and practices that have shaped their negative beliefs about blacks in a world in which whites see themselves as the bona fide members.[136] This is why, as John Berger demonstrates, "the relationship of what we see and what we [believe] is never settled."[137] In other words, because what we "see" is, for the most part, influenced by what we believe, the way we "see" or don't see is predisposed by what we already believe. Because blackness is believed to be the invisible and unrecognizable standard that continues to negate and marginalize a black person, "to see him[/her/them] as black is not to see him[/her/them] at all. His[/her/their] presence is a form of absence."[138] Regardless of class location, through the hermeneutics of the graphicality of blackness, blacks are positioned in a world that forces them to be like Ralph Ellison's "invisible man" who is "seen" and yet not "seen."

After all, no individual or group that is positioned outside of whiteness can sustain itself properly.

What Is at Stake for Blacks?

The construction of a black identity as a bodily mark, an open site of otherness, imposes itself on blacks who try to abide by such an imposition. The bodily mark has a "high social profile," in the sense that it affects how the racialized body is observed and responded to. In addition, the bodily mark of race conditions blacks to the worst effects of the others' gaze and paves the way for the grouping of blacks into a racialized category, which in turn shapes and determines how blacks are positioned in a world that offers them no true self-consciousness but lets them see themselves through the revelation of whiteness. In entering this discussion, we need to draw from W. E. B. Du Bois's "double consciousness" as one of the key problems of blacks' existence, which lends itself to the significant question: What does it mean to be black in the United States, to have an identity that first and foremost is determined by the color of your skin? This issue, I think, can be imaginatively responded to by turning to Frantz Fanon's *Black Skin, White Masks*. Fanon declares that the black person has difficulties in developing their sense of self.

Blacks draw their power from either performing whiteness, to undo "blackness," or to outdo blackness. In both ways, it is a certain refusal of prescribed identification. Indeed, to undo "blackness" is another way to be positioned as the ex-colored man as is depicted in James Weldon Johnson's *The Autobiography of an Ex-Colored Man*, where the black man imitates whiteness and "passes" for white. In performing whiteness, does he do so naturally, without, to use Fuss's words, "that coefficient of play, of imitation,"[139] characterizing whiteness? Is it possible to separate the imitation from what is not imitated, which in this case is blackness? Does he (the black man) still remain largely outside of whiteness because there is no authenticity behind the performance? So, is he pierced by a sensation of not having a "true" identity? To avoid the harsh realities of living in a blackphobic society, the black man submits himself to another kind of ridicule, to a racial in-betweenness, *not black, not white*, which, as Michael Jackson as an artist exemplifies, still signals an unavoidable blackness revealed by the performative function of race culturally identified in his dance style.

Nonetheless, the singer's in-betweenness as an ever-changing and self-contradictory subject position maintains identity continuously at arm's length and keeps it uncertain. It is exactly identity that is deferred by the work of identification, identity that remains in a state of exile, "gathering place." In other words, Michael Jackson's racial in-betweenness, *not black, not white,* is in constant interpretations, caught in, in Fuss's term, "a system of cultural relays"[140] that make his racial identity complex and irresistible to debates. This leads to name-calling and othering as in "Michael Jackson is a freak or is weird." Weirdness, in the face of blackness, in no uncertain terms, pervades the tabloids. Furthermore, weirdness or freakiness is subject to the most extreme form of disparagement because blackness constructs a body that is already defiant of social norms.

On the other hand, the outdoing of blackness is a part of the newfangled discrete variant of African American culture, a "crucial site in the struggle over power, identity, and meaning"[141] that progressively reconfigures itself through rap and hip-hop music, dance, dress, and Ebonics as foils to white social norms and leaves antiblackness in place. Touré's *Who's Afraid of Post-Blackness: What It means to Be Black Now* makes use of the term "postblackness." "Postblackness," indeed, "points . . . to the end of the reign of a narrow single notion of Blackness."[142] It resignifies the end to "blackness" constructivism as pathology. Maybe, it is to embrace blacks' pathology "without the pathos; to create a transvaluation of pathos itself";[143] to move blackness away from the distinguishing norms of recognition as a bodily mark. Yet, what unites blacks with each other is not merely a bodily mark, the unmistakable blackness, "like itself," its outsideness; to be sure, it is the visceral pain that accompanies blackness outsideness that blacks share, which Achille Mbembe attempts, in his lecture at Duke University, to explain as "the politics of viscerality." As I understand it, "the politics of vicerality" is another way to think of how racial violence, for example, is played out "in our viscera, in our experience, and our internal-felt self," which, by extension, is a form of anxiety for blacks because it is there, in the body, that the actual outcomes of racist discourses and acts are realized.

In any event, my concern here is that through cultural practices, epistemologies, visual representations, and the matrices of power and discourse, blacks, for the most part, have internalized cognitive and evaluative schema that replicate whiteness, and it is not easy for any black person, even if he is the King of Pop, not to uphold an austere regime of self-censorship. One reason for this is that blacks depend on such a representation for their existence. Even if blacks work hard at creating "another" identity, as is the case of Michael Jackson, in the end, it is not how one defines oneself, but how a racist society constructs and defines blacks that matters. What comes to mind is how a black identity, for instance, was defined by the one-drop rule (of blood), which established that a person "having any African blood in their veins" is black and created the pressure for blacks who pass as whites to assimilate whiteness. We get from James Weldon Johnson, in *The Autobiography of an Ex-Colored Man*, that while passing is an important means for enjoying white privilege, the psychological cost of passing is very often greater than the reward. It is a case of self-alienation. The case of Anatole Broyard is illustrative. Broyard "wanted to be a writer, not a black writer. So, he chooses to live a lie rather than be trapped by the truth" of blackness, "an identity that other people have invented and he had no say in."[144] He shed his black identity to become a writer, as Henry Louis Gates Jr. remarks, "who writes endlessly about shedding a past and an identity."[145] This is a good example of the psychological debts of running away from blackness to take on whiteness.

On the other hand, "what is it about whiteness," as the cultural critic Kobena Mercer asks, "that makes the white subject want to be black?"[146] I suppose, these days, it is hip for some urban white kids to "act black";[147] that is, to willfully repeat the stereotypes of African American pop culture and adopt a "black" persona in their verbal communication, dress, hairstyle, and music with the hope to take on some form of "honorary blackness." This is to say, as Mercer does, "a kind of strategic self-othering in relation to the dominant cultural norms."[148] In some cases, it may be a desire on the part of whites to outdo blacks in their "blackness" and to exceed the logics of blackness as a notable determination to make it more "other" than the Others,[149] which is to say, of course, "do blackness" and identify, for example, with the hip-hop culture.

An important question: Can "honorary blackness" be extended to "race changing?" To get at the heart of this matter, let us take the case of Jane Lazarre's *Beyond the Whiteness of Whiteness: Memoir of a White Mother of Black Sons*. To speak, as Lazarre does, of the tensions between having white skin and rejecting whiteness and taking on blackness (honorary blackness) as her social identity is of great signification. In other words, as Lazarre sees it, her social identity as "black" is hidden by her white skin. Is her "crossing over" or "passing over" to blackness an example of "race changing"? And even though Lazarre's actions are well meant, to "cross over" racial boundaries, or "crossing" in every sense, is a privilege reserved only for whites.

"Honorary blackness" is not conditional, itinerant, or temporal, as is the entry of blacks into "honorary whiteness," which is a racially charged category wrongly projecting the inertia of race and its ontological status. And while paradoxically, "honorary whiteness" claims also to be colorblind—that is, not to see race—it signifies racial difference precisely through its framework. "Honorary whiteness" is in fact more about passing as the "right kind" of black, those who work hard not to make whiteness apprehensive and to repress the notion "to rock the boat" in a sea of whiteness. Even though nothing good can spring from "the sea of whiteness," "honorary whiteness" inscribes and prescribes that blacks can simply never be white. In a word, *to be like* whites is never the same as *to be* white. And while passing these days is about securing a license for entry into "honorary whiteness," as with the several examples I have already provided, "black is black."[150] It is true that blacks can enter "the white world," as Cheryl I. Harris cogently puts it, "albeit [it is] a false passport, not merely passing but trespassing."[151] It is not surprising, then, that if "honorary whiteness" can be bestowed, it can also be withdrawn.

It is hard for a black person to "cross over" because to be "black" is determined not from the "inside" but is overdetermined from the "outside." Once again, blackness outsideness as overburdened and saturated by racist interpellations such as "Look, a Black! See that Black! I am frightened!" cannot be disavowed. The certainty and undoubtedly "fact of blackness" is what Jared Sexton calls with Orlando Patterson "social death,"[152] "the social life of social death."[153] In other words, blacks' lives are not yet lived in a world where whiteness is the norm. We do need to repeat, here, that a norm is never originary; it is a response to the anti-normative—in this case, blackness, which precedes whiteness. In other words, blackness is *ante*-normative.

Consider, on this score, that "honorary black," as Mercer puts it, "encodes an antagonistic subject position on the part of the white subject in relation to the normative codes of [whiteness],"[154] and "honorary blacks," however, still enjoy the countless privileges that come with white skin. As far as I can tell, "honorary blackness" does not actually signal an ontological shift in whiteness; that is to say, these "honorary blacks" cannot feel the pains that come with blackness as a bodily mark. Keeping in mind that race is inscribed on the body, blacks are unable to transcend their race as the signifier that works to promote ill treatment of them. Other identity markers such as gender, class, sexuality, speech and language impairment, and disability have been put out of articulation because of race, a matter of racial law, an all-encompassing affinity to a black identity. So, what does this say about the respect for identities (in the plural) as is prescribed by identity politics whose present phase is multiculturalism, where the emphasis apparently is no longer on cultural assimilation (the melting pot) but the recognition and celebration of differences?[155] Yet, differences among blacks, women, and sexual minorities, for example, have to be disregarded in the name of the politics of difference.

In fact, Michael Jackson's videos, from *Beat It* to *Thriller* with various forms of ensemble dance, are made to "heal differences," in David Brackett's words.[156] But, in reality, while race defines one's cultural identity and one is made to feel that cultural pride would prove and make good one's difference in skin color, in fact, it is an endless reminder that one is different.[157] In this respect, difference is comprehended as cultural specificity; that is, as what is culturally different about an individual whose meaning, at the very least, is tied to race as the signifier. Or, put slightly differently, identity becomes synonymous with difference (otherness) as one illustration of how multiculturalism, for example, developing from a racialist ontology, cannot resist the trappings of promoting cultural otherness. This would mean, significantly, that we do agree with Walter Benn Michaels's conclusion that cultural recognition "is a form of racism."[158] What we have here is another form of the "new racism" veiled with cultural reasoning, the redemptive project for the toleration (and toleration here is the key) of cultural differences as obligation. It is, in other words, that culture is the metonym for race.

Blacks who try to deviate from the cultural norms of whiteness by developing their own sense of style in their clothes, hairstyles, walk, and talk, as attempted willful acts of resistance, which are self-affirming and sustaining and which amount to "be black," are not to be taken for granted. And even though acts of resistance are inevitable within relations of domination, for the most part, these acts are taken to be "ghetto" in nature. As a result, these acts are indeed not without their critics and, for the most part, confronted by oppositions, sometimes even from other blacks. And if it is important to draw this out, it is precisely to point out how resistance to whiteness, in terms of other ways of knowing and being in the world, returns blacks to racist stereotypes even from members of both their ascribed group and other racially marginalized groups.

Michael Jackson's self-identification process, a severe redundancy of artifactual racial otherness of the sort that it made possible, for example, with hair straightening and dyeing, and countless plastic surgeries, is criticized with a great amount of harshness. However, what is revealed—a kind of unsurprising revelation—is that Michael Jackson's act of self-expression is read as outside the recognizable norm of race assignment, *not black, not white*, as another form of continual misidentification, playing a foundational role in the dialectic of *not black* ("other") and *not white* (the self's "other") while concealing the essentially "ambivalent structure of identification"[159] for blacks, which can lead to social and psychological harms. It also, too often, as with the case of Michael Jackson, leads to oversimplifications such as assuming that the singer is deliberately destroying his African physiognomy in order to "become" "white." I try to dissect this oversimplification by examining Michael Jackson and racial identification in the next chapter.

Chapter 3

Michael Jackson and Racial Identification

Michael Jackson seemingly moves from being a cute black boy to being neither male nor black in his adulthood—that is, according to some critics. Certainly, we use identity to construct our lives. Identity provides a nexus for membership into groups based on, for example, race, gender, sexuality, ethnicity, nationality, disability, and religious affiliations. Yet, these identities are always already questionable. Even though people are constructing identities all the time (gay and punk, for example), for Michael Jackson, having a black American identity is important. How this "having" becomes a part of "being" black is an essential question. In an interview with Oprah Winfrey on February 10, 1993, Michael Jackson made a public announcement: "I'm a black American. . . . I'm proud to be a black American. I'm proud of my race." Leaving aside, for the time being, Michael Jackson's announcement, the emphasis on being black American, which reads the doubling of subjectivity, black and American, "two souls . . . in one dark body," stands in for what W. E. B. Du Bois calls the "double consciousness,"[1] which can be extended to Frantz Fanon's idea of "implicit knowledge," of living one's life in two ways: one on the surface (outside) and the other hidden (inside) even from one's self.

It is clear that Michael Jackson's pride of being black is at "the center of his deconstruction"[2] of race, as is expressed in his songs, videos, and dance performances. As the youngest member of the Jackson Five, he "marked the assertive mood of 'Black Pride' cultural movements," with performances such as "I Want You Back" and "ABC."[3] Certainly, his song "Black or White," for example, is not about him confirming his racial identity, but about refusing the constraints of racial identification. "I am tired of this stuff. . . . I am not going to spend my life being a color," he wearily acknowledges, in an effort to dismiss racial norms and reconstruct a racial identity, seemingly *not black, not white*. This would be all well and good, but in the United States, race is inescapably identifiable. We all remember the one-drop rule (of blood), which deemed black anyone "having any African blood in their veins" no matter how white they looked. Nowadays, individuals are identifying themselves as mixed race and, as such, do not identify as "truly black."[4] Given that mixed-race individuals do not consider themselves "truly black," should they be spared the stigmatization of blackness?[5] It is hard to say. One thing for sure is that it is very hard to bypass America's history of the one-drop rule. In this respect, Michael Jackson's body, seemingly *not black, not white*, still carries the marks of America's history of race on his body, his skin, his surface, and, as a subterranean "force"[6] in the form of the unstoppable disciplinary power of whiteness, reducing the black body to abnormality.

Michael Jackson does not have a problem with the representation of race, but with how race is presented—that is, the immediate prereflective and prelinguistic existence of what is constructed as blackness, which is what race is. Race is on the surface of the body and a means of social control. Indeed, race functions as a disciplinary regime, and racialized subjects are fashioned through racial discipline. In other words, the means through which this disciplinary formation is introduced and continuous is through a specific form of power that produces the racialized subjects. All blacks can be said to fulfill "a kind of performative racial passing";[7] that is, the means through which racial discipline is "regulated and sustained."[8] While discipline and the performative essentials of race might seem to delimit ways of being "raced," as is seemingly the case for Michael Jackson, it is imperative to see how the artist attempts to elicit new modes of racial "becoming," *not black, not white*, which thereby cast him off as "weird" or a "freak."

What is striking is that Michael Jackson merely asks society not to "black[en] or white[n] [him]." These words read as Michael Jackson's intimation to move beyond race because race is, as he claims, "where your blood comes from."[9] However, blacks belonging to a group whose blood is "bad" has figured so prominently in the history of race relations in the United States. And while it is true that the first time we see our blood, it always shocks and horrifies us, the "one-drop rule" (of blood) carries the American history of racism. On the opposite side of this racial spectrum, whiteness is defined as wholesome and pure, which is what black lesbian feminist Audre Lorde calls "mythical norms."[10] In order to maintain the racial hierarchy, the concept of whites as pure serves to make the distinction between whites and blacks, which, of course, has racist implications. It means that Michael Jackson is "a slave" not to racial normalcy and cultural inscriptions, but to his own sense of his racial identity as "different, non-identical, and non-identitary."[11] In a word, Michael Jackson tries to move away from the assigned normalized category of race, and in his self-fashioning, he seems to be *not black, not white*. In the end, Michael Jackson's self-fashioning, nonetheless, works in the production and presentation of him as a racialized subject.

It is precisely for this reason that the following question imposes itself: If Michael Jackson is *not black* and *not white*, what is he? Because he is positioned between the " 'other' of 'being' " (not white), he is already "another" because blackness is already "*not*" being, or being "*not*." In a sense, Michael Jackson aspires not to be "*not*."[12] Not to be "*not*" positions him in a racial in-betweenness. This ambivalent self-identification or, in this case, disidentification of the subject from himself is the consequence of a normalizing whiteness that discursively differentiates between black and white racial belonging. To be black is to be outside of whiteness, another way of saying to be "outdoors." As Sara Jane Cervenak and J. Cameron Carter, taking about Toni Morrison's *The Bluest Eyes*, put it, being black is "an irrevocable and physical fact, defining and complementing our metaphysical condition."[13] In a word, blackness remains outdoors/outside; that is, exposed, "overdetermined from the outside," even when brought indoors/inside.[14]

Remember the case of the actor and playwright Ossie Davis; when he was six or seven years old, two white police officers ordered him to get into their car. They drove him to the precinct where they kept him there for an hour, laughing at him and eventually pouring cane syrup over his head, which provoked more laughter because he "looked like a silly black boy."[15] Eventually, he was given some peanut brittle and was sent home.[16] This is a perfect example of blackness when brought indoors is always outdoors. There is no end to blackness outdoorness. Take the case of Michael Jackson's Neverland Ranch: it a space of domesticity and Michael Jackson's fortress. But the doors of this fortress were forced open by the police and the place ransacked. Even if the police obtained a warrant to search the premises, they violated both the place and body of Michael Jackson (as I said before, they took pictures of his genitals) as evidenced in Michael Jackson's alleged child molestation charges. Blackness makes the difference of being indoors and to be surveilled; that is, to be outdoors. To be black is to be without cover. As soon as blackness enters the indoors, the Kantian practical reasons go through the window, and blackness remains outside, outdoors.

Is Michael Jackson an other "other"? An other "other" is a person, in the words of Diana Fuss, "who do[es] not quite fit into the rigid boundary definitions of (dis)similitude, or who indeed may be left out of the Self/Other binary altogether."[17] Because of Michael Jackson's ostentatious otherness made possible through hair straightening and plastic surgery, which, some scholars have argued, have diminished Michael Jackson's "African features,"[18] I want to suggest that he is an other "other": *not black* (other), *not white* (other). This is one way of looking at Michael Jackson's artifactual identity and discussing how the new model of a racial identity that he seeks to construct produces an otherness of the "other." Of course, this makes sense since the otherness of the "other" can only be contemplated because blackness is already "other" and Michael Jackson cannot escape blackness as cultural inscription. The "twoness" that W. E. B. Du Bois talks about is, in Michael Jackson's case (an other "other"), like "two souls in one dark body."[19]

When it comes to the nonnormative construction of Michael Jackson's raced identity, it is useful to draw a parallel between race performativity and "gender/queer performativity" as theorized by Judith Butler in *Gender Troubles* and *Bodies That Matter*. To say, then, that race is performative is to say that it is a certain kind of presentation, which becomes reified and realized through repetitive performative and daily acts.[20] The question that remains is that given the ontology and epistemology of race in the United States and its modalities of visual performance—that is, not what race is but what race does—is it possible to neutralize/deconstruct the performative function of race that "inferiorizes" blacks? Whether race performativity can have any, in the words of Seth Silberman, "assumable relationship to [that] person's life or consciousness"[21] is important. Indeed, race performativity is materialized out of its repeated performance and produces the results of that which is seen and named, which, in this case, is blackness. Blackness is made to be, in practice, the marker for a black identity, operating as a "becoming," which always assumes the status of nonbeing. In this regard, "performativity," as Judith Butler explains, "must be understood not as a single or deliberate 'act,' but, rather, as the reiterative and citational practice by which discourse produces the effects that it names."[22] The representation of blackness as racial discipline produces race as a bodily mark. In so doing, it sets multiple systems of power relations that regulate and sanction the black body.[23] In this regard, power must be understood as creating the subject as well as presenting the very condition on its existence.[24]

My attention to the racial self-fashioning of Michael Jackson provides for another account of how race is not lost; it is never lost; and it is always at the forefront of identity formation as a bodily mark that prescribes ways of "seeing" and "knowing" all there is to know about blacks. And while Michael Jackson is positioned on the margin of normalcy, as we know from deconstruction, that which is relegated to the margin is often at the center of thinking itself. That is to say, in the case of race, race gives significance to the ways in which blacks, through laws, epistemology, and cultural practice, are positioned as the "other" in the United States. For sure, Michael Jackson's racial identity has prompted tremendous debates about the ways he has destroyed his African physiognomy and unfixed "race on the body."[25] In this sense, race is viewed as essentialist; that is, "a belief in the real, true essence"[26] of blackness, "the invariable and fixed properties, which define the 'whatness' "[27] of blackness as opposed to the "whoness" of blackness—that is, who blacks are. As I have mentioned before, the "whoness" of blacks are not yet known to the white world, and when it is known it will be reflected in blacks' actions in the world. When this happens, "I can say I'm the light of the world," to borrow from Michael Jackson's song "This Is It." Even so, the "whatness" always takes precedence over the "whoness" of blackness.[28] In the words of Michael Jackson: "This is real."[29]

Fred Astaire, observing Michael Jackson's dance moves in "Billie Jean," describes him as "a hell of a mover" and "an angry dancer. I'm the same way. I used to do the same thing with my cane."[30] Astaire's comments are meant in the spirit of congeniality. Certainly, Michael Jackson's dance "is a series of 'rhythmically patterned movement performed by a sentient being,'" which "is a succinct depiction of a complex process of embodied creative expressions that have many levels and purposes."[31] However, Margo Jefferson, in her bleak outlook, views Michael Jackson's dance as "a young man who can't control his energies."[32] Others see his moves as "the angry black man" who is "working something out."[33] Why shouldn't black men, or even anyone, be angry when racism in all of its multidimensional forms is more resilient than ever? It is my fervent hope that this anger will propel all of "us" to go against racism. But "us" does not signal that the "us" is all the "same" in the fight against racism and to heal the world from this "usual disease," in Harper Lee's apt phrase in *To Kill a Mocking Bird*,[34] so as to secure a better future for all of us.

Notwithstanding that these overstatements of Michael Jackson's dance moves and superfluous vocalizations, as it is, show that blackness is always already policed by the white gaze, making blacks into "the problem"[35] and barring them from being on their own terms. Again, this is how Fanon explains it: "It's cold, the [Negro] is shivering, the [Negro] is shivering because he is cold, the little boy is trembling because he is afraid of the [Negro], the [Negro] is shivering with cold, that cold that goes through your bones, the handsome little boy is trembling because he thinks that the [Negro] is quivering with rage, the little white boy throws himself into his mother's arms: Mama, the [Negro] is going to eat me up."[36] Blacks, as a result, are forever exposed to all kinds of epistemic, ontological, and targeted "violence," understood "as a violation of one's being"[37] that should not be violated but is violated. What sets in motion the violence directed at blacks is the visuality of race; that is, its outside/outdoor appearance, its surfaceness in relation to the body, and its physiological features as a social phenomenon. At the same time, it is this violence that sustains blackness, and without it, whiteness would lose its preeminence.[38]

Frantz Fanon's analysis in *The Wretched of the Earth* and Michel Foucault's in *Discipline and Punish* help us to recognize how the body, the state, and violence are linked with America's history of institutionalized violence, which counted on "men to kill some white people to keep them white and to kill many blacks to keep them black."[39] A black person who entertains the very possibility of crossing over racial boundaries must be policed at whatever cost. And since whiteness is the norm, it makes sense that specific epistemologies, ideologies, and practices are in place to systematically sanction and protect white privilege. Michael Jackson and his quandary of identity, besides demonstrating the problematics of self-identification for blacks in the United States, provides a useful starting point to analyze the preeminence of whiteness and the specific ways blacks experience their being through normalized whiteness.

Given this, racial identification, in Fanon's words, "becomes a pathological condition"[40] in which blacks' subjectivity becomes subjugated by a gaze that is directed through the episteme of whiteness. For the most part, this condition can be transformed into a melancholia and a perversion, which inadvertently takes on an unusual form of racial identification. This experience of subjugation leads to an identity "crisis" and a misidentification, as is the case of Michael Jackson, where the "self's other" (not white) and the "other" (black) have become implicated. And while blacks become strangers to themselves—that is, "not to be an Other to oneself, but to be without any stable reference point in the world, to be separate ultimately through one's radical immanence to oneself from the world,"[41]—the subject, hence, becomes an unsettled agent, in between sameness (whiteness) and otherness (blackness). This, for blacks, is experienced first as corporeal, the material foundation of one's social and subjective conditions.[42] Secondly, one's image starts and ends viciously disjointed. In this disjointedness, according to African American philosopher George Yancy, "one ceases to experience one's identity from a locus of self-definition and begins to experience one's identity from a locus of externally imposed meaning."[43] In other words, one is "forever in combat with [one's] own image"[44] as the essential "other" of whiteness.

Michael Jackson's preoccupation with racial in-betweenness, *not black, not white*, an otherness within the "other," a body that is overdetermined, unrepresentative, and escapes strict description, in no uncertain terms, signals blackness. Indeed, Michael Jackson's self-fashioning has promoted anxiety among the masses. As we know from Judith Butler, some modes of appearance for category, such as race, "are marked and some are unmarked."[45] That is, in Butler's words, "some stand out, such as blackness, as visible social signs, whereas whiteness, which is no less social is nevertheless part of the taken-for-granted visual field, a sign of its presumptive hegemony."[46] While for Michael Jackson racial identification expresses itself in the form of the multiplying of identity, operating as a narcissistic manifestation of the "self's other" (not white) and the "other" (not black), which represents a form of racial liminality, his racial identification is related to the other cultural representation of alterity that implicates him as wanting to be "white," which goes against strict strictures about representing the "truth" of the visibility of race as a form of difference discursively marked on the body.

To say nothing of Michael Jackson's desire not to anchor himself in racial particularity, he cannot avoid being trapped in the doubling of otherness, which is not dominated by a longing to undo blackness and move toward whiteness but by a longing for racial ambiguity. Michael Jackson's performance and resistance to impose racial definitions is not locked in a symbiotic relationship of subordination (blackness) and domination (whiteness), but it seems to display an otherness of the "other" or an other "other." Michael Jackson's seemingly racial in-betweenness, *not black, not white* still signals blackness, and he continues to be seen through what Fanon calls the "corporeal malediction" of his unavoidable blackness.[47] Hence, like every black person in America, Michael Jackson must live the color line, the racial divide, which bears witness to the existential dilemma at the very core of his sense of "self."

In this chapter, I will examine how Michael Jackson is positioned between the "self's other" and the "other." Indeed, because of Michael Jackson's manufactured otherness through self-fashioning, which includes alterations of hair straightening and plastic surgery, I want to suggest that he is an other "other." In other words, even though Michael Jackson works on constructing another identity, the polymorphous uncertainties of his self-identification process, all operating in complex and different directions, are often simplified as him wanting to be "white." Part of my intention is to demonstrate that Michael Jackson's appearance deconstructs and challenges the corporeal notions of "natural bodies" and fixed identities. However, his race identity is not lost; it is never lost.

Jackson and Self-Fashioning

Let's take at our starting point that blackness is a social and subjective identity and the locus of identification.[48] At once, it is viewed as a sign of deficiency, disapproval, and lack. Michael Jackson is determined to break away from the wretched construction of blackness so he reconstructs another image, *not black*, *not white*, bordering on racial in-betweenness, an otherness within the "other," which undoubtedly indicates blackness. As I mentioned above, the King of Pop continues to be seen through what Fanon describes as the "corporeal malediction" of his inescapable blackness, which, as a category of analysis, is a way of showing that although Michael Jackson's identity is seemingly not stable—it is in flux—it disturbs and unsettles because it does not conform to its bodily marking and positioning in the realm of the either/or race category (black/white),[49] which deems him as not quite human.

However, this form of reading Michael Jackson continues through journalistic references of, and commentary upon, Michael Jackson as lacking humanness, to use the words of Gilles Deleuze and Félix Guatteri, a "body without organs."[50] It is for good reasons Sara Ahmed and Jackie Stacey, in *Thinking Though the Skin*, wonder "[h]ow bodies come to be identified as having organs in the first place."[51] Indeed, even if blacks want "to be" (being)—and "not to be" (nonbeing) is never a universalistic concept—they are positioned in such a way, "not to be" (nonbeing), that they are constantly dehumanized. In fact, if blacks were to be seen as human, they could go beyond the boundary of race, and like whites, they could be viewed as raceless. However, blacks are not, in Toni Morrison's words, "worthy to be treated as whites."[52]

The actress Elizabeth Taylor once compared Michael Jackson to E.T. because of "their mutual alien-ness, their distance from the planet earth, their ambiguous sex."[53] Michael Jackson's various parts on-screen as a nonhuman "other" include those of a scarecrow in the 1978 *The Wiz*,[54] a werewolf and a dancing zombie in his *Thriller* video, and a Robocop-like metallic figure in *Smooth Criminal*. Michael Jackson also appears as a thirty-foot-tall statue in his 1995 promotional video for his song "HIStory,"[55] which allows many to confirm that he is not quite human.[56] To sum up, Michael Jackson is often described as animal-like, readily positioned in the realm of nonbeing (not human), and made into thingliness "in the order of things." Here is how Patrice Douglas and Fred Wilderson explain it: "Being black, or . . . black(ened) being . . . submits my being to the perpetuity of political ontological breaking with and by inescapable gravity and darkness, such that, on orders of time and space both macro and micro—being, life, existence, knowledge, ethics, as they are framed by the permanence promised by capital 'D' Death (social death) and the temporariness inherent in lower-case 'd' (corporeal death)."[57] By way of explanation, blacks arrive in this world already blackened.

Against the irrationality of blackness and its social positioning, a black person is always ahead of himself, not in the same way in which Simone de Beauvoir sees it, "as projecting [themselves] toward something, toward the future,"[58] but in the sense that they are continually already marked, complete, certain[59] in their blackness, and it is rather difficult for them to function outside of race. This might lead us to recognize that, unlike the existentialist assertion according to which existence comes before essence, essence (race) precedes and, at the same time, sustains a black person's existence. In other words, race constitutes who the subject is in a way that frames whites' views of blacks. With Fanon, one can say again, "I come back to one fact, wherever he goes, the Negro remains a Negro."[60] Sealed in their blackness as a nonbeing (not human), they are something else.

In her work *On Michael Jackson*, Margo Jefferson borrows Keith Haring's words and states that "it would be much cooler if [Michael Jackson] would go all the way and get his ears pointed or add a tail or something, but give him time."[61] This is a rather disturbing comment, even more so if one takes into account her appreciation of Haring's comment as "refreshingly nonjudgmental."[62] And even though some of us remained startled by such offensive statements, the internet shows an image of Michael Jackson dressed in a white satin tuxedo, flowing hair, and heavy makeup, accepting his trophy from the Rock 'n' Roll Hall of Fame. Next to his picture is a still from the 2001 film, *Planet of the Apes*, showing one of the leading apes played by Helena Bonham Carter "in heavy ape-make-up and ape costume, dressed in a shimmering disco suit."[63] Depending on one's *ways of seeing*, according to Kathy Davis, "the resemblance between the images is unmistakable: their faces and poses are alike, their hair is similar, they are wearing the same kind of clothing."[64] As the proverbial saying goes, "seeing is believing"—that is, only distinct evidence is convincing. Fittingly, the uncritical thought is that visual perception engages the world in an objective way and is never answering to any subjective influences. It is the definite and tangible understanding of reality. While "seeing is believing" is simply "false seeing" because of the objective way of understanding the reality of race, I want to propose here that seeing Michael Jackson as a monkey is another form of "false seeing."[65] It is, in fact, a form of willful blindness with the purpose to denigrate. However, I don't think that many have yet caught up with the fact, as the zoologist Desmond John Morris reveals, that all human beings "share 84.4 [percent] of our genetic makeup with the chimpanzee."[66]

"Willfulness," Sara Ahmed explains, is "asserting or disposed to assert one's will against persuasion, instruction, or command; governed by will without regard to reason; determined to take one's own way obstinately self-willed or perverse."[67] As a way of moving away—far away—from willful blindness, there is a dire need for an alternative definition for "seeing," which is called "reseeing." Reseeing would involve not only retraining the eyes to see differently, which is outside of immediate sensory perceptions, but also moving away from "false seeing."[68] But first, we would have to unlearn what we have learned to "see" about the black body. It would require understanding that truth-claims of race as a marker promote differences that lead to racialized discourse and practices. The unlearning, then, would be, in the postcolonial theorist Gayatri C. Spivak's oeuvre, "one's loss"[69] so as to extricate one's dominant ways of seeing and knowing all there is to see and know about the black body, which returns it to its presumed animality. The form of psychic and ethical risk for the white subject would be a good example of what James Baldwin means when he suggests "to earn one's death."[70]

Another example of blacks depicted as "not to be" (nonhuman) is the posters of Barack Obama as a monkey, or as an African witch doctor wearing tribal regalia.⁷¹ In an anxious attempt to demonstrate their disgruntlement of having a black president and to "[take] the country back" and "[return] the American government to the American people,"⁷² white right-wing ideologues and the Tea Party furthered the idea of the black man as a nonhuman. *Who are "the American people"?* is an insightful question posed by Bruno Bosteels. "How does a people become a people? Does a people become only that which it *is*? If so, then what *is* it? How can we know: (1) What a people in general *is*? (2) What this or that people is? (3) What we ourselves are?"⁷³ Besides these questions is another underlying one: What is it that defines "the American people?" Indeed, whiteness is essential for the construction of "the American people" as white. Although there was a cultural practice and a social code already in place that determined whites as American, with the Naturalization Act of 1790,⁷⁴ American citizenry is white because it is institutionalized. The Act, of course, allowed only whites to be citizens of the United States, forging a single American identity amongst its diverse multicultural and multiracial population. Indeed, whiteness is the standard against which blacks are measured and deemed as inferior by virtue of their blackness. There is no other vantage point for many whites to imagine otherwise because, as George Yancy reminds us, "to imagine otherwise is seriously truncated by ideological and material forces that are systematically linked to the history of white racism."⁷⁵

Blackness, positioned as "outside" of what constitutes an American identity, is viewed as a threat to the social body. Any analysis of blackness needs to inquire into what renders this kind of a priori racial knowledge possible. Just as Judith Butler in *Gender Troubles* argues in opposition to a sex-gender differentiation in which sex is the natural, univocal, and material basis of gender, culturally created and performative, it should not surprise us, at this juncture, that the binary opposition of whites as civilized and blacks as uncivilized needs to be deconstructed and recognized as a culturally constructed hierarchy that puts blacks at the bottom and fixes them in a place of alterity whose boundaries are continually conferred by an arsenal of dehumanizing practices. In the end, for Michael Jackson, coming to terms with the existential dilemma of self-definition in a society where whiteness is the norm becomes problematic.

The outcome is always looking at oneself through the eyes of the culturally constituted white gaze, which is inescapable and forces upon blacks an unusual weight. Whiteness has been the definitive marker for acceptability within "The Great Chain of Being,"⁷⁶ providing the fundamental structure for the present formulation of race. It also provides, which is definitely ignored, a consideration for how whiteness is fastened to itself as a "possessive investment"[77] in itself. This is precisely what makes whiteness unraced and unmarked, the invisible norm. In the United States, whiteness maintains its presumptive hegemony "through symbols, images, discursive structures, foundations, and epistemologies."[78] In the face of whiteness, the underlying dynamic at work, here, is that blackness "being what it is not and not being what it is,"[79] or, put differently, "a certain way of not being a being, which it posits simultaneously as other than itself,"[80] allows blacks to react to whiteness and, in some cases, to imitate whiteness. Blacks, imitating whiteness, in Homi Bhabha's words, "reveals something in so far as it is distinct from what might be called an *itself* that is behind" the imitation.[81]

It is not surprising blacks, in an attempt to resolve their blackness with what is perceived "to be" (human)—features that are basically assigned to whiteness—have propelled some blacks, as Kathy Davis points out, "to alter their noses and lips through cosmetic surgery."[82] In this sense, there is no *"blackness-for-itself"*; that is, a blackness that is conscious of its own consciousness, because "blackness" has not arrived as yet. Certainly, the black being is not yet known to the world, or as Fanon would say, "no one knows yet who [the black] is,"[83] and when it is revealed, *blackness-for-itself*, touching the "other," feeling the "other,"[84] would revolutionize the world and society would advance. Fanon takes this one step further: "Black consciousness [would] be immanent in its own eye. . . . My Negro consciousness does not hold itself out as a lack. It is. It is its own follower."[85] In Fanon's theory, blackness as the *same* will continue to be the case because whiteness is still the norm acting on blacks prior to any action they may undertake.

In all western societies, physical beauty standards are based on whiteness. Even though cosmetic surgery is treated by most plastic surgeons as a beauty concern (improving appearance),[86] it is in reality a form of race refashioning and can lead to pathological behavior, as the multiple plastic surgeries that Michael Jackson (and many) underwent attest.[87] Indeed, Michael Jackson's plastic surgery stirs up "bad news" for him because many view, for example, his "nose job" (to have more of a "white" nose) as trying to look "white" or, in Kobena Mercer words, "'becoming white'—a deracializing sell-out, the morbid symptom of a psychologically mutilated black consciousness."[88] However, I want to point out that "to be," "to be like," or "to become" white would indeed involve a "whitening process." Michael Jackson would have to learn, in Harper

Lee's fitting phrase, "the ways of white people"[89]—the actions, practices, and outlooks that are characteristically allied with whiteness. This would not be a simple task.

For good reasons, the 1960s motto of the Black Power Movement, *Black Is Beautiful*, which contra the idea of black as ugly, emphasizing the need for blacks not to do away with African-identified features such as lips, nose, and hair by, for instance, straightening their hair, but keep it natural, "merely provide[d] a raw material for practices, procedures and ritual techniques of cultural writing and social inscription,"[90] which, for Mercer, itself is "cultivated."[91] The word cultivated comes from the medieval Latin word *cultivat*, meaning "till, prepare for crop," "to devote one's attention to," to looking "good," which is why Mercer can say, "nobody's hair is ever just natural but is always shaped or reshaped by social convention and symbolic intervention";[92] it is cultivated. Can acts of self-grooming/self-improvement "constitute 'political statement' or racially inflected acts of 'symbolic intervention'"? If is it true that in a culture where self-grooming/self-improvement is practically a moral imperative, is it evidently "natural" for anyone to want to be "cultivated," "to devote one's attention to" looking one's best? Is a black person having a nose job, for example, to make one's nose appear more "white," a form of self-improvement?

Certainly, Michael Jackson's nose job is viewed by some as him wanting to look "white," notwithstanding his confession in *Living with Michael Jackson* that the nose job he underwent was to help with his breathing and singing. However, we cannot disavow that "African features," through the European lens, are seen as ugly. While it is argued that Michael Jackson's plastic surgeries are about a sign of black, to borrow from Cynthia J. Fuchs, "self-hatred,"[93] and "an unnatural act that entails negating his essential [racial] identity,"[94] Greg Tate, for one, is correct: "There are other ways to read Michael Jackson."[95] In Michael Jackson's biography, he claims defiantly, "It's a matter of choice: I can afford it, I want it, so I'm going to have it."[96] In the end, his plastic surgery is, according to him, to "look better."[97] In fact, there is a moral argument for wanting to "look better;" to enhance one's physical appearance by, perhaps, having cosmetic surgery so as to look younger, to "look better." Certainly, to "look better" is always defined by the cultural ideals of what it means to "look better," and there is an unease and an apparent need to care for the body, a sense of its "vulnerability and exposure."[98] Given that the black body is always racially marked, or in Sara Ahmed and Jackie Stacey's words, "'seen to be damaged' such as black skin,"[99] what is imperative here is that Michael Jackson's body can never "look better." His "white" skin is, as the saying goes, "skin deep," and it becomes the site in which the desire for another identification (not black) and the impossibility of a "white" identity (not white) is present.[100] Michael Jackson's embodied blackness is always done in, overworked.

In the case of Michael Jackson, with the plastic surgeries he underwent, what he can hope for, at best, is pseudo-recognition; that is, a white mask. In fact, this is the trick of whiteness as structured in everyday life. As George Yancy has shown, "it is to give the appearance of fixity, where the look of the white subject interpellates the black subject as inferior, which in turn, bars the black subject from seeing him/herself without the internalization of the white gaze."[101] Hence, the black body has to police and regulate itself because it has internalized the white gaze, with "an inner compulsion and subjective conformation" to whiteness.[102] This is, in part, what W. E. B. Du Bois is getting at when he talks about "the double consciousness," this sense of always looking at one's self through the eyes of whites, shaping one's subjectivity as "mixed up" and fragmented, which, in particular, is one of dislocation from one "true" identity.

To this end, even though Michael Jackson's skin became "whiter"—"less ebony, more ivory," as Michael Awkward puts it[103]—the rumor was that he wanted to be "white" and not "black." Yet, in an interview with Robert E. Johnson of *Ebony*, Michael Jackson denies this.[104] As it is, as Atticus Finch reminds us in *To Kill A Mocking Bird*: "You never really understand a person until you consider things from his point view . . . until you climb into his skin and walk around in it."[105] There is no denying that there is in fact a change in Michael Jackson's appearance as he has grown, in that "the glossy sheen of his complexion appears lighter in colour than before; the nose seems sharper, more aqualine,"[106] or what Terri Eagleton in *The Guardian* describes as an "over-chiseled nose."[107] Similarly, Kobena Mercer describes the nose as "less rounded and 'African,'"[108] and Kathy Davis concludes that it is "whistled to almost nothing."[109] In addition, Mercer complains that Michael Jackson's "lips seem thicker as less pronounced,"[110] which, as Davis sums up, "gives his face a skeletal look,"[111] past the point where there is no return. How Michael Jackson's body is read, narrated, produced, and remembered is fascinating. All of this—the politics of Michael Jackson's self-fashioning—is interpreted by his critics as undoing race, unfixing "race on the body."

Michael Jackson's body politics is provoking many anxieties about the "truth" of race on the body. The "search for truth," as Macarena Gómez-Barris and Herman Gray warn us, "is also what television, news, documentary, and reality programming depend on for their authority."[112] In the end, these mainstream media outlets, for the most part, support and uphold rather than unsettle and challenge dominant systems of representations. Not without worries, there is a pretense, at least, to impartial and objective news coverage.[113] In short, Michael Jackson's body, woven out of "thousand details, anecdote, and stories,"[114] is subject to all kinds of negative readings and conceptualizations. These negative readings of Michael Jackson's body demonstrate, in no uncertain terms, "how the body marks difference, as well as being marked by difference"[115] as it becomes a site for racial identity, which he unsuccessfully attempts to erase. To fully understand the "quandary" in which Michael Jackson's racial identity is articulated, a different ethic of reading Michael Jackson's racial performance is needed.

In the documentary *Living with Michael Jackson*, interviewer Martin Bashir seems obsessed with Michael Jackson's attempt to refix race on the body and the "truth" of race, "its veracity, its representability, its historicity."[116] In fact, the "truth" of race is pinned down to blackness "as overdetermined from the outside," the outsideness of blackness, which Franz Fanon describes as the visuality of the body—its surfaceness, in itself, a social phenomenon that has produced and upheld a convincingly negative understanding of race. Bashir, injecting "words like poison into the conversation"[117] with Michael Jackson, points mercilessly to Michael Jackson's physical appearance—light skin, thin lips, straight nose, and so on—which, he points out, is different from when Michael Jackson was a child. If Michael Jackson's "metamorphosis" suggests that he does not want to be "black" but "white," it is too simplistic to argue that he is unfixing "race on the body."[118] On many occasions, Michael Jackson announces that he would very much like to look like the African American diva Diana Ross.[119] And while this comment provoked some speculations as to whether Michael Jackson was contemplating a sex change, it did not dissolve in the least the highly heated debates about his racial "metamorphosis." This is not unusual. Charles Mills lets us know that America is structured in such a way that it is hard not "to bring race in,"[120] which Cornel West explains and describes as *Race Matters*. This is one reason why it is worrisome that some scholars suggest that this is not about race and assume that "race" as a referent is "outside" of race thinking. These misleading approaches skirt the racial issue and obliterate the fact that race indeed mattered and continues to matter. Certainly, the interrogations around Michael Jackson's body allow for thinking about a black identity as "overdetermined from the outside." But the danger lies precisely in the problems that the outsideness of blackness poses for blacks. Michael Jackson's attempts to construct an identity on his own is subject to all kinds of ridicule directed at him.

If Michael Jackson wants to be "white," it not surprising. "However painful it may be for me to accept this conclusion, I am obliged to state it: For the black there is only one destiny. And it is white."[121] As Fanon explains, the enormous amount of privilege that comes with whiteness necessarily triggers an unconscious desire to be white or a phantasmal whitening through, for example, what Fanon calls "lactification" of the black race. Because there is no escaping the fact that race is epidermalized, how race is seen and treated in the visual realm—that is, the outward appearance in relation to the body and its physiological features—is paramount. The unfathomable site of Michael Jackson's body as a form of a radicalized difference from the essentialized concept of racial identity is indeed distressing for the masses because it is seen as "unnaturally" instigated. To make the point that there are different standards for blacks and whites who have undergone plastic surgeries, it is useful to think of the French body artist Orlan, who like Michael Jackson deconstructs "the notion of a natural body and fixed identities."[122] Of course, Orlan's radical act of changing her appearance through plastic surgery in the name of art is not harshly criticized. But Michael Jackson's surgical reconstructions definitely are. What these two examples show is that a white person is freer "to experiment with her or his appearance—and this includes indulging in the 'surgical fix'—[and] the same experiment takes on a different meaning when undergone by a black person."[123] And while we are all disciplined, in the Foucauldian sense, and abide to norms and values of whiteness until we become self-disciplined, we are socialized into thinking that "white features" are what define ideal beauty. This is symptomatic of the thriving market for skin-bleaching cream and hair-straightening cream in black communities, which reveals a "subjective enslavement to Eurocentric definitions of beauty,"[124] operating in concert with hegemonic cultural codes of whiteness[125] that fasten blacks to that corporeal decorum.

Any attempt is foreclosed by blacks "to throw off the burden of that corporeal[ity]."[126] That is to say, "the body as it feels," which "is experientially distinct, if inextricable, from the body image and the discursive construction of the body that are culturally imposed, one way or another,"[127] on a black person who is being fixed by the white gaze. The body image, then, dislocates, relocates, and surpasses the corporeal schema. The corporeal schema is the way in which the body's agency is manifested in the historical world as a universal given of human perception, which is foundational for human presence and being-in-the-world with others.[128] The French philosopher Maurice Merleau-Ponty points out that both the self and the world are constructed through the corporeal schema. In other words, the corporeal schema is the image that we construct and reconstruct about ourselves as we move about in society.

The corporeal schema should be seen for its normativity,[129] which is based on whiteness and maleness. More so, within the experiential frame of the bodiliness of racism, a black person has difficulties in developing their corporeal schema—that is, the corporeal schema fails and the body is surrounded by an antagonism that comes with an "implicit knowledge" about the black body. This knowledge is discursively constructed within a racist society out of "thousands of anecdotes and stories" about a black person, which are ascribed to them by the white alienating discourse. One of the effects is an uncertain self-identification, a disavowal of the self. With extraordinary persistence, Fanon depicts this as a negating experience. And given that "the body is surrounded by an atmosphere of certain uncertainty," it responds to and imitates the pejorative white gaze and exceeds the "corporeal schema."[130] Hence, below the corporeal schema there is, on the one hand, the "historico-racial schema" and, on the other, the cultural and discursive "racial epidermal schema." Given that the "historico-racial schema" is what a black person must use in order "to construct a physiological self" for themselves, "the historic-racial schema" is thrown into disarray. Consequently, the "historico-racial schema" has been supplanted with the "racial epidermal schema," which is culturally fashioned by racist discourse and "is the definitive structuring of self and of the world," creating a "dialectic between [the black body] and the world" that firmly fix the positionality of blacks.[131]

The very appearance of blackness in the face of whiteness is always already an antiblack phenomenon,[132] or, as Calvin Warren calls it, "onticide"; that is, "a certain murderous operation through ontology."[133] This is one reason why ontology does not allow us to comprehend the being of the black man. Not only must he be black, but he must be black in relation to whites, with no ontological resistance to whiteness,[134] thus reinforcing his blackness. How the black body is acclimatized by race—that is, in its fixity–brings us to an important observation that a black person is, as Fanon puts it, "a slave not of the 'idea' others have of [him/her] but of his/her own appearance."[135] Once again, we are reminded of Michael Jackson's confession, "I look in my mirror and it took me by surprise. . . . I can't help it if I wanted"[136] "to be" (human). Indeed, nothing changes, because Michael Jackson's "inside" (the insideness of blackness) is the same as a black person's "inside," which cannot be separated from the "outside" (the ousideness of blackness). Achille Mbembe theorizes the suffering of the black body—its pain, its grief, and its outrage—in his disturbing "politics of vicerality" to show that the racist trauma is played out in the visceral. Indeed, the "inside" impacts the "outside."

Race as a visual presentation and a social phenomenon that has produced a persuasively negative understanding of race does take into consideration blacks who "pass" for whites. We do remember the landmark case *Plessy v. Ferguson*. Even though Plessy "passed" for white, he was asked to leave the carriage for whites and ride in the carriage for blacks. And even though passing is now passé and replaced by "honorary whiteness," race and its broader cultural dynamics entrap blacks in the realm of corporeality and position the black body as a foil to the social body. It stands outside of the norm of recognizablility (whiteness). In the case of Michael Jackson, the singer seemingly looks "white" but cannot "pass" for white. In this sense, "passing" means that Michael Jackson assumes a white identity in order to escape being black in a blackphobic society. If that is the case, Michael Jackson would then have to learn the ways, attitudes, and behaviors of "white folks." In other words, Michael Jackson would have to learn how, to borrow from Linda Martín Alcoff, "to experience [him]self as white";[137] that is, his relation to whiteness and the routinized and unconscious habit of always asserting his superiority over blacks, which is an expression of whiteness. Because whiteness is internalized and reproduced, blacks have no choice but to present an unrestrained predilection toward whiteness and to express their ambivalence toward their own blackness.

Whiteness, indeed, does not stand apart from the exterior inscription of whiteness upon the body. For this reason, a poor white person learns the attitudes and behaviors that are tied to whiteness as a fundamental defining signifier of white superiority. Surely, the principal task of white superiority is not a demonstration that, as Oliver C. Cox puts it, "white is superior to all human beings but to insist that white must be supreme."¹³⁸ We do remember how white supremacist ideology unified erudite scholars in robes in the hall of academia and poor whites in the hood of the Ku Klux Klan (KKK).¹³⁹ The upshot is that to "pass" for something that you are not is to be tolerated by those for whom you are "passing." Tolerance, in this milieu, is that the tolerators (whites) have to put up with the passers (blacks).

The continuing chronicling of Michael Jackson's so-called white features is that "blackness" is always already anchored in his distinctive style and gestures, making him inauthentic. Accordingly, Michael Jackson is fraught by a "self" that is constituted, reconstituted, and deconstituted; it is a fragmented "self." Michael Jackson is, in the words of Henry Louis Gates Jr., "not only estranged from whites—he is also estranged from his own group and from himself."¹⁴⁰ Belonging to a group affords one with an identity and minimizes the weight of self-knowledge, of understanding who you are.¹⁴¹ That said, Michael Jackson's skin becoming whiter cannot be imagined as him wanting to be "white." Skin, in this sense, is assumed to be the sign of Michael Jackson's interiority; that is, what it means for him to be "black" or "white." Even if Michael Jackson is viewed as "white" on the outside, because his blood is "black," it is a blood that never dries. Michael Jackson is, as DMX says it best, "the flesh of my flesh, the blood of my blood."¹⁴² To put it differently, as Hélène Cixous's *The Third Body* does, "he is in my flesh, and he is in my eyes, and he is the marrow of my bone."¹⁴³ In a word, Michael Jackson can never be "white." To be white is "to be" like whites. However, his skin is also expected to reveal the truth of the "other" and to give us access to his being or, in this case, nonbeing (not to be). Michael Jackson's body is "pure text" to be studied and discussed. "To be" (being) or "not to be" (nonbeing) always remains "the question." In a blackphobic society, a black person is always "not to be" (nonbeing).

While bell hooks, rightfully, identified blacks' desire for lighter skin as a result of a "racist imagination" and "a colonized black mindset"¹⁴⁴ cannot be ignored,¹⁴⁵ today, passing is no longer about looking white; it is about getting a license for entry into "honorary whiteness." It requires freeing oneself from the labels associated with blackness and being presented to a white society in a way that make whites feel unsusceptible and less anxious. It is like joining a private club; once you have become a member you must abide by the rules. So, if Michael Jackson passes for "white," he will project an inauthentic whiteness, a whiteness that can never be outed and remains "in the closet," to borrow the title of one of his songs.[146] Furthermore, we need to be reminded that he would have to adhere to a specific form of whiteness, which unremittingly accompanies the interior "whitening" process.

Looking white depends on the looker given that when the white *look* is directed at blacks, it always reduces blacks to the object of the *look* and blacks encounter the "other" through the *look*, producing an ontological condition for blacks that frames their way of being in society. In this sense, even if Michael Jackson looks "white," looking "white" disturbs the meaning of "looking black," and black is already a disturbing designation. That disturbance sometimes euphemizes some deeply antagonistic problem usually related to "looking black." So, if Michael Jackson is being *not black*, this disturbs the meaning usually assigned to being black (as nonbeing for whites), and if to be black is already a sign of disturbance, his identity as *not black, not white* doubly disturbs. However, this double disturbance might constitute an opening for "an-'other'" possible black identity. "An-'other'" possible identity can never feel good because it disturbs and unsettles the social body. It is a life livable in "social death."[147]

Notwithstanding all of Michael Jackson's success, he was confined to black entertainment. As a black entertainer, he performed at the Super Bowl in 1993; he was invited to the White House by both Presidents Ronald Reagan[148] and Bill Clinton. George Bush Sr. saw him as a role model, a good example for young blacks.[149] An invitee to the White House was and is expected to behave like an American. However, Michael Jackson was not expected to behave like an American but like a black American. Blacks as always "in expectation" to be black conjures up Fanon's eloquent summation: "When people like me, they tell me it is in spite of my color. When they dislike me, they point out that it is not because of my color. Either way I am locked into the infernal circle."[150]

It is not surprising that Michael Jackson finds himself in the company of the two most controversial African American leaders, the civil rights activist and reverend Al Sharpton and Louis Farrakhan of the Nation of Islam.[151] The latter was name-checked on two of the hip-hop group Public Enemy's albums, *It Takes a Nation of Millions to Hold us Back* and *Fear of a Black Planet*.[152] When Michael Jackson died in 2009, Al Sharpton gave the most heart-wrenching eulogy at his memorial service on July 7, 2009. Sharpton is remembered for his words to Michael Jackson's three children: "[There] wasn't nothing strange about your daddy. It was strange what your daddy had to deal with, but he dealt with it anyway. He dealt with it for us."[153]

As Greg Tate's "'I'm White!' What's Wrong with Michael Jackson" notes, even if Michael Jackson is changing his physical appearance, his becoming "whiter," in the end—the outside transformation of skin/flesh from "black" to "white"—is not a good reason to put forward that Michael Jackson wants to be "white." In fact, Michael Jackson's skin becoming "whiter" has been explained as a skin disorder called vitiligo.[154] Vitiligo sufferers' psychosomatic recognitions may very well be invested in "skin."[155] Indeed, the recognition of "self" in skin color was historically made illegal with the implementation of the "one-drop rule." As that law stated, a person did not, need not "look black" "to be" black.[156] This might be something that many Americans may not want to revisit. But how the United States remembers its racist past is important since it has shaped its future on race and racial thinking. In this regard, America's racist history must not be disavowed because, as the great poet Maya Angelou reminds us, in the poem she read at Bill Clinton's 1993 inauguration, "On the Pulse of the Morning," "history, despite its wrenching pain cannot be unlived, but if faced with courage need not be lived again."[157]

What is even more paramount is that Michael Jackson's skin disorder, "which often leads [its sufferers] to [experience] social embarrassment and psychological turmoil,"[158] is stigmatized. Is it because Michael Jackson's skin color reminds us of the role skin color played and continues to play in the United States' racist history? Certainly, skin color is a social and corporeal attribute ascribed to blacks to position them both as distinct from whites and as less than whites. The "less than" is comprehended as a form of cultural lacking and establishes another way for whites to invent the social and existential realities of racial thinking, which works to powerfully construct and support a specific account of blackness that is premised on *likeness*—that is, a physicality that a black person shares with all blacks, fixing race on the body. *Likeness* becomes a matter of collective characteristics that take away from blacks their individualities because they are not perceived as unique individuals but rather as belonging to a homogeneous group. In this way, *likeness* unites blacks through a physical bond and, in the face of the white social body, makes them hypervisible and exposed; that is, "overdetermined from the outside." Michael Jackson's skin as the site in which the desire for race identification and the likelihood of another possible identity is played out disturbs and unsettles because it challenges *likeness*.[159] Reducing this racial struggle to Michael Jackson's desire to be white is distressingly unproductive. What this reduction signifies in the cultural unconscious is Michael

Jackson's desire to undo his blackness. But, in the racist society in which he lived, blackness can never be undone because there is no possibility of racial transcendence.

Michael Jackson, seemingly "transwhiteness," which might not be the most appropriate term to talk about his complex racial positioning, cannot be considered transformative. It cannot avoid the script of a particular morphological body given that blackness can never be successfully concealed behind an apparently white physicality. (Remember the case of Anatole Broyard and Alice B. Rhinelander.)[160] Based on this observation, Hank Stuever, a journalist for the *Washington Post*, says it best: "A black man is still a black man, underneath it all, no matter where life takes him even if that man is Michael Jackson."[161]

When Michael Jackson spoke in 2002 at Al Sharpton's National Network in Harlem, he confessed, "I just look in the mirror—I know that I am black."[162] Here, we can recognize the transmutability of the flesh. Michael Jackson's skin's surface does not merely delimit or contain the imaginary morphology of his individual self but actually enables access to the symbolic as a place from which both internal (repression, disavowal, and projection) and external (the gaze of the other) perceptions,[163] which permanently fixes him in the manner "in which a chemical solution is fixed by a dye."[164] Michael Jackson's identity as the site of both internal and external perceptions is achieved, as Fanon explains, in "a slow composition of [him]self as a body in the middle of spatial and temporal world . . . , [which] creates a real dialectic between [his] body and the world."[165] At a quick glance, Michael Jackson's appearance, *not black, not white*, troubles the normalizing operations and surveillance techniques of a persuasive concept of race. And because he refuses these strict racial categorization (black or white), his body, no doubt, is a body that can be conceptualized as "the third body," in-between black and white, an other "other."

Many scholars have argued that Michael Jackson's body gestures, dances, and choreographic performances, when on stage, refuse racial belonging, which is applauded by those who refuse to recognize that in the United States race continues to give credence to the oldest and most persistent problem of race presentation as a bodily mark that congeals as the "other" or, in Simone de Beauvoir's words, "reduces [blacks] to pure facticity."[166] Going against all arguments that Michael Jackson forfeits his black identity, his performances on stage and in videos show that the ontological status of race is not far removed from how race is presented.

In fact, his "verisimilar self-presentation in videos such as *Black or White* draws directly from 'the rich black heritage that gave him his musical and dance style,'"[167] which is rooted in the Afro-American tradition of Soul.[168] Anyone who watches Michael Jackson's performances is moved by his style. Certainly, "the power of Soul as a cultural form," as Kobena Mercer points out, "lies in the passion of the singer's voice and vocal performance"[169] and is never lost in his performance.

Michael Jackson's vocal performance is characterized by "breathy gasps, squeaks, sensual sighs, and other wordless sounds,"[170] which, according to Mercer, "has become his stylistic signature. The way in which this style punctuates the emotional resonance and bodily sensuality of the music"[171] has a close similarity to what, in Roland Barthes's "new scheme of evaluation," is described as "the 'grain,'"[172] which "is the body in the voice as it sings."[173] In this sense, "the emotional and erotic expressiveness of the voice is complemented by the sensual grace and sheer excitement of Jackson's dancing style."[174] As a rejoinder, this, in Michael Jackson's words: "I try . . . to put in song. Put in dance."[175] As Mercer explains, it is a "cultural form and sexual ritual, a mode of decoding the sound and meaning articulated in the music,"[176] which, in Michael Jackson's words, "I put in my art to reach the world."[177] Michael Jackson's artistry is, as Hortense Spillers would say, "a site of irresistible sensuality,"[178] or, as Halifu Osumare's title reads, a site of *dancing in blackness*.

Indeed, Michael Jackson's style is rooted in black cultural forms, "the incarnation of complete fusion with world, an intuitive understanding of the earth," and "no white man," according to Fanon, "no matter how intelligent he may be," can ever truly understand (self-understanding) Michael Jackson's style.[179] If it is confession time, Michael Jackson would simply turn to the Presbyter/confessor, if he had one, and say, "Africa I have kept your memory [/] Africa you are inside me."[180] On the Oprah Winfrey show in 1993, he refers to himself as a "slave to the rhythm," words borrowed from Grace Jones's song "Slave to the Rhythm."[181] Jones, a black female performer, in her musical, dance, and other forms of aesthetic expressions, is considered a threat to the avant-garde "white, male, heterosexual music industry."[182] This is not surprising. In fact, in a press conference in Harlem in 2002, Michael Jackson accused the chairman Tommy Mottola and Sony music of "systemic racism against Black performers and song writers."[183]

Blackness is always perceived as a threat. The only threat, in my estimation, is a black woman fighting against how she is positioned; on the one hand, as exotic and fetishized, and on the other hand, as fearful and repulsing. Race as a signifier is pegged to the other signifiers—gender, sexuality, and class, for example—creating her complex positioning. Either way, she cannot escape what Thelma Pinto describes as the Sarah Baartman syndrome derivative of the white male gaze.[184] In 1810 in London, Sarah Baartman, a black South African woman, was on exhibition for the white male gaze because of her "exotic" features.[185]

Even as a child, Michael Jackson's staging performances incited similarities with the godfather of soul James Brown, another great black singer Jackie Wilson nicknamed Mr. Excitement,[186] and Stevie Wonder. Above all, his "looping walk in African American style," to borrow from Gates,[187] which is "inside him" and gets out in his video and performances on stage, cannot be missed. One remembers Michael Jackson's performance of *Billie Jean*. In a word, his blackness can never be lost. What Maggie Nelson, in *The Argonauts*, says about "Wittgenstein's idea that the inexpressible is contained—inexpressibly!—in the expressed"[188] is another way of describing Michael Jackson's style. However, because Michael Jackson's body operates socio-discursively through an absence or a lack, "it cannot desire, but is, instead, desired."[189] In other words, being racially othered affects a black person at the level of his own subjectivity, which is always under erasure. However, the process of erasure always leaves its mark.[190]

Given that the "other," in this case, is always ascribed a racial identity, it is no wonder that Michael Jackson attempts to achieve the unachievable by reconstructing his racialized identity, *not black, not white*. It unsettles and plays on whites' fears and vulnerabilities by presenting an identity that is positioned outside the norms of recognizability, as between two races, black and white. What is important is that his racial identification goes against the presentation of race as a sign of its inherent "truth." In the United States, to be either black or white is prompted by obligatory norms.[191] Accordingly, Michael Jackson's racial in-betweenness, even though it might have opened up a possible way of thinking about race identity along new lines—because his racial in-betweenness still signals blackness—his otherness of the "other" unsettles the social body. It is in this way, the constraints imposed on Michael Jackson's attentiveness, "to be" (being) queer is "not to be" (nonbeing). Weirdness becomes the metonym for "queerness," another way of labeling what Michael Jackson himself calls his "strange eccentricities."[192]

Michael Jackson's Otherness of the "Other" and Its Problematics

The mistake is that we think we know something about Michael Jackson because of the many fictions he devises. Judging from his lived experience, he is nevertheless incapable of convincing himself that he is not white. He is unwilling to accept the harsh consequences of being black in a society that normalizes whiteness, so he tries to forge new meanings for the black body that unsettle its fixity and negative interpretations. In this regard, he vigorously attempts to move between racial spaces, *not black, not white*, and presents a sort of racial in-betweenness, an otherness of the "other." It is not surprising, then, that the persona of Michael Jackson has intrigued many scholars. According to Cynthia J. Fuchs, "whenever he appears in public—say on stage for 'Motown 25,' on television with Oprah Winfrey for their momentous interview, in Monte Carlo at the 1993 World Music Awards—his history is recounted through video imagery, reconfirming that his body is the site of a visibly identity, an effect of erasure, repetition, and resurrection."[193] It is indeed a body that is discursively constructed, deconstructed, and reconstructed, culturally imposed and refuted, and undoubtedly bounded by blackness as culturally assigned.

Because the construction of blackness has ironically relied on an absolute contempt for the lived complexities of blacks in the United States that have always been reduced to otherness, Michael Jackson's identification process as "a variation, a deviation, and a spacing"[194] in relation to racial classification is far from simple. If his body always appears as a discernably changing identity, "an effect of erasure, repetition, and resurrection,"[195] it is a body in all its seemingly self-contradictory articulations that remains black, a static and inescapable reality. And while blackness is an infraction of a constructed otherness, it cannot resist being under surveillance. In other words, a black person is persistently, to use the title of one of Michael Jackson's songs, a "man in the mirror,"[196] haunted by a "self" that is persistently constituted and reconstituted by the tenacity of the white gaze, operating amid presumptions about race that do not see blacks as equal to whites.

Hence, it is important for whites to position themselves also as "different" from blacks. This form of differentiating, or what Calvin Warren calls "ontological cutting," demands remarkable epistemic violence,[197] which, as Fred Wilderson submits, is "a paradigm of ontology."[198] I have given the name of systemic whiteness to this form of violence. For whiteness to remain invisible, it needs to produce the "other," blackness. In this sense, whites project what Diana Fuss identifies as an "alienation effect" onto blacks, who are "enjoined to identify and to disidentify simultaneously with whites, to assimilate but not to incorporate, to approximate but not to displace."[199] It is within the context that racial identification for Michael Jackson "carries an ontological and epistemological valence, such that the question, Who or What am I? becomes a question of being and knowing, a question of desire."[200] Another way of putting this is to ask who or what Michael Jackson is, which at the heart is the question of feelings, thinking, and knowing; in other words, of being black. The fixing of race on the body does have implications for racial transcendence proper.[201] Michael Omi and Howard Winant, in *Racial Formation in the United States*, explain this phenomenon as a racial project—a project that supports the systems and institutions advancing and upholding whiteness. In a world that is structured by such a negative imperative, in Jared Sexton's warning, "above all, don't be black"[202] becomes paramount.

Certainly, Michael Jackson's appearance of racial in-betweenness aligns with "the postmodern discourse that the body is changeable"[203] and thus must be seen for its rhizomatic potentiality. Furthermore, it deconstructs and challenges the notions of natural bodies and fixed identities as prearranged and controlled. Robert E. Johnson once described Michael Jackson "as beyond category."[204] Michael Jackson's disquieting racial ambiguity is consistent with his claim: "I wouldn't help it even if I could,"[205] which is not conceptualized, at least for him, "as an awkward or deliberate failure."[206] Certainly, Michael Jackson, for the most part, attempts to deal with his situation and the image he takes on. In fact, the image is not created by Michael Jackson but is the image that was already there waiting for him.[207] Yet, this image is sometimes enough to mark him as enigmatic and illusory. Terri Eagleton describes him as blurring "the distinction between facts and fiction."[208] In this view, there is no "real" or authentic Michael Jackson who can ever "become black." In the face of whiteness, blacks have no true role in their "becoming." His personhood is wiped out, canceled out as unreal. His attributes are deemed nonhuman. This cancellation comes in the form of a judgment which bears on Michael Jackson's sense of belonging to the "real."

While the black body is already formed, the plasticity of Michael Jackson's body—that is, how his body "takes form" and "gives form" in its self-definition/self-fashioning—makes Keith Haring conclude that

Michael Jackson is now "a trans-human, a cyborg."[209] If Donna Haraway is correct that a cyborg is "a hybrid creature, composed of organism and machine,"[210] why shouldn't there be bodies that do not principally take a human form, "a condensed image of both imagination and material reality, the two joined centres structuring any possibility of historical transformation"?[211] Indeed, rumors were traveling that Michael Jackson slept in a hyperbaric sleeping chamber and that he was obsessed with the "Elephant Man."[212] Furthermore, Michael Jackson confesses in an interview with *Ebony* magazine that he continues to be called a scarecrow.[213] But Michael Jackson is not just a scarecrow because he played the scarecrow in *The Wiz*. Another way of reading this is that a black person in a blackphobic society is always transformed into thingliness, absolute nothingness. This nothingness, according to Sara Jane Cervenak and J. Cameron Carter, "bespeaks but the undercommon otherside paraontology, namely, a modality of life unmoored from ownership, (en)titlement, groundedness, and settlement."[214] It is in this condition that a black person can declare, as Frantz Fanon did, facing the white man, "All I wanted was to be a man among other men,"[215] which is also to say, in the words of Michael Jackson, "I can't help it if I wanted to"[216] "be a man." Indeed, Michael Jackson enters the world full of imagination and thought. Like all blacks in the United States, a world which "yield[s] him no true self-consciousness, but only let[s] him see himself through the revelation of the other world"[217] and bars him of any participation as fully human. His encounter with the other world, "the only honorable one,"[218] in the words of Michael Jackson: "I'm gonna make a chance/For once in my life/It's gonna feel real good/Gonna make a difference."[219]

And even though what constitutes a black identity is never fixed, Michael Jackson is considered a traitor to his race, as is expressed by several tabloids. Certainly, in Michael Jackson's quest to transcend racial boundaries, he is the precise embodiment of James Weldon Johnson's "ex-colored man," a liminal figure living on the margins of racial normalcy, neither black nor white, the embodiment of a fragmented self, fractured and dislocated repeatedly. In this regard, Michael Jackson's body is doubly registered and viewed as an error, which cannot be defended in the Nietzschean joyful sense of "restored reason." "To err is to stray," Sara Ahmed tells us; "to err is to go the wrong way,"[220] to stray from the usual path of normativity. Michael Jackson must be "normalized" and disciplined. The normalizing and disciplining of Michael Jackson will, in part, be the focus of chapter 4.

Chapter 4

Michael Jackson's Nonconformity and Its Consequences

There are many attempts to "explain" the King of Pop Michael Jackson; that is, to "read" him as if he were a text to be read and discussed. Whether it is the tabloids, journalists, scholars, or the public, Michael Jackson has often been named a "weirdo" or a "freak," partly because of his refusal to abide by normative identity categories, such as race, gender, and sexuality, and assimilate himself into a specific social group. This nonconformity is best exemplified in Prince's song "I Would Die 4 You" in the ways it challenges these fixed identities. As the singer says: "I'm not a woman/I'm not a man/I'm something you'll never understand."[1] Of course, in this society, this "fluidity" is not allowed. One's identity must conform to the rigid either/or categories such as black/white, disabled/abled, gay/straight, and woman/man. This is one of the reasons why there is so much pressure on transgender people to identify as either a man or a woman.

Notwithstanding the fact that these oppositional binaries work in tension with one another, we warm up so willingly to these categories. And given that one is always impacted in some ways by the category that one does not belong to, I discovered in James Baldwin the most extraordinary acknowledgment that "we are all androgynous";[2] that is, in his phrase, "each of us helplessly and forever, contained the other—male in female, female in the male, white in black, black in white,"[3] and gay in straight, straight in gay. Baldwin concludes, "We are part of each other."[4] Baldwin's acknowledgment, of course, would put identity politics and the politics of recognition on the defensive.

Certainly, identity categories function as normative standards in the construction of subjectivity, which, as Joseph Vogel reminds us, is "an ever-mutating process of becoming, fashioned through," using Stuart Hall's words, "memory, fantasy, narrative and myth."[5] The uncertainty of Michael Jackson's race, gender, and sexuality identities, *not black, not white, not woman, not man, not gay, not straight* (the "nots" of identity's fixity within normative categories) that he seemingly displays, which challenges and disturbs these rigid identity categories, is enough for his critics to cast the King of Pop as a weirdo or a freak.[6] While, to use Michael Jackson's words from his song "Will You Be There," it "seems that the world has a role for [him],"[7] to call him a freak is a dishonest representation and an epistemological ignorance and misunderstanding of the King of Pop. As James Baldwin rightfully points out, "freaks are called freaks and are treated—in the main, abominably—because they are human beings who cause to echo, deep within us, our most profound terrors and desire."[8] As the saying goes, this certainly "hits close to home."

Over the years, Michael Jackson's seemingly weirdness or freakiness metric[9] accumulativeness includes his living with his chimpanzee, his close relations with animals he rescued from zoos and circuses (Louie the llama, Bubba the lion, and Muscles the snake),[10] and his wearing of a black surgical mask does not help.[11] In his *Leave Me Alone* video, Michael Jackson also dances "with an animator's fantastic rendition"[12] of the bones of the Elephant Man, the most celebrated "freak" in history. To try to comprehend the hullabaloos of Michael Jackson as weird, Joseph Vogel's reflection on "[dishonest] custodian of black life and wealth, especially males, in America"[13] is helpful. Michael Jackson's "weirdness" ricochets his queerness, another name for what Jackson himself calls his "strange eccentricities"[14] or "queer utopia," as Susan Fast puts it.[15] However, his "weirdness" is at the center of all discussions but is discussed uncritically. A critical examination should impose itself since Michael Jackson, the iconic figure, does not exist in a solipsistic state free from litigious media's conscription. What the public sees on the TV or at the movies, reads on the internet or in the newspapers and magazines, matter a great deal.[16] In fact, an account of how "media framing" works is important for any analysis of how the media produces a specific image of its subject and how it corresponds to a particular kind of discourse to indoctrinate its audience. In a word, "media framing" defends its agenda and, in Judith Butler's words, "produces the effect that it names."[17]

Certainly, some famous people or cultural icons can, for the most part, rely on the media framing them in such a way that it heightens the public curiosity about them and confirms their "normality." Consider, for example, "Babe Ruth's boozing through Frank Sinatra's association with alleged mobsters."[18] These wide swaths of incidents have always been acceptable and moreover confirm the "normality" of celebrities. Interestingly, with Michael Jackson, this is not the case. Let's make this point in a different manner. We can say with Susan Fast that "Jackson's queerness was quickly turned from utopia to dystopia by the media."[19] How is this allocation possible? Is it because the media "perpetuate[s] White America's racial disquiet"[20] about blackness? Does this have to do with Michael Jackson's refusal *not to be* that which has been ascribed to him? In *The Black Image in the White Mind: Media and Race in America*, Robert Entman and Andrew Rojecki provide an important account of the media and race. They explore how much "subtle material pertinent to Black-White relations structures all media production,"[21] and their "impacts on Black-White relations."[22] The fact that whites mostly act "as experts in network news"[23] and are usually incapable of transcending their racialized habitus[24] sheds some light on the reasons why ordinary citizens, journalists, documentarists, and even academics are united in their conservative posture and reactionary response to Michael Jackson as a racialized subject.

Furthermore, critics—conservatives and liberals alike—obsess over Michael Jackson's race, gender, and sexuality identities as well as over his plastic surgeries or any physical changes, whether they pertain to his features, his skin, his nose, or his hair (all of this supposedly casting him as *not black, not white* and exemplifying his refusal to conform to either/or race categories or gender assignments). His wearing of a surgical mask and his *Thriller* video let us see how living beings can undertake "metamorphosis." One of the most remarkable examples is in the singer's metamorphosis into a werewolf and a dancing zombie in *Thriller*, suggesting that he is not quite human. The tabloid nicknamed the King of Pop "Wacko Jacko," which, given its racist genealogy, Michael Jackson rightfully despised.[25] However, he cannot exist outside of such naming. In other words, his own experiences are marked by weirdness or freakiness. What makes Michael Jackson's "(ab)normality" demonstratively different from other celebrities is that his artifactual otherness departs from the reality that race is an identity readily visible on the body. Is this departure disturbing because Michael Jackson's skin/flesh returns America to its racist history of the one-drop of black blood rule?

Above all, Michael Jackson is a "natural" living being who, nonetheless, in the eyes of his distractors, lacks precisely the human character, the precise human reality, and these detractors even go so far as to outright claim that he "has lost touch with reality."[26] This loss is ostensibly demonstrated in Michael Jackson's most remarkable and controversial self-fashioning, characterized by an allegedly perverse identity stuck in-between opposites: unnatural and natural, black and white, woman and man, mother and father, gay and straight. And while this complex matrix is the definitive metamorphosis that his phenotype underwent,[27] one can imagine Michael Jackson like Orlando in Virginia Woolf's *Orlando*: "I'm sick to death of this particular self. I want another," from "the two thousand and fifty-two"[28] selves that are available to him. Michael Jackson's desire for another "self" for himself, or to be another "self" for someone else, in the face of the unremitting whiteness, is inevitable, in that he wants to be a "self," but he cannot be a "self" for himself. The social or ontological claim that everybody can be a "self" is not true for blacks because "what is often called the black [self] is a white man's artifact," as Frantz Fanon reminds us.[29]

Michael Jackson's ambivalent self-identification or, in this case, disidentification of the subject from himself is a willful demonstration, not so much between opposite identity, in terms of race assignment. *Not black, not white*, coexisting at the same time on the body as an enigmatic site of race ambiguities, creating a "third body" out of the entwinement of Michael Jackson's ambiguous race, which nonetheless underscores the materiality of the racialized body, marking "the body prior to its mark"—and it is the practice through which the body "becomes signifiable"[30] as black—is important. That is to say, blackness, in its phobogenic state, a process of "epidermalization" to which Frantz Fanon refers,[31] renders race logical and conjures all kinds of anxiety for the social body. One of the results, in its vicious after-effects, is lost on the "third body"; that is, a body that is "out from" the either/or racial binary, positioning Michael Jackson as a "three-dimensional" man.

Epidermalization is what makes race perceptible, and it works through a form of disciplinary power that makes "the individual a racial subject."[32] It concerns "itself to immediate everyday life" and the struggles around racial difference and the production of an identity that is marked on the skin. Furthermore, epidermalization "categorizes the individual, marks him by his own individuality, attaches him to his own identity, imposes the law of the truth of race [on] him that he must recognize and others have to recognize [on] him."[33] This is precisely one of the reasons why Michael Jackson's racial in-betweenness marks him as a weirdo or a freak.

From a different perspective, Michael Jackson's "weirdness" is just another way of him being [ec]centric. "Ec" comes from the Greek work *ek*, meaning in English, "out of," "away from," "outside of." The ec in eccentric is its "outside of" the centric, the center of what is "normal." To be eccentric is to be ek, outside of the "normal," leading cultural critic Richard Corliss to declare that Michael Jackson's "eccentricities gave him an otherworldly cast."[34] This "outsidedness of the norm" is also negatively translated by others into "a trans-human, a cyborg,"[35] and "a sleek jagwar."[36] To borrow from Donna J. Haraway, "the boundary between human and animal is thoroughly breached."[37] So, when a black person is viewed as another sort of living being, in this case not quite human because of America's history of dehumanizing blacks, it carries with it a form of epistemic violence. That is, in the eminent Gayatri C. Spivak's terms, "the remotely orchestrated, far-flung, and heterogeneous project to constitute [blacks] as other"[38] provoked a negative reading of the King of Pop. Accordingly, many remain distrustful of Michael Jackson and judge him unnecessarily harshly. No wonder he says with great remorse, "Before you judge me, try hard to love me."[39] However, we cannot ignore that there is a double standard when it comes to the media's scrutiny of celebrities. White celebrities' "weirdness" is devoid of such ridicule. Certainly, Michael Jackson's announcement in his aptly titled song "Black or White"—and in the very line, "It don't matter if you're black or white"—is indeed very wrong. It does in fact matter if you are black or white.

Even though Seth Clark Siberman is called by Libby Copeland "a Jackson junkie,"[40] Siberman is right to remind us that Michael Jackson did not invent weirdness.[41] Still, it is possible to try to give an account of how "media framing" works with the help of Judith Butler's *Frames of War: When is Life Grievable?* in order to help us understand: (1) the many ways in which the media's rhetoric, language, ideology, and discourse produced an implicit image of Michael Jackson as "weird"; and (2) how this image corresponds to racist discourses that indoctrinate many Americans. One does not have to be a psychoanalyst to recognize that Michael Jackson's exposure to this kind of name-calling (freak, wacko, or weirdo) makes him vulnerable to such name-calling, which establishes a vital feature of the speech act, through which he acts because the speech is acting upon him and which, following Judith Butler, I will call the performative power of naming. In fact, it is useless for him to try hard to train his ear not to hear the *name* he is called. The public expects him to behave "weird" and he obliges.[42] Indeed, there is an anxiety for Michael Jackson of having been called a name, a name he himself did not know and has never chosen. Once he is named weird, he can never be seen in a different light. He must be the poster boy for "weirdness." In fact, he incarnates the "weirdness" to which all blacks are subjected and hailed. "Am I that name" is for blacks the quintessential question.

Basically, it is not a secret that weirdness or freakiness in the face of blackness is always subjected to the most excessive form of derision because blackness already constructs a body that is defiant of social norms; a body operating at a limit that resists normalization and provides a text, which is unsettling and disorienting to whiteness. And given that "whiteness," Sara Ahmed tells us, "orients [the black body] in specific directions, affecting how [it] 'takes up' space, and what it 'can do,'"[43] disorientation can create an unending "crisis" for whiteness. I use "crisis" here as Giorgio Agamben defines it: an "instrument of the rule"[44] promoting and upholding the insistence that whiteness must be superior to blackness.[45] Certainly, the facticity of blackness fixes and objectifies the black man. In the particular case of Michael Jackson, where identity is reduced to skin, the surfaceness of the body is doubly objectified, *not black, not white*, which positions him in a peculiar racial in-betweenness that forecloses any chance for racial hybridity.

At the same time, given that Michael Jackson is positioned as an other "other," his liminal racial identity, which is visible in its failed performance of race, unsettles, frightens, and disturbs. This does not depart from the multivalent and reliant processes of racialization in the United States that marked a black person, in the Fanonian language, as "overdetermined from without."[46] As George Yancy puts it, a black identity is continuously before now "fixed, complete, given."[47] To put it differently, they are "being dissected under white eyes, the only real eyes." They are "fixed" by their "own appearance."[48] Simply because of their social appearance as a race being rather than their personal human qualities, it makes it difficult to operate outside the process of racialization.[49]

For Robert Miles, racialization is "the representational process whereby social significance is attached to certain biological (usually phenotypic) human features on the basis of which those people possessing those characteristics are designated as a distinct social collectivity."[50] It was a process used by the colonists to position blacks as "raced beings" rather than "human beings," which continues today. That said, like all blacks, Michael Jackson cannot escape America's practice of the "fixing and classifying of racial boundaries,"[51] taking as its foundation "physical identity formation,"[52] which imagines race as a social construct to be fixed on the body. The opposite holds true for whiteness as the invisible norm. Not that whiteness is invisible to blacks—for blacks, there is an ontological specificity of whiteness as terrifying.[53] Given that whiteness is unraced and unmarked, a black person is forever confronted by what W. E. B. Du Bois describes as a "peculiar sensation," this "double consciousness, . . . this sense of always looking at one's self through the eyes of others," shaping blacks' subjectivity as "mixed up" and fragmented, inner/outer, self/other, and, in Michael Jackson's case, attempting to present another "me."

Michael Jackson appears to be viewed negatively as a "body without organs,"[54] which positions him outside of the realm of the "normal." In fact, that which is "normal" is inevitably natural and becomes the source of "truth." This emphasis on naturality is another way to transform the subject or social being into, as Judith Revel observes, "a new instrument of control."[55] This leads Stuart Hall to acknowledge: "It is one thing to position a subject or a set of people as the other of a dominant discourse. It is quite another thing to subject them to that kind of 'knowledge' not only as a matter of imposed knowledge and domination, by the power of inner compulsion and subject confirmation to the norm."[56] Judith Butler clearly knows this; she reminds us that a norm acts "on us from all sides, that is, in multiple and contradictory ways."[57] Given that Michael Jackson unsettles racial norms, for example, he is considered a freak or weird.

How does Michael Jackson's "weirdness" or "freakiness" challenge identification as well as misidentification—that is, the doubling of "otherness"—that informs his racial self-alienation? Does his "weirdness," anchored in being neither black nor white, an other "other," create anxiety because of its subverting potentiality that he must be resisted, restricted, or worse, punished and humiliated in order for society to safeguard the realm of normality? I raise these questions to think about locating Michael Jackson's "weirdness" within a larger framework of self-fashioning.[58] Even for those who hold firm the notion of Michael Jackson as a freak or weird and try to make him into something wanton and overlook his cultural achievements,[59] he "changed culture all over the world"[60] and achieved worldwide eminence. On this score, Dave Marsh's announcement that "Jackson . . . has become a necessity . . . for those who pretend to know about American music"[61] rings as essential. Furthermore, Michael Jackson, as another reviewer notes, "practically invented a new genre of mass entertainment, and made himself into the most popular performer in the history of American music,"[62] which accomplished similar fervor in his appearance in *Captain EO*,⁶³ a film released on September 12, 1986, at Disneyworld's EPCOT.

In *Captain EO*, Jackson "emerges as the hero of Captain EO, the archetypal postmodern figure of utopian potential."⁶⁴ Richard Corliss describes "the first half of the film as 'an energetic rehash of the Star Wars space battle,' and the second half as an 'elaborate Michael Jackson video.' "⁶⁵ Notwithstanding that the general-public was enthralled by the film, in Corliss's conclusive remarks of the film, he describes it as "being sugar but no spice."⁶⁶ The film is also dismissed by Carl Miller as "academically or philosophically inconsequential."⁶⁷ This is to say that philosophy (as it is narrowly understood) or academia, for that matter, are the only reliable modes of thinking critically. It very disconcerting to think that the general public cannot read. In fact, the university is the educational microcosm or the place to develop and advance a precise kind of knowledge, and it functions as the status quo, the communal order, the prevailing norms. Because of all this, the university can put a restriction on thought that is outside of western institutionalized learning and dismiss any form of indigenous knowledge, for instance. Partly, for this reason, Henry Louis Gates Jr. acknowledges that the university is an establishment of legitimation—establishing what counts as knowledge and what counts as culture.⁶⁸

In "Michael Jackson: The Peter Pan Pop," *Newsweek* refers to Michael Jackson as "The Peter Pan of Pop"⁶⁹ and, in the same breath, enlarges the conception and disharmonic reference of him to report that "Michael Jackson remains something of an enigma."⁷⁰ This stance is readily taken on by journalists, scholars, and the general public with narratives "all running in complex and different directions,"⁷¹ which often reduce Michael Jackson to weirdness or freakiness. Here is how Ken Tucker of *Entertainment Weekly* puts it: It is "impossible to deny the creepy subtext of a 34-year-old, crotch-grabbing, *Dangerous* guy [Michael Jackson] who says he most likes to hang out with 'animals and children.' "⁷² Going against Tucker's unnecessarily harsh remarks, Carl Miller, rightfully so, points out that "Jackson is the literal embodiment of the cyborg, in a manner that bypasses 'bizarre' in favor of 'progressive' and 'utopian.' "⁷³ In spite of Miller's remarks, it seems impossible for Michael Jackson to extricate himself from this constructed weirdness. However, we must decry Tucker's comment as pernicious.

In this chapter, I will look at how the polymorphous uncertainties of Michael Jackson's self-fashioning, all operating in complex and different directions, uncritically simplify him as "weird" or a "freak." Indeed, I want to show that "weirdness" or "freakiness" in the face of blackness is subject to the most excessive forms of derision—because blackness constructs a body that is already defiant of social norms. In other words, blackness coupled with "weirdness" or "freakiness" is forever perceived as *bad* and *dangerous*. Jackson must be disciplined and "normalized." I will take my cue from Michel Foucault's *Discipline and Punish*, in which at "the heart of all of the disciplinary systems functions a small penal mechanism,"[74] which identifies that what is reflected normal behavior is essential. In this way, what is indeed paramount is how the disciplinary process functions to punish and correct bodies that do not conform to societal norms.[75] I am interested, here, in how race functions as a discipline regime.

Michael Jackson and "Weirdness" or "Freakiness"

For a long time, Michael Jackson has been viewed as weird. This is to be upheld when the fate of Michael Jackson is revealed in Hackett's *Newsweek* article "Michael Jackson Puts on Ears" (September 29, 1986). The title of this article reminds us of how a black person, an uppity black "'clean cut' Negro, well-dressed and groomed,"[76] always "puts on ears." What is one to make of such a title? In his 1997 journal entry, artist Keith Haring cautions that Michael Jackson did not yet "get his ears pointed or add a tail or something, but give him time."[77] This comment epitomizes the othering of Michael Jackson as not one of "us" but one of "them." He can indeed never be a part of the "us," even if he is the King of Pop.[78] Even when Michael Jackson, as a godlike figure (the lamb of God) bestowed on him by his many billions of faithful fans, which he gleefully embraces, Hackett cannot but ask rhetorically, in a sardonic mode, "Has Michael Jackson finally gone off the deep end?"[79] Such speculations are fueled by some regrettable incidents such as Michael Jackson dangling his baby from the fourth-floor balcony of the Hotel Adlon to please his cheering fans wanting to see his baby. However, his critics, of course, interpreted his behavior as "weird." And when I say this, I am thinking about how, in Silberman's words, "Michael Jackson dangles the freak we so comfortably expect."[80]

Notwithstanding the moment when Michael Jackson puts his child and himself totally at risk, on grounds that famous blacks are continuously policed by the media, that incidence, for sure, adds to the view of him as weird. Furthermore, the public was outraged. Michael Jackson had to issue an apology, referring to the incident as "a terrible mistake"; in the same apologetic tone, he concluded, "I offer no excuses for what happened." He added, "I got caught up in the excitement of the moment. I would not endanger the lives of my children."[81] Who wouldn't get "caught up in the moment" when thousands of fans scream outside of one's hotel window. Michael Jackson was indeed lucky that the incident occurred outside of the United States. If it were in the United States and the police were notified, it could have resulted in his arrest. In the United States, there is a history of whites calling the police on blacks. We remember well the infamous case of Dr. Henry Louis Gates Jr., as I mentioned before. In fact, on July 20, 2009, Lucia Whalen, a white woman, informed the police that she had seen two black men (one of the men being Dr. Gates) on the porch of Dr. Gates's home. Dr. Gates was thereafter arrested by Sergeant James Crowley, a white police officer, outside of his own home in Cambridge.[82]

The perception of Michael Jackson as a freak reached its climax in 2005 when he was accused of child molestation and he showed up at his trial "dressed in blue print pajamas and looking more spectral than ever."[83] He was reported being at the "Cottage hospital in Santa Ynez with a serious back problem," but the Court Judge Robert S. Melville insisted that if Michael Jackson did not show up for the trial within the hour, he would issue a warrant for his arrest and forfeit bail.[84] The way this episode was reported by the media is unforgettable. Michael Jackson's arrival at court was described as "a spectacle, a high-tech ministerial show, . . . a tragic large-scale example of what results of a black man who defiles his 'place.' "[85] This comes as no surprise to anyone who has charted the genealogy of America's racist history. Michael Jackson's ridicule started way before the alleged child molestation charges. Joseph Vogel writes, "It was not long after the successes of *Thriller* (including a record haul of eight Grammy awards in February 1984) that the tide began to turn against Jackson."[86] Why was this? Is it possible that the entertainment world, which is known for its racism and its multidimensional form of discriminatory practices, did not react well to the success of Michael Jackson, who, as James Baldwin puts it best, "having turned so many tables"[87] in his race, gender, and sexuality presentations, was then, as the King of Pop, at the center of the entertainment world? A black sin which, in Baldwin's words, is "not swiftly forgiven."[88] More importantly, Baldwin goes on to say, "All that noise [about Michael Jackson] is about America, as this dishonest custodian of black life and wealth; the blacks especially, males in America."[89] Certainly, how blackness puts a black person in the imminent danger of being socially lynched cannot be disputed.

Michael Jackson's persona, his racial in-betweenness, his ambiguous gender and sexuality, and his "strange eccentricities" expose the damages of the otherness of the "other" and the paranoid logic of unfixing identity that threatens the social body. All of this seems impermeable enough to label him as weird or in some cases as a freak. This might have prompted Libby Copeland in "One Strange Case" to describe him as an alien; his "face looks as if it's made from puzzle pieces that weren't meant to fit together," she writes.[90] The contempt directed toward Michael Jackson was not without significance and persisted for a long time. Margo Jefferson, for example, compares him to Gloria Swanson, played by Norma Desmond in the 1950 American film *Sunset Boulevard*, whom Jefferson insensitively describes as "a travesty looking very much like an aging transvestite, a freak."[91] Jefferson's juxtaposition of transvestitism with freakiness opens a space for reflective thinking about exclusion and marginalization of bodies that are positioned outside cultural norms and social bodily practices. Once again, the emphasis is on the visually unpleasing body, *the body* that is outside of the normal, which is no different from *our body* that is aging. While the focus, here, is on *the body*, when *the body* (i.e., a body that is outside of the norms of recognizability) is replaced with *our body* (i.e., a body that is no longer youthful), it rushes us into the lived experience of our aging body, *essentially speaking*, reconfigured by, in the words of Diana Fuss, "scars, disfigurements, discolorations, damages, [and] loses."[92] Only in replacing *the body* with *our body* can we recognize the "freakiness" of *our body* in its aging process and its expected demise, which presents a more complex view of freakiness that does not have the same averseness in the way freakiness is used to denigrate Michael Jackson.

The interference of freakiness with a range of cultural and historical issues is not taken into consideration in Jefferson's attempt, in her short chapter on "Freaks" in her book *On Michael Jackson*, to both report and analyze what she describes as the "freaks" of our society to bring about the notion that freaks can be divided into two broad categories: the "freaks of nature, outside the boundaries of the normal"[93] and the "self-made" freaks.[94] In this spirit, Julian Vigo warns us that "Jefferson makes little effort to tease the problematic historical discourse of freakery from the present,"[95] to draw on how culture constructs freakery, and to locate freakery in its broader historical context. Vigo notes, "for the late twentieth century freak was often a role model for others to follow. . . . It is about embracing difference and rendering it both spectacle and normal."[96]

Jefferson, for whom being a "freak" is to stray away from normality, nonetheless labels Michael Jackson as a "self-made" "freak." What a person is in life, to a large extent, is constituted by the social practice of naming, which returns us to Judith Butler's important analysis of how and why "discourse produces the effect that it names."[97] Michael Jackson cannot refuse such a practice. In other words, he has to reckon with this name-calling and the destiny of cultural marginalization and abjection that it calls up. The likelihood of another possibility for him, in this sense, other than his weirdness or freakiness, is foreclosed.

One of the most telling examples is found in the discussion presented by Terry Eagleton on Michael Jackson: "Jackson's freakish body represents the struggle of fantasy against reality, the pyrrhic of culture over body."[98] Sadly, Michael Jackson is read as a " 'freak" with double alterity because his freakiness is located in his blackness, which is already defiant of social standards and positioned outside of the standards of recognizability based on whiteness. Jefferson's comparison of Michael Jackson to Phineas T. Barnum's gathering of "freaks" from the early nineteenth century cannot be ignored.[99] For Michael Jackson to be labeled a " 'freak" is a summon by the other to be the "self" that the other wants him to be. In his conscious or unconscious responses to the projection or desire of the other, he cannot help being on the side of freakiness/weirdness because what is stronger than him is the other's relation to non-freakiness. This response, however, can only lead to the corporeal modality of physical reductionism and abjection of his bodily positioning.

Julia Kristeva's description of abjection "as an extremely strong feeling which is at once somatic and symbolic, and which is above all a revolt of the person against an external menace from which one wants to keep oneself at a distance, but of which one has the impression that it is not only an external menace but it may menace us externally from the inside"[100] can help us to think about how a black identity is culturally constructed as abnormal against a white identity as normal and, in the end, about how blackness performs its abnormality as an identity that threatens the social body. This is another way to organize racial hierarchy in the United States. Frantz Fanon, in *Black Skin, White Masks*, perspicaciously draws our attention to western discourses and shows how the reciprocal hermeneutic relationship between the physical and the social upholds whiteness as normal, as the seemingly natural state from which the black identity, for example, is a social, moral, and aesthetic foil.[101] Furthermore, whiteness is defined as the undetectable standard against which blacks are judged in constituting their identity, existence, power, and representation. Surely, for this reason, whiteness as the standard is unendingly emphasized and upheld within systems, structures, discourse, epistemology, and ideology, which Foucault defines as "the polymorphous techniques of power."[102] This form of power marks the continual determination of whiteness to inaugurate and argument its authority[103] over blackness outsideness.

Indeed, Michael Jackson is made out to be a "weirdo." Well-crafted choreographies with titles such as *Michael Jackson's Boys*[104] and *Michael Jackson and the Boy He Paid Off*,[105] bringing "together [a] notion of corruption as a monstrous inner to explain him as a monstrous other,"[106] a "weirdo," did not help. Also, the British journalist Martin Bashir, who oversees the documentary *Living With Michael Jackson*, exacerbated Michael Jackson's identification as "weird." In order to get another view of Michael Jackson other than what Bashir presents, it will do well to look at *The Michael Jackson Interview: The Footage You Were Never Meant to See*. The latter is from the footage that Michael Jackson also openly taped while Bashir was interviewing him for *Living With Michael Jackson*.[107] This is indeed a good example of "a camera behind a camera," a claim to another "truth," dancing the dance of attempting to get to the "real real," the unchanging "truth," as you will, if you truly want to grasp the adept unethicality and cunningness of Bashir.

While the documentary is an important form for meaning construction to take place because of the way it draws "on narrative structures and characterisations of their subjects,"[108] one simply cannot rely on it to get to the "truth," even though the documentary presumes a truth prerogative. In opposition to the views presented in *Michael Jackson's Boys*, as the title suggests, the documentary *Wacko About Jacko*,[109] in which Michael Jackson's heterogeneous UK fans in the documentary, at whatever cost, support and defend their idol, a god, "gone astray in the flesh,"[110] is essential. According to *Entertainment Weekly* on June 25, 2009, "Jackson's fans are among the most loyal"[111] and the singer is deified by them. Of course, Michael Jackson's fans, in this case, are labeled "emotivists," in that "[e]motivism grounds moral judgment in people's opinions and in how they feel" about Michael Jackson.[112] So, when his fans attempt to defend him from what they consider as malicious gossip working to tarnish the image of their hero, they are labeled as emotivists. In this sense, to be an emotivist is to be vulnerable, to be "taken in" by Michael Jackson's fame and stardom. And while we do know that vulnerability has been culturally coded as female because women are considered a vulnerable group that needs protection, the assertion that Michael Jackson's fans are made vulnerable by him who, to borrow from Vigo quoting Jefferson, "hides behind a mask of cosmetic surgery, skin lightening, and increasing 'effeminization' "[113] has no support and is equally flawed.

Going against Jefferson's bleak outlook, most of all, Vigo reasonably concludes, "many of Jackson's fans identified with him due to their own marginalization."[114] Like Michael Jackson, they are themselves positioned outside of the "normal." Certainly, his fans, and so they must be, embrace him as one of the most gifted and talented entertainers ever, not as a freak or a weirdo. In the end, in *Living With Michael Jackson*, Jackson tells us "I sing for my [fans] and they cheer for me. It's about love." The love shared between Michael Jackson and his fans exists on a manifest level considering the millions of albums he has sold and the many lives he has touched. Make no mistake, the love between him and his fans is deeply entangled. This is why he can say wholeheartedly, "where there is love, I'll be there."[115]

When Michael Jackson confesses in *Living With Michael Jackson* that he likes to hang out with children and animals, this is one of the responses from his critics that must be repeated: It is "impossible to deny the creepy subtext of a 34-year-old, crotch-grabbing, *Dangerous* guy who says he most likes to hang out with 'animals and children.' "[116] Is this so unusual? For Michael Jackson, children and animals are innocent. They want nothing from you, except your love.[117] Love is a persistent theme in Michael Jackson's lecture at Oxford University; it is "the foundation of all human knowledge, the beginning of human consciousness."[118] At one point, in *Living With Michael Jackson*, Jackson tells Bashir outright, "when kids come to [Neverland Ranch], they want to stay with me." Bashir's response to such a revelation is, "That is entirely wrong." For Kathryn Flett, on the other hand, "it's like getting to live at Disneyworld with Mickey as your host . . . complete with milk and cookies and story time." Flett, indeed, asks the right question: "Does it really make [Michael Jackson] mad, bad, and dangerous,"[119] in other words, weird or a freak? Of course, for the faultfinders, the unsophisticated answer is a simple *yes*.

Like Nietzsche's Zarathustra on the mountaintop, searching for a way to build a new world, Michael Jackson sits at the top his favorite tree at his Neverland Ranch[120] thinking about the many problems of the soul and produces mind-blowing lyrics for "*everyone and no one.*"[121] Let us look at Michael Jackson's "Man in the Mirror": he takes a political stand and wants to change the world. Perhaps, from the top of his tree, he "sees the kids in the streets with not enough to eat" and "no message could have been any clearer." This, above all, is Michael Jackson's desire to change some of the hardness in the world, like hungry children on streets "with not enough to eat." But in order to bring about these changes, you have to start with, as Michael Jackson contends, "the man in the mirror" and ask "him to change his ways/And no message could have been any clearer/Take a look at yourself and then make a change." This indeed is not the romantic Michael Jackson, sitting and asking himself, "How did love slip away?"[122] However, "Man in the Mirror" bears the trace of Michael Jackson's overarching concern for love, power, and poverty, for example, that influence the human condition.

"Man in the Mirror," for all its heavy themes of the pain and suffering of children, is quite uplifting.[123] Indeed, the song is positive in its message and it inspires one not just on a quest to know the world but also, like Michael Jackson, to try to change, when you can, the many suffering of children and people in general. Like Nietzsche's Zarathustra, Michael Jackson is "the advocate of suffering."[124] It is no wonder that underprivileged kids are invited by Michael Jackson to Neverland Ranch. Of course, who else but Martin Bashir would say that Neverland Ranch "is a dangerous place for vulnerable children to be," or, as he further elaborates, "what I'm saying is that children who are vulnerable should not be going into the house of a billionaire superstar where they sleep in his bed. That is entirely wrong." To put it differently, it is weird. Martin Bashir, the self-appointed spokesperson for traditional family structure quarrels with Michael Jackson for not adhering to these values.

Indeed, a nagging fear of Michael Jackson's contra normative family values appears to be on Bashir's mind. He asks Jackson: "Do any of [your] children's mother[s] live with you?" and when his response is "no," Bashir further asks, "Is that difficult?" Michael Jackson's response of "why should that be difficult?" prompts Bashir to ask further still: "Are the children not looking for their mother?" And while Bashir's answer is embedded in the question he finally asks, and the question itself is formulated in such a way as to impress upon its wrongness with a capital "W," Michael Jackson seizes on the opportunity to answer Bashir's question: "Many babies live with their mothers, and they don't have fathers around them." However, in the mind of Bashir, a single male-headed household like that of Michael Jackson's destabilizes traditional family values.[125]

In any case, when Michael Jackson himself started to spread the rumors that he sleeps in "a hyperbaric chamber so that he can live to be 150 years old,"[126] it became the cover story for the *National Enquirer* on September 16, 1986. Of course, gossipmongers wanted to know: "Has Michael Jackson finally gone off the deep end?" as George Hackett had asked.[127] Michael Jackson was obviously amused: "I can't believe that [the media] bought it. . . . It's like I can tell the press anything about me and they'll buy it."[128] Perhaps his hoax was "to arouse a restless public's interest."[129] Seth Clark Siberman (quoted in Copeland) states that "Michael has long had an interest in us thinking that he's weird."[130] Indeed, Michael Jackson is *in* this world, but he ceases to be *of* the world.

Undoubtedly, Michael Jackson can write his own *Ecce Homo*. He is the man who stands on the gate of compassion and constantly knocks, knowing that there are many Pontius Pilates adding to his crucifixion. Unlike Nietzsche's *Ecce Homo* that starts off with "Why I am so Wise," Michael Jackson's could start with "Why I am so Misunderstood" while sitting at the top of a tree in his ranch, like an uncaged bird in its natural habitat, narrating his way back to tranquility[131] with the freshness of life itself, and in a gentle outburst he would confess, "I like livin' the way."[132] However, Michael Jackson is misunderstood because he acts in a way that does not respect the social and cultural rules of bodily behaviors, and as a result, he must be disciplined and normalized. "Normalization," John Caputo and Mark Yount acknowledge, "does impose homogeneity"[133] and is continually used to evaluate and control people because one must be recognized as a member of a particular identity category (as an either/or). But in the case of race, for example, Michael Jackson is *not black, not white*, and this unsettles racial norms. In fact, his racial in-betweenness positions him outside of the norm of race recognizability. As such, he is always in danger of misrecognition, which has a cultural, epistemological, and material foundation. The point is, misrecognition occurs when an identity does not adhere to the either/or category. And, in the case of Michael Jackson, race identity, for example, appears as heterogeneous and unfixed. For this reason, Michael Jackson must indeed be disciplined and normalized.

The Disciplining and "Normalizing" of Michael Jackson

Michel Foucault lets us know that an individual "is amputated, repressed, altered by our social order" of normality and "is carefully fabricated into it, according to a whole technique of forces and bodies"[134] through which subjects are made. Michael Jackson's racial identity, *not black, not white*, his racial in-betweenness, for one, unsettles "the keepers and seals, those who know what the world needs in the way of order and who are ready to supply that order"[135] through the behemoth webs of disciplinary power. Given that race functions as a disciplinary regime and blackness is produced through racial discipline,[136]—a "highly rigid regulatory frame," in Judith Butler's words[137]—such a regime supplies the order that produces a racialized body that conforms to the recognizable norms of blackness or, in Foucault's phrase, "the discourse of truth,"[138] putting the restrictions on race conceived within the norms of recognizability as a bodily marked. In this sense, race performativity as a cultural practice cannot be "multifaceted, fluid, and individualized,"[139] as is the case with Michael Jackson. There is a specific way of being black.

While race performativity is never a single or deliberate action but rather a discursive practice that produces the results of that which is seen and named, any attempts at a different performance of race as Michael Jackson does violates the law of race. This conjures up the Greek play *Antigone*, in which the eponymous character violates the law of kinship. As Judith Butler writes in *Antigone's Claim*: "Antigone has already departed from kinship, herself the daughter of an incestuous bond, herself devoted to an incestuous love for her brother, and how her actions compel others to regard her as "manly" and thus cast doubt on the way that kinship might underwrite gender."[140]

Kinship in the family is important. Certainly, in the family, we kin in various ways. However, if the family as a community pertains specifically to the black community, then there is a specific way of being black, a likeness (all blacks look alike or, to use Jean-Luc Nancy's words, blacks as "beings in common"[141]) that is based on a look, a bodily mark. In Fanon's leitmotiv, *Look, a black*, the *look* serves as a discipline devised to make the black person conscious of themselves as black and discipline them until they become self-disciplined into their blackness. On this score, how racial discipline, as a form of "the specific technique of power," in Foucault's words,[142] becomes a mechanism of "normalizing regulatory ideals that generate the very [body] that race governs,"[143] bringing into existence how race as a social construction is supposed to function. And if Judith Butler is correct that "thinking the body as constructed demands a rethinking of the meaning of construction itself,"[144] it is significant to note at this point that in the United States, the construction of race as a form of disciplinary power premised on the rule of white men was evident from the beginning of indentured servitude[145] and extended into the slave regime where it took on a ruthless form of corporeal punishment, in the form of severe whipping, mutilations, and killing of slaves, a legacy that lives on through the Reconstruction period and the Jim Crow South through the spectacles and rituals such as lynching.[146] The biopolitical rights of those in power (white men) were absolute and indispensable.[147]

While for Foucault power is not complete, nor does it occur in opposition to resistance, how race is constituted within the wider workings of racial discipline and performative requirements cannot be disavowed. For sure, blacks have always worked to resist the power of whiteness (the Black Power Movement and hip-hop culture, for example). However, a black person's attempt to resist race assignment as a bodily mark is always foreclosed. They are met with all kinds of resistance outside of the "self" and are returned to themselves as a foil to the social body. Because the black body is always policed, it is safe to say that race assignment, as an example of disciplinary power, is indeed productive for whiteness preeminence. It is no wonder that Michael Jackson's racial in-betweenness, *not black, not white*, provokes such strong debates over his race and an "ongoing cultural anxiety over the polymorphous ambiguities"[148] of his racial identity. Michael Jackson must be "normalized."

The arrest of Michael Jackson on November 20, 2003, for allegedly molesting children and the media's overshowing of the mug shot taken at his arrest are highly significant: "It was a particularly harsh image which emphasized the radical distortions of [Michael Jackson's] feature and skin."[149] What in my view is the most disturbing aspect of this portrayal of Michael Jackson as a freak of nature is that supposedly reasonable and intelligent people can be so easily swayed by apocryphal narratives. It is ghastly when commonsense replaces imagination. On this score, Michael Jackson must be resisted, restricted, or worse, punished and humiliated in order for society to safeguard the realm of normality. Indeed, he must be "normalized" and disciplined into what are registered as the norms and values of society.

Taking everything into consideration, one of the strategies to "normalize" and discipline Michael Jackson was to assault his body image. For this purpose, the police made a mockery of the Fourth Amendment of the American Constitution's right to privacy—that is, "the right of the people to be secure in their person"—and boldly photographed and displayed Michael Jackson's penis as part of the evidence in the alleged child molestation charges against him. During the gross violation of Michael

Jackson's rights to privacy, he pleaded with the police with a heavy heart: "Please, do I have to go through this?" and desperately cried out, "Make them stop."¹⁵⁰ Furthermore, he tried to plea his innocence, "Don't treat me like a criminal, because I am innocent."¹⁵¹ Given that in this case, the "I" cannot be referenced without a "them" circumscribed and intractably presented as criminals, the dyadic relation between the "I" and the "them" cannot be ignored. "I am not a criminal" means the opposite: "I am a criminal." Of course, Michael Jackson's affirmation is completely ignored by the authorities because in this case the "I" lacks any kind of authority. "To speak," as a black person, according to Fanon, "is to exist absolutely as other"¹⁵² and to lack authority. In this sense, when a black person speaks out against any kind injustice directed toward them or other blacks, blacks are always under fire. Take the case of Oprah Winfrey. Winfrey came under fire because she drew similarities between the murders of the fourteen-year-old Emmett Till in 1955 and the seventeen-year-old Trayvon Martin in 2012.¹⁵³ So much for freedom of speech. This illustrates an important point. Blacks do have "speech," but it is never attached to this thing called "freedom."

In returning to the disciplining of Michael Jackson, in his unproven child molestation charges, his penis, we are reminded, unlike "hair samples, finger prints, or human tissues," was used as evidence to determine that a crime was committed.¹⁵⁴ This is not without importance. We can speak of this as an additional practice of, in the words of Fred B. Wilderson III, "policing blackness."¹⁵⁵ We remember the case of Ms. Rhinelander, who, in order to prove that she was black, was instructed by her lawyer and the judge "to bare her breasts to the jury."¹⁵⁶ Certainly, policing blackness, Wilderson goes on to say, "is what keeps everyone else sane."¹⁵⁷ There are several accounts of white women calling the police on blacks because blackness as a threat to "public safety" is a part of the white psyche. Thus, blackness must be constantly policed. I have already pointed to several examples of what I call "commonsense racism." High increases in crimes and violence, for example, are explained commonsensically through race, and this commonsense racism is expressed in official and unofficial daily practices, ideologies, and discourses. In the United States, "governing through crime" is a good example of "commonsense racism." Blacks, for the most part, cannot protect themselves against the spectacle of "commonsense racism"¹⁵⁸ and are forever vulnerable to such an atrocity.

A true anomaly of this kind of "commonsense racism" is found in the manner in which the police are structurally placed to fight whites' inherent ways of "seeing" blackness and to protect whiteness against its own endangerment from, and fear of, the black body. By virtue of whiteness, in whites' imaginary, the policing of blackness in the form of excessive police hostility toward blacks "is not a form of discrimination."[159] Assigning hostility to the object of police hostility, in this case blacks, is a strategy that continues to reiterate and uphold the policing of blackness and hampers any kind of compromises proper. In this respect, "the victim is twice victim, once as wronged in a criminal act, and a second time by effacement, albeit legally of the injury that had been suffered, an effacement whose publicity offends the victim."[160] The ill treatment of the superstar and icon Michael Jackson by the police resurrects the age-old question of what counts as evidence, justice, and due process, and this is, indeed, a good example of "commonsense racism."

In this occurrence, Michael Jackson is the one who is deemed a monster. But unlike Mary Shelley's *Frankenstein* who is given a voice and can speak for himself, Michael Jackson is not and cannot. The sort of bodily pain he experiences is incommunicable. Ronald Judy identifies this incommunicability as "muteness"; that is, "to be inarticulate, to not compel, to have no capacity to move, to be without effect, to be without agency, to have no thought" and it cannot be explained with words.[161] Michael Jackson's experience, then, for which there is no immediate articulation, is prediscursive. It comes before words. It is afterward, in a press conference titled "Jackson sets the record straight," which is *italicized* (you can't see it), broadcasted live on CNN, that Michael Jackson states: "They served a search warrant on me which allowed them to view and photograph my body, including my penis, my buttocks, my lower torso, thighs, and any other areas that they wanted. . . . It was the most humiliating ordeal of my life. . . . But if this is what I have to endure to prove my innocence, so be it."[162] Sadly, "it" is never "it," whatever that "it" is. It is an impossible "it."[163]

Blacks' experience with the police is forever fraught with the very fact that they do not have the comfort of leaving their blackness behind. Hannah Arendt argues that "race, politically speaking, [is] not the beginning of humanity but its end. . . . Not the natural birth of man but his unnatural death."[164] And even though the word "racism" was not in use during the colonial period, as George M. Fredrickson reminds us,[165] the historical evidence points to the ill treatment of blacks at the time that clearly establishes an unnamed practice that is today called racism.[166] In other words, the symbolic identification of the phenomenon through naming does not stop racism, as an established system in practice, from actually existing and happening before it takes on a name. Analyzing racism, in the form of how the body is positioned within the very imperativeness of racism—that is, the bodiliness of racism—is important for this discussion. Indeed, the "howness" of the body's constitution is demonstrated in racial profiling and the shooting of blacks by the police. Racism, in this sense, is performative. It does what it sets out to do, which is to assimilate blacks into their otherness. Given that blacks are physically and mentally exhausted from perpetual racist assaults stemming from their otherness, their behavior might take on an act that is not the product of a free will, like Michael Jackson, for example, making changes to his body with the use of plastic surgery.

A black person is centering their appearance as a raced being, and the social ways in which one appears in the world is significant as a person "overdetermined from the outside."[167] Race, because of its corporeality, its noticeable appearance, confirms the ontology of race and repudiates any form of negotiation proper. Seeing that a black person is "always already fixed, complete, given,"[168] they do have, in the words of Judith Butler, "an ontological status that preexists any appearance . . . and social status as well."[169] They are not separate from their social appearance as a raced being. And to remove the constitutive power of the social category of race, as the discourse of colorblindness[170] attempts to do, is to remove blacks as well. This form of "re[moving]" promotes a different mode of racism today in the United States, which I call racism without "seeing" race; that is, a deliberate withdrawal from visual perception. Of course, this does not mean that one forgoes what one is always already socialized to think about race, which, in no uncertain terms, evokes all kinds of predetermined and guaranteed attitudes and beliefs about the black body, resulting in racial profiling, police harassment, and the killing of unarmed blacks. Further, Osagie K. Obasogie, in *Blinded by Sight: Seeing Race through the Eyes of the Blind*, helps us to think through the fact that whites who are legally blind do not have to "see" race as a visual representation in order to be impacted by racist conditioning that forms and maintains truth claims about blacks and other nonwhites.[171] It follows from this view, then, that we must attentively tend to race matters in the United States.

The "techniques of recording" Michael Jackson's statement where the "lie detection" experts listened to the tape only to declare that "the stress in Jackson's voice shows that he is lying"[172] is not surprising. Based on Michael Jackson's appearance as a black person, when the black body is placed under the panoptic white gaze, as Sara Ahmed puts it, "the 'body' itself [is] the 'site' of social stress."[173] Certainly, Michael Jackson's announcement in the media, drawing attention to his ghastly treatment by the police, evoked serious concerns about blacks and the laws, reminding us of what Frantz Fanon diagnosed as "the lived experience" of blacks. Jared Sexton's comment in "The Social Life of Social Death" that a "black life is not lived in the world that the world lives in, but it is lived underground"[174] is a concern that is practically summed up by the title of one song in Jay-Z's 1996 album *Reasonable Doubt*: "Can I Live." In this rendition, Jay-Z asks the age-old question four times, "Can I live?" which, without a doubt, draws our attention to the status and nature of black lives, their lived experience[175] infused with everything that literally breaks and disturbs their livability. In the end, for them, their life is a "death-in-life," which can be discussed in terms of "ontological death"; that is to say, the loss of their personhood,[176] or what Fanon, in *Towards An African Revolution*," calls a "daily death," the "North African Syndrome."[177] In the United States, this is, for sure, the black syndrome, which was well established centuries ago, starting from indentured servitude to slavery, Reconstruction to Jim Crow South, and which is now upheld and maintained by racial profiling and mass incarceration—the symptoms of antiblack racism. Indeed, blacks are "always positioned [and treated] as slaves."[178] This holds true even for the King of Pop.[179]

Certainly, child molestation is a serious issue. Even so, it cannot be treated as something separate and apart from the laws and institutions that construct and define race, gender, and sexuality norms and values. For instance, in his work, "A Foucauldian (Genealogical) Reading of Whiteness," George Yancy explores "how members of a society are trained to perceive themselves as having a certain sexual nature through the deployment of theories and practices that define that nature and so determine the realms of the normal and the abnormal."[180] Yet we must be cautious of the operation of "truths" about sexuality that control and stigmatize the racialized body as essentially a sexed being. I think this takes me to my single point of uneasiness here. With the media's reporting of Michael Jackson's child molestation charges, where his penis is treated as evidence, I cannot help but repeating here that morality and ethics are converted into an exasperating medium of a familiar black racial aesthetic.

Displaying Michael Jackson's penis in order to humiliate him recasts the focus on child molestation to the hypersexual illegitimacy attached to black masculinity within the framework of heteronormativity and the larger racial discourse regarding the sexuality of black men as a menace to the white social body. The mythical norm of the black penis plays into whites' fears, vulnerabilities, and hypersensitivities of the imaginary threats of black masculinity. In Michel Cournot's *Martinique*, Cournot gets to the heart of the issue. Quoting Cournot, Fanon writes: "The black man's sword is a sword. When he has thrust it into your wife, she has really felt something. It is a revelation. In the chasm that it has left, your little toy is lost. . . . Four Negroes with their penises exposed would fill a cathedral. They would be unable to leave the building until their erections had subsided; and in such close quarters that would not be a simple matter."[181] This is not without significance. In Michael Jackson's alleged child molestation charges, "the Santa Barbara District Attorney had wanted the physician to measure the size of his genital" but his lawyer at the time, Johnnie Cochran, objected. Was this to be convinced that Dr. Palé was correct when he says "the average length of the penis among the black men of Africa rarely exceeds 120 millimeters (4.6244 inches)"?[182] Even in death, Michael Jackson's penis continues to take center stage. Michael Mario Albrecht writes, " 'The recent release of autopsy report confirmed that at the time of his death, Michael Jackson was uncircumcised,' a statement which ostensibly differed from the 1993 account of his penis by the boy Jackson allegedly molested."[183] Indeed, the penis is a metaphorical substitute for the black man. He is always in relentless endangerment of symbolic and literal castration.

The disciplining of Michael Jackson is not an error. Through normalizing, in the form of racial disciplining, the discursive power establishes and produces raced bodies.[184] At the moment, when the biology of race as a foundation for racial knowledge has been attacked from the left through the discourse of race as a social construction and the right through the discourse of colorblindness, fixing the "truth" of race on the body is fundamental.[185] There is a particular racial etiquette, a particular performance of blackness that has to measure up to whiteness and thus is reduced to otherness. Michael Jackson, for one, wants to rid himself of the stigma of color, to become what dialecticians term an "absolute being; a being that stands in the way of human being or a human way of being."[186] This makes sense. Indeed, W. E. B. Du Bois, for one, understands the restless *souls of black folk*.[187]

Epilogue

Reflections

In this book, I take up the challenging task of thinking about the King of Pop Michael Jackson and the quandary of a black identity.[1] I began by discussing how a black identity, understood in Fanonian terms as "overdetermined from the outside"—that is to say, "of being black outside"[2]— cements a black identity that is tattooed and fixed on the body, and that rests on a regulating compulsion that poses all blacks as identical. These are what I call the distinguishing norms of recognition, the fact of blackness, which purports blacks to be treated as a fixed unity, annihilating, for example, their gender, sexual orientation, able-bodiedness, language and speech impairments, and class differences. In other words, race is comparable and intertwined with what black feminist Hortense Spillers once described as "impermissible origins."[3] And while Spillers's exploration of race, gender, and sexuality shows that race functions as the signifier that is pegged to the signified (gender and sexuality),[4] I would also add that other identity markers such as class, disability, age, and ethnicity are also signified. In other words, despite the fact that blackness does find different expression in whiteness, aporetic differences among blacks, which, in their full complexities, remain unique and particular to a black person, have to be disavowed, concealed, or denied. This, in itself, is over and against the individuation of blacks, of them becoming independent of blackness outsideness as a disciplinary devise to make blacks conscious of themselves as black[5] and reduces them, as I have already argued, to the burdened life.

In his complex masterpiece *Black Skin, White Masks*, Frantz Fanon helps us understand the difficulty of a black person's attempts at delineating a "corporeal schema" that is continually already anchored in a "historico-racial schema." Thus, a black person has to rely on the "legends, stories, history, and above all historicity"[6] woven by a racist society so as to craft a physiological self for themself. This is a hard task because the historico-racial schema is misinterpreted and replaced by what Fanon calls the "racial epidermal schema"[7]—a culturally fashioned schema that today expands to clothing (the hoodie), loud music, and a whole array of characteristics not only fixing racial differences but also identifying all blacks with a distinctive category comprising physical, emotional, and intellectual outlooks, which in turn are marked as cultural defects. We can see, then, the need to break with these shibboleths of identity politics and confront the apparent problematics they present for the recognition of a black identity.

For those of us who have been trained in the critique of identity politics, it is essential to say that the flaunted recognition of a black person's multifaceted identities, the "me" that is visible, is one's race identity, which leaves the other identities "unvoiced, misseen, not doing, awaiting their verb"[8] as if race were the only site where struggles appear. At any rate, because race is the signifier that is pegged to these other signified, race is like a *watchman*, in Harper Lee's sense:[9] it antagonistically keeps watch and has blacks under surveillance to make sure that they do not stray too far from their race assignment. Alexander G. Weheliye's *Habeas Viscus*, coming to this question from a different perspective, is concerned, for his part, with "an alternative way of conceptualizing the place of race"[10] and the presentation of blackness. Indeed, blackness presentation as an inescapable bodily mark and its prosthetics of identification (i.e., a hoodie and loud music) solely defines a black person's identity, which is, partly, informed by media framing. This is why, for good reasons, one can say, "blackness functions as a constant underlying mark of racialization as does no other racial designation."[11] Essentially, the evidence before us is that blacks' devalued status is expressed in the old maxim "skin deep"; that is to say, it is "located [o]n the body and the space it occupies,"[12] barring any likelihood of slippage between the historically obligatory imago and how blacks live the reality of their identity as fixed on the skin/surface.

The black body, something other than oneself, in a word, is "a site of discursive, symbolic, ontological, and existential battle."[13] In other words, my body makes of me continuously a person who suffers. And so it did, in fact, for Michael Jackson in the UCLA Medical Center as he lay dying. Even in death, the scrutiny of Michael Jackson's body/corpse could not be resisted,[14] and it took on a life of its own. Michael Jackson may be dead (a living beyond death), but his "body continues to perform the myriad contradictions," as Michael Mario Albrecht reveals, "in regards to his identity,"[15] calling into question his race identity and vitiligo condition[16] to fuel the fire of his disputed desires to be "white." And if it is possible for a black person to make his skin "white" and thus, as Fanon puts it, "to throw off the burden of that corporeal malediction,"[17] Michael Jackson's white skin/flesh does not change the fact that he is black. In life, he continues, for example, to "dance in blackness,"[18] which, as I have already revealed, leaves its mark. In Claudia Rankine's words, "despite everything the body remains"[19] black and can never be at "home" where whiteness is the norm.

In this book, I attempt to provide particular insights into a black identification process. That said, I draw on the problematics of an essentialized blackness and the specific implications that are associated with blackness. This leads to the crucial question: What does it mean to be black in America? My response to this question, in its postulation, draws on the groundbreaking work of the philosopher and psychiatrist Frantz Fanon's anticolonial exposition in *Black Skin, White Masks*, in which he asks this other question: "What does the black man want?"[20] In short, ontology does not permit us to understand the being of the black man in the face of whiteness.[21] And because of how the body is racialized, blacks encounter the racist world through their bodies. The problem of identification for blacks as fixed on the skin/surface, as it is, serves to position blacks as unlike whites, incomplete and inferior. In this sense, blacks "want to want" what is denied to them, which is mutual recognition is not without signification. In other words, as I have already discussed, an absence of recognition for blacks produces the condition of a black person to know thyself (yourself) and to focus on self-care, a personal kind of ethic that is premised on holding on to one's truth, one's self, in a polity of instrumental rationality that goes against self-knowledge.

In fact, the actual neurotic structuring of whiteness produces a black identity that is marked on the body, a body as the locus for exclusion and out of control, which must be regulated and controlled through racial discipline. And since whiteness robs blacks of their subjectivity, cutting them off from truly developing any sense of "self," the black "self" does not exist. Rather, what does exist is a conclusive construction of the "self" and of the world—conclusive because it harvests a real dialectic between the black body and the world.[22] Indeed, a black person is *in* the world but not *of* the world and is "locked in his [or her] body,"[23] which is "a fatal way of being alive."²⁴ The phenomenological or lived experience of blacks, in the words of W. E. B. Du Bois, "is the history of this strive"²⁵ which, as I have shown in the previous chapters, continues to write itself. In fact, even though how blackness is lived is reactivated in new ways, it continues its old ways of pinning blacks to a specific form of suffering that interferes with their will to "know themselves" outside of race as a bodily mark. This, in its single-mindedness, generates great anxiety for blacks and creates an unprecedented kind of disorder. Given that, in the black world of disorder, "where the saner you are, the madder you are made to appear,"²⁶ *things fall apart*.²⁷ This is why Fred Moten can say, "the lived experience of blackness is, among other things, a constant demand for an ontology of dehiscence, a para-ontology."²⁸

However, the lived experience of blacks is driven and depicted most often in the guise of an "unasked question"—"How does it feel to be a problem"²⁹—which I have already discussed. In fact, this question is constantly asked and "presented or re-presented under the sign of absence, displacement, nonpresence"³⁰ directed to blacks from whites. Given the trajectory of the question from whites to blacks, "the question," in Nahum Chandler's words, "destroys itself."³¹ Blacks are not the problem. Along this line, it is a blackphobic society that makes them into the problem, a problem that cannot be ignored. In this sense, blacks are in "a black hole. But then again it could be white."³²

In his life, Michael Jackson tried to resist racial identification and attempted a polytrophic self-fashioning, *not black, not white*, in which his otherness was always doubled, a different way of *being* in the body. That is, the black body as it "looks" in its abandonment of the distinguishing norms of race assignment is positioned outside of the either/or category, presenting a threat to the social body. It is one reason that Michael Jackson's change in skin/surface from "black" (not to be) to "white" (to be) provoked many controversial and acrimonious debates around the belief that the singer was savaging his African physiognomy. Indeed, if one were to ask *what is an African physiognomy?*, one would be quickly confronted with the clash of *skin* and *blood* as depicted in America's history of the one-drop rule. It is thus important to remember that the bodiliness of racism is a huge part of America's history.

As I see it, a change in Michael Jackson's physicality is not about *being*, a *being* that he cannot access, but about "becoming," a dynamic kind of "becoming." It is the Nietzschean will to power: not power over others, but over himself; it is a being that is interacting with epistemology, ethic, ideology, and everyday customs that uphold whiteness as the cultural standard. "Becoming," in Nahum Chandler's words, "would remain always at stake in that which is not yet born, in that which always arrives on the threshold of historicity too late or after the fact."[33] Certainly, one, following Judith Butler, does "not arrive in the world separate from a set of norms that are lying in wait for [one], already orchestrating [one's] gender, race, and status, working on one."[34] So, then, Michael Jackson cannot truly decide who he wants to become because, like all blacks, whiteness as the norm acts on him "from all sides, that is, in multiple and sometimes contradictory ways."[35] Michael Jackson, like Pecola Breedlove in Toni Morrison's *The Bluest Eye*, cannot escape whiteness and, accordingly, as she does, fully internalizes the mythical norms of whiteness as beautiful and pure.[36] Blackness is a foil to whiteness and, the black, in the words of W. E. B. Du Bois, is a "dark, uncertain, and [an] imperfect decent."[37] Blackness contra whiteness is, for one, an act in which the black body is torn asunder. In Michael Jackson's case, *not black, not white*, as is expressed in his words, "Beat me, hate me/You can never break me/Will me, thrill me/You can never kill me/Sue me, Sue me/Everybody do me/Kick me, Kick me/Don't you black or white me,"[38] cannot be disavowed. These lyrics exemplify the singer's refusal of race assignment, "the not self" which has been ascribed to him and his attempts to self-fashion another "self."

Because Michael Jackson's racial in-betweenness escapes the fixity of the either/or (black or white) racial categories and challenges the notion of natural bodies, he is read by some scholars as a post-racial subject, transcending racial boundaries, leading to the conclusion that Michael Jackson is not quite human. If the postulation of the English poet Alexander Pope "to err is human, to forgive, divine"[39] is correct, it is not surprising that his erring such as the dangling of his baby from the fourth-floor balcony of the Hotel Adlon is for many unforgivable.

Some misconstrued behaviors, or "his way of being in the world," what he calls his "strange eccentricities,"[40] his situated subjectivities (race, gender, and sexuality ambiguities), for example, provide for a negative reading of the King of Pop and name-calling. Such *calling* never identifies that which was before but brings into existence how Michael Jackson as a subject "becomes a subject only through his response to the call:"[41] Look, Michael Jackson! What is it "we" are looking for? Is there some kind of certitude that "we" will find what "we" are looking for? Certainly, what "we" are looking for, "we" do find, even without the help of the media, lost in speculation, which unfairly awarded Michael Jackson the racist epithet "Wacko Jacko."[42] I have already drawn on several examples of Michael Jackson's lived experience as outside of what society considers as "normal." As I see it, Michael Jackson's performance of his identity, overdetermined by his "abnormalities," is not primarily an act of his will to be outside of what society considers as "normal," but his unrelenting need to refuse, for example, the truth of race as a determinant for a set of rules, in this case, as either black or white.

And while, as I have already shown, Michael Jackson must be normalized and disciplined into race recognizability, which is definite and precise, certainly, he cannot say with confidence, "I am always searching for the black" because wherever he goes, the black man remains black,[43] even if he is the King of Pop. To put it differently, the comedian Chris Rock, in one of his shows, says, "go and marry a fucking Kennedy and see how black you are." Listening to Chris Rock, I did feel the need to hide my amusement. That is to say, I did not want to kill myself laughing. In Fanon's words, "laughter had become impossible"[44] due to fact that "I already knew that there were legends, stories, history, and above all historicity"[45] about blacks that positioned them as less than whites. The abolitionist David Walker confesses: "I would wish, candidly, however, before the Lord, to be understood, that I would not give a pinch of snuff to be married to any white person I ever saw in all the days of my life"[46] because she is white. Walker concludes: "And I do say it, that the black man, or man of colour, who will leave his own colour (provided he can get one, who is good for any thing) and marry a white woman, to be a double slave to her, just because she is white, ought to be treated by her as he surely will be, *viz*: as a NIGER!!!."[47] It is for good reason that Walker destroys the mythos of white women as an object of desire. The ploy of whiteness, nonetheless, is "to insist that whites must be [desired]."[48] Therefore, as Fanon puts it, "The sexual myth—the quest for white flesh—perpetuated by alienated psyches, must no longer be allowed to impede active understanding."[49]

In fact, black men's relationship with white women, in the words of Ruth Frankenberg, "frequently reduce[s] them to sexual beings."[50] This characterization supports the terrifying myth according to which, in Harper Lee's words, "all Negro men are basically not to be trusted around women,"[51] which is to say, white women. As Evelynn Hammonds's inspiration from the great Lorraine O'Grady establishes: "White is what woman is; not-white (and the stereotypes not-white gathers in) is what she had better not be."[52] This helps us to understand further the woman question: What is woman? In this regard, one might turn back to the queen of soul Aretha Franklin singing at the Kennedy Center Honors in 2015, "you make me feel like a natural woman,"[53] which draws our attention to the very abyss of the denaturalization of black women, positioned outside of natural womanhood and as the "other" of the "others." Indeed, there is no end, no limit, *to out*, to the outsideness of blackness. I have already drawn on how black women are positioned outside the gender norm that is founded on whiteness.

The act of Michael Jackson entering the institution of marriage in 1994 and 1996 with Lisa Presley and Debbie Rowe respectively, both white women, was seen as another way for him to whiten/lighten the race. In Fanon's terms, "the race must be whitened"[54] by marrying white.[55] On that basis, if Fanon is correct that a black man marrying a white woman "is a form of recognition that Hegel had not envisaged"[56] and is left unattended, in a genealogical and deconstructive mode, to imagine with Fanon, "Who but a white woman can do this for a [black man]? By loving [him] she proves that [he is] worthy of white love. [He is] loved like a white man. [He] is a white man. Her love takes [him] onto the noble road that leads to total realization. . . . [He marries] white culture, white beauty white whiteness. When [his] restless hands caress those white breasts, they grasp white civilization and dignity and make them [his]."[57] However, if it is true that in the moment of intimacy, the black man is often "reduced to a sexual being" and he experiences his being through whiteness, or, to put it differently, he is not allowed to enact his desire as a part of the "us" (whites) and is dissected and fixed as a part of the "them" (blacks), how then can the black man and the white woman be, in Michael Jackson's words, "one and the same,"[58] the inessential other for the white man?[59] And while the "them" provides for the presence of the "us," the evidence is here. It is unalterable. I read it exactly as it is that white women are not positioned outside of whiteness as a "them." In a word, she can never be counted as a part of the "them."

Michael Jackson's marriage is viewed by his critics as a sham in order to "pass" for heterosexual.[60] However, the focus on his sexuality does not derail other facets of his identity, such as his gender and race ambiguities. Certainly, identities matter and have *real* implications. *Real*, as Linda Martín Alcoff explains, "works to counter a view that interpellations of social identity are always chimeras foisted on us from the outside."[61] And while my focus in the book, especially chapter three, is on

Michael Jackson's race in-betweenness, *not black* (the "other"), *not white* (the self's "other"), which, as I have shown, is that Michael Jackson is an other "other," I move away from the notion that his racial in-betweenness destabilizes the strict dichotomy (black and white) to turn toward Homi K. Bhabha's idea of "a cultural hybridity that entertains difference without an assumed or imposed hierarchy."[62] Michael Jackson is outside of the self (white) and other (black) dialectic as an other "other," which is in conflict with the either/or of racial category and unveils other problematics for a black identity as social regulation; that is, the allocation or assimilation of blacks to their ascribed racial group.

Because racial discipline is used as a device to discipline individuals into the strict either/or racial category, and Michael Jackson is positioned outside of the either/or category, the media constantly portrays him in superficial and sometimes very harsh ways, reinforcing the notion that he is weird and/or a freak. Anticipating the media's performance, one might say the media is simply doing what it does best, which is to denigrate blacks on a regular basis. One example is how the media continuously shows the "black face" as the criminal, and regardless of what blacks do, the interplay of race and crime constantly already criminalize blacks and disempower them. Take the case of Michael Jackson in the alleged child molestation charges; he was already deemed guilty even in the absence of concrete and fully worked-out evidence.

Indeed, Robert Entman and Andrew Rojecki's *The Black Image in the White Mind: Media and Race in America* is a compelling and helpful guide to understand the relation of the media and race and how it is challenging for the mainstream media to work through its racialized habitus. Their portrayal of black people "is always hedged in by the cognitive process of synecdoche, metonymy, and projection"[63] and hampers it from presenting blacks in a more neutral light. We must thus see the importance of The Voice of the Nation (WVON)-AM radio, the black talk radio in Chicago, which focuses on issues that are important to blacks and frames blacks in a positive light. Catherine R. Squires reminds us of the importance of black talk radio. Yet, she notes that it is "largely ignored by media scholars."[64]

Michael Jackson's self-fashioning seems to present another way for some scholars to label him as "post-race/nonracial." This development, in its racialist ontology, provokes a description of Michael Jackson as a post-racial subject and thus, in this sense, a post-racial future is on the horizon for the United States as a whole—a democratic experiment, which, nonetheless, continues to subjugate blacks and other marginalized groups. I have elsewhere discussed how the post-racial discourse is deployed for a wide gamut of purposes, including the maintenance of the presumptive hegemony of whiteness. Notwithstanding the fact that post-race has developed from a racialist ontology, it has mightily espoused and flooded, in many ways, the discourses in which it continually flows: "I don't see race." Yet within the particular schemas of "the declining significance of race"[65] and "the end of racism,"[66] the post-racial discourse cannot be readily resignified or designified and to picture that its treacherous overtones can be easily rearticulated into a seemingly empathetic idiom wrapped in an exhaustive self-congratulatory wishful thinking, a sentence such as "I don't see race" needs to be understood as mere attitude. The prevalence of such an attitude, as I see it, is, at best, a severe form of Sartrean "bad faith,"[67] a form of self-denial and lying to oneself[68] and, at worst, what Charles Mills describes as an "epistemology of ignorance."[69] And while the locus of power, in this respect, legitimizes and extends the interests of those served by the ongoing effects of such operational power, post-racial, we would have to agree with Barbara Fields and Karen Fields, "turns out to be—simply—racial; which is to say racist,"[70] or, in George Yancy's summation, an "astonishing and repulsive lie."[71]

Even though the post-racial discourse died a natural death with the election of Donald Trump, some scholars shamelessly continue with these shenanigans that there is "a declining significance of race" and "the end of racism."[72] To question post-racialism is to show how racism fixes race on the body. Blacks in New York City, for example, still cannot secure a cab with ease.[73] Cornel West in *Race Matters* narrates such episodes from a first-person perspective: "I waited and waited and waited. After the ninth taxi refused me, my blood began to boil. The tenth taxi refused me and stopped for a kind, well-dressed, smiling female fellow citizen of European descent. As she stepped in the cab, she said, 'This is really ridiculous, is it not?' "[74] As Nahum D. Chandler reminds us: "We cannot pretend to *speak* of these things. We reach a limit"[75] that makes speaking inarticulate and we do not want to speak. And, while in Thomas Carlyle's words, "silence is the element in which great things fashion themselves together,"[76] we do speak endlessly, without stopping to ask the question *why*. And, as Toni Morrison reminds us, "since why is difficult to handle, one must take refuge in how";[77] so, the question is not *why* are blacks immobile in their lived existence as the "other" and "reduced to pure facticity"[78] but *how*. Indeed, *how* can blacks overcome their epidermalization, that is, the exposed surface/skin, "throw off the burden of that corporeal malediction,"[79] and, above all, as Peter McLaren puts it, "choose against whiteness"?[80] In fact, whiteness, in the words of Ibram X Kendi, "was 'stamped from the beginning'"[81] of the United States becoming a nation. If stamp is inspired by the Greek word stembein,[82] in my reconstruction of *stembein*, *stem* is to *emanate from* and *bein* is *comfortable*, then whiteness as stamped, in this sense, emanates from comfort.

Whiteness as the norm bars a black person from comfort and forces them to admit to one's own blackness as a *lack*. At the heart of the admission of their blackness, which is structured as a verbal act by which one affirms the "truth" of what one is—"I am black. My blackness is a lack"— one then binds oneself to that "truth," submits to whiteness, and, at the same time, amends one's relationship to oneself. Thus, to "choose against whiteness," it is important to draw attention to the fact of how whiteness has constructed blackness. In this context, I want to use material from literature that deals with underived fiction not as an opposite to the "truth," but as a way of getting at the "truth"—in this case, blackness constructivism.

In this context, we would have to go through Aimé Césaire's *A Tempest*, where Caliban, the black slave, is able to resist blackness. On this view, Caliban, addressing Prospero (the master), lets him know, "For it is you who made me doubt myself";[83] that is, in Césaire's exposition on *Discourse on Colonialism*, "to have an inferior complex, to tremble, to kneel, despair, and behave like [a] flunky."[84] The act of self-recognition for the slave, which the master hopes will never arrive, is significant in the encounter of Caliban with Prospero in *A Tempest*. Caliban's words to Prospero are truly illuminating: "Every time you summon me it reminds me of a basic fact, the fact that you've stolen everything from me, even my identity."[85] In other words, Caliban's lack of self-knowledge bars him from the freedom of the *will* to know himself.

A culture that makes it easy for whiteness to draw its power from its proclaimed ontological neutrality so that the white subject is raceless and unmarked and, in turn, positions blackness as this "other" thing that is raced and marked is a good illustration of how blackness is compared to whiteness and is reduced to pure physicality, which has a "high social profile" in the sense that it affects how the racialized body is perceived and responded to. A trope for the lived experience of blacks on which Michael Jackson draws, in his song "They Don't Care About Us," that blacks "are victim[s] of police brutality" is not without significance. Certainly, the killing of unarmed blacks by the police, which was the impetus for the Black Lives Matter movement, is the definitive aspect of the bodiliness of racism—that is, a body located within racism, as shown in previous chapters.

Seeing blackness outsideness as it is constructed locates and collapses all blacks in the economy of likeness as a site for otherness, as I have already argued, demonstrates that blacks cannot overcome their epidermalization. In other words, the inscription of meaning onto skin/flesh, as Fanon's famous scene of a white child crying out, "Look, a Negro! . . . . Mama see that Negro! I'm frightened"[86] illustrates, is the scene of the ordinary racial encounter. Ordinary comes from the Latin word *Oro* or *Ordin*, meaning order. The old French word *ordinarie* means usual, and in the fifteenth century in the English-speaking world, *ordinary* acquired the meaning of "belonging to the usual order or course." In short, ordinary is the standard. And, of course, in the white child's statement, "Look, a Negro! . . . Mama see that Negro! I'm frightened,"[87] to be sure, in the words of Nietzsche's Zarathustra, the teacher of affirmation, the Negro is "a forest and a night of dark trees: but he who is not afraid of [his] darkness, will also find rose slopes under [his] cypresses."[88] However, the *looking* perfunctorily returns the black person to themself in "bad faith."[89] The black body is phenomenologically returned to them as a foil to the social body. What we see, here, following Teresa de Lauretis's observation, is that "it is there, in the body, that the 'real effects' of racist discourses,"[90] which is inevitably "woven out of a thousand details, anecdotes, stores,"[91] and performances that are "real-ized." This is what Fanon calls blacks' *expérience vécue* (lived experience).[92]

So, in taking up Fanon's charge that "the Negro suffers in his body quite differently from the white[s],"[93] I rely on Teresa de Lauretis's concept of "difference embodied," which she defines as "the division or incoherence of the subject based on the materiality of the body which the traumatic inscription of race renders incongruous and in excess of the body ego."[94] In fact, difference embodied is something that blacks try to escape with little or no success because of the fixity of blackness on the body. The singularity of a black identity as a bodily mark fails to recognize that, in the words of Touré, "the number of ways of being Black is infinite. Where the possibilities for an authentic Black identity are boundless. What it means to be black has grown so staggeringly broad, so unpredictable, so defuse that blackness itself is undefinable."[95] Blackness as both "is" and "ain't"[96] can help us to conceptualize the enormous amount of diversity among black people. Michael Jackson, for one, reminds us how diverse blackness is in his attempt at self-fashioning.

If, as Frantz Fanon states in *Black Skin, White Masks*, for blacks "there is only one destiny and it is white,"[97] the only thing that blacks can hope for is a white mask since blacks can never be white. It is thus interesting to note that in a feature article published in *Black Voice*, "Are We Proud To Be Black," the author criticizes "beauty pageants, skin-bleaching cosmetics and the curly-perm hair-style epitomized by [Michael] Jackson's image and consider[s] these trends as the signs of a 'negative' black aesthetic."[98] In other words, for example, hair straightening, cosmetic surgery, and skin bleaching are also seen as, in Kobena Mercer's words, "a diseased state of black consciousness."[99] It seems to be, in fact, a proper example of the scars of whiteness, leaving its mark and damaging blacks' psyche as they attempt to find expressions on the skin, on the surface, which cannot be ignored. This is another way to arrive at the fact that blackness is not self-contained. In this sense, blacks must mimic whiteness, which condemns and positions them as *less than* whites. Indeed, blacks' action is a prescribed action, following as it does the guidelines of whiteness, which inject them with an irrational fear of being rejected from whiteness.[100] However, blacks, as George Yancy reminds us, "must remain attentive to and resist against oppressive modes of being whitely-in-the world."[101]

While Mercer moves quickly into his diagnosis of the black condition, in that blacks' "wretched imitation" of whites "amounts to a diseased state of black consciousness,"[102] we have to extend it a bit further. In the Fanonian sense, it can be interpreted as a neurosis, a process of alienation that must be uprooted. This is one reason why an emphasis on, to quote Trey Ellis's title, a "new black aesthetics,"[103] or Grey Tate's summation, a "postliberated aesthetics,"[104] has unfolded in black popular culture. Stuart Hall's significant question, "What is this 'Black' in Black Popular Culture?" focuses on how culture is opened up "to the play of power."[105] Hall writes: "Black popular culture is a contradictory space. It is a sight of strategic contestation. But it can never be simplified or explained in terms of the simple binary oppositions that are still habitually used to map it out: high and low; resistance versus homogenization."[106] Even so, black popular culture refutes the guidelines of whiteness prescription, which returns blacks to racist stereotypes.

In order to think about black consciousness, or, in this case, "double consciousness," Patricia Hill Collins discusses "the social construction of black feminist thought" and draws our attention to the fact that "subordinated groups identity with the powerful and have no valid independent interpretation of their own oppression."[107] Like all subordinated groups, blacks can never be at home with their blackness and experience their own blackness outside of whiteness. And while a "new black aesthetics," in which the "new" "would always only arrive by way of a second time or even an apparently secondary time,"[108] can open some possibilities for the overcoming of a "negative blackness," a resignification of blackness is paramount. Indeed, the "re" of "resignification" would be in deep dialogue with the Fanonian dialectic of whiteness as pure and blackness as a lack, which forecloses any black person to position themself against the materiality of the racialized body as a pathology and a deep-seated threat to the social body, in part, is to be overcome. Often, of course, blackness is seen as negative, in that blackness makes whiteness weak, but, in honest contemplation, blackness can have another effect of grace, charm, and beauty away from its fetishism. And to know that *black is . . . black ain't*, the reclaiming of blacks' self-hood by embracing blackness and rejecting internalized ways of equating blackness with *lack* would be necessary for blacks' self-realization and the possibility of a "new" way of thinking about blackness. However, as long as whiteness is the privileged norm, blacks will merely emulate the norms and values of whiteness.

The aforementioned remarks return us to the working of whiteness on the black psyche as they see themselves through the white gaze, as is expressed in "an atmosphere of certain uncertainty" that surrounds the black body.[109] W. E. B. Du Bois and Frantz Fanon both point to the fact that blacks are equipped with what the latter describes as an "implicit knowledge" and the former, in Lacanian terms, as the double consciousness,[110] " 'split subject' or 'barred subject'—all written with the same symbol, $—consist entirely in the fact that a speaking being's two parts or avatars share not common ground: they are radically separated."[111] That said, whiteness normativity, a contingent set of practices that fashions itself against the anti-normative (blackness) and the culprit for projecting onto blacks always a false sense of self, we very well know—and to know is to see—that by the ripping away, or the de-normalizing of whiteness, blacks would eventually advance to another self, a self of "their own" and not an "other" to "their own"; that is, a self "always contingent on the presence of The Other,"[112] looking for some form of recognition.

The choreographer Billie T. Jones undoubtedly knows this when he poignantly admits: "I was so confused about my identity. I attributed all the negative things to black dance."[113] Jones is not the exception, but the rule. Certainly, the construction of blackness as a lack allows for Jones's scenario. This would partly explain how rarely a black person is allowed to think outside of race. They have to avoid the first-person single "I" altogether in the existential here and now. In this sense, "I" is nothing. "I" cannot invoke and scrutinize the "self," a "self" of their own, which calls forth the fictional character Pecola Breedlove in Toni Morrison's *The Bluest Eye*. Morrison tells us that "each night, without fail, [Pecola Breedlove] prayed for blue eyes. Fervently, for a year she had prayed."[114] Blue eyes, an attribute of whiteness, would make her beautiful like whites. The young Breedlove, as the desiring subject wanting *to be* (a condition of becoming being) like a white girl (Shirley Temple or Mary Jane), continues to find herself in the metaphysical situation of *being* an object among other objects deprived of the "I," the first-person experience, which is independent of race. If "I am white: that is to say that I possess beauty and virtue, which have never been black."[115]

In a reconstruction and not a description of *The Bluest Eye*, I image how blacks, having the "bluest 'I,'" would propel whites in listening and learning blacks' ways of seeing and being in the world; a white person would be able to know, "ontologizing, and evaluating outside of whiteness,"[116] and see a black person "'I' to 'I.'" It would be a space where blacks and whites would recognize each other as transcendental subjects equal in "a world of reciprocal recognition,"[117] in which the Hegelian dialectic is replaced by the anti-Nietzschean dialectic in the form of the will to power: not power over others but power over oneself. This would answer Fanon's call in *Black Skin, White Masks* "for an ethics of mutual identification"[118] in which blacks would overcome their epidermalization, and, like the white self, knowing "itself as not enslaved, but free; not repulsive but desirable,"[119] the black self would embark on "a progressive fulfillment of destiny"[120] *to be* (human) instead of *not to be* (nonhuman) perhaps can lead to a "new humanism." What this "new humanism" would entail is beyond the scope of this book. However, I want to point that the "new humanism" would not be on the side of blacks or whites but would be nonaligned and, in part, would be imagined as a project of moving away from "thinking white," which is taken to be a step away from where whiteness is at the moment. If there is to be a social and political world based on equal recognition, it would mean to put the norms and values of whiteness behind us.

But first, whiteness as the norm would have to be denormalized/decentered—that is, a whiteness that remains outside of normalized whiteness and works to transform both the consciousness of blacks (enslaved by their inferiority) and the consciousness of whites (enslaved by their superiority), which, in no uncertain terms, pervert humanity to such an extent that it demotes humans' goodness. Both blacks and whites would work together in a common project to de-normalize whiteness as a basis within which a "post-white" subject could be posited and imagined. But this would require whites to enter the process with blacks and work at healing themselves from white privilege.[121] Like in El Greco's 1557 painting, "Healing the Man Born Blind," the blind man is healed not with words but with touch and love,[122] whites, bracketed in close proximity to the "other," in the words of Fanon, would be able then "to touch the other, [and] to feel the other."[123] That is to say, for whites not to be the "other," but to be "in" the "other" so that the myths of blacks as *less than* whites would be "destroyed at all costs."[124] This is one way in which a "we" can emerge in solidarity where blacks, other racialized ethnic groups, and whites can work to denormalize whiteness. Certainly, the denormalizing of whiteness, then, would have to be followed continuously and responsibly as the "indispensable condition for the quest for human completeness."[125]

So, what is the future for blackness? To pose this question is to show that as long as whiteness is the norm, blackness is always postponed and is "yet to come"; that is to say, no one knows yet what black is.[126] I know exactly what Fanon says about this revelation. For Fanon, as I noted earlier, "knows that fear will fill the world when the world finds out. And when the world knows the world always expects something of the [black] person."[127] This is a good reason why Fanon "is afraid of the fear that the world would feel if the world knew."[128] In thinking with Fanon, to rethink what blackness would be like on its own, free from its comparison with whiteness, would be to put forward a rejection of the comparison, where neither blackness nor whiteness is superior. The King of Pop Michael Jackson acknowledges, "I am the black man,"[129] and attempts to let the world know that *Black Is . . . Black Ain't*. And most importantly, when blacks arrive—like Caliban, the black slave in *A Tempest*—they can eventually say to Prospero, the white master (as Caliban does):

> [Whiteness,] you are the master of illusion.
> Lying is your trademark.
> And you have lied so much to me
> (lied about the world, lied about me)
> that you have ended by imposing on me

an image of myself.
Underdeveloped, you brand me, inferior,
That's the way you have forced me to see myself.
I detest that image! What's more, it's a lie!
But now I know you, you old cancer,
And I know myself as self.[130]

A black person, in the act of reclaiming one's blackness as an identity to celebrate, will work through their double consciousness and would eventually say, "I am proud of my blackness. I am proud of who I am." Indeed, a black person, knowing oneself as a "self," can now take care of oneself, self-care, and be identifiable not as a menace to the white social body. Now, blacks and whites can look at each other "I" to "I" and "relate across our human difference as equals."[131] This was not the case for Michael Jackson. In Aimé Césaire's delicate words, "death has delivered him"[132] from the "bad faith" of whiteness. I see his *face* in the *stars*.

Notes

Introduction

1. For a more comprehensive examination of Jean-Michel Basquiat's *Irony of Negro Policeman*, see Nathan Brown, "The Irony of Anatomy: Basquiat's Poetics of Black Positionality" (2016, 11). Also, see the front cover and page 65 of *Jean-Michel Basquiat: Now's the Time*, edited by Dieter Buchhart, 2015.

2. Hartman 1997, 58.
3. Moten 2017, 226.
4. Morrison 2017, 58.
5. Fanon 1967, 109.
6. Fanon 1967, 60.
7. See Homi Bhabha, *The Location of Culture* (1994, 53–56). Also, see Marjorie Garber's *Vested Interests: Cross Dressing and Cultural Anxiety*, where she focuses on a "third" space created by transvestite activity. For her, this "third" is "a mode of articulation, a way of describing a space of possibility" (1997, 15), which for her, because of its binary logics of male/female, provides little room for creative, counterhegemonic self-expression. On the other, I think it challenges normative gender performativity and creates Judith Butler's gender troubles. However, in the case of blacks it creates race *trouble* in which such "trouble is put into action" (Ahmed 2015, 182). Blacks become actional. I will return to this point in chapter 2, "Blackness and a Black Identity."
8. Foucault 1972, 18.
9. Racial sameness assumes that all black people are alike.
10. Fanon 1967, 111.
11. Fanon 1967, 173.
12. Du Bois 2003, 5.
13. Awkward 1996, 179.
14. Lévinas 1979, 66.
15. Lévinas, 297. In Emmanuel Lévinas, *Ethics and Infinity*, the "face is what forbids us to kill" (1985, 86).

16. For more on nanoracism, see Achille Mbembe, "The Society of Enmity," 2016.

17. Butler 1993a, 2.

18. See Denise Riley, *"Am I That Name?" Feminism and the Category of Women's History*, where Riley points to the avid need for the category "woman" for any feminist philosophy.

19. *Black Is . . . Black Ain't* is the title of Marlon Riggs's 1994 documentary.

20. However, this process is not prior to blacks' encounter with whiteness, but is constitutive of whiteness as a specific power relation.

21. Fanon 1967, 116.

22. Rankine 2014, 7.

23. Du Bois 2003, 5.

24. Fanon 1967, 111.

25. Butler 1993a, xii.

26. Fanon 1967, 111.

27. Fanon 1967, 111.

28. The history of whiteness in the United States is edifying. For instance, historically, the Irish, Jews, and Italians were not considered white. This was not because these white ethnic groups were not phenotypically white. The Irish, of course, were not white because of their culture; and eventually to become white, they had to be culturally whitened—that is, follow the norms and values of whiteness. See Noel Ignatiev's *How the Irish Became White* (1995). For a discussion on how the Jews became white, see Karen Brodkin, *How Jews Became White Folk and What That Says About Race in America* (1998). Nonetheless, I think a more pressing question to ask is how blacks entering in the United States, even before undergoing the naturalization process, automatically became black and are susceptible to racial discrimination in all of its forms.

29. Fanon 1967, 109.

30. Fanon 1967, 60.

31. This reminds us of Hannah Arendt's example of a man accused by the Party during the Stalinist era as a factory saboteur. He acknowledges that he was not a saboteur, but he goes on to say that since the Party is always right, if the Party says that he is a factory saboteur, he must be a factory saboteur.

32. Sartre 1979, 69. Also, on this point, see Frantz Fanon's *Black Skin, White Masks* where he writes: "Let us have the courage to say it outright: It is the racist who creates his inferior. This conclusion brings us back to Sartre: 'The Jew is one whom other men consider a Jew: that is the simple truth from which we must start. . . . It is the anti-Semite who makes the Jew'" (1967, 93). This analogy shows that it is indeed the same kind of epistemic violence that whiteness imposes on blacks and other nonwhites.

33. See Frantz Fanon, *Black Skin, White Masks* (1967).

34. Du Bois 2003, 3–4.

35. See William Julius Wilson, *The Declining Significance of Race* (1980).

36. See Dinesh D'Souza, *The End of Racism: Principles for a Multicultural Society* (1995).

37. Patterson 1982, 176.

38. Indeed, there are a wide variety of extremely different defenses of blacks' inferiority, ranging from religion to philosophy and literature and politics. We do remember Thomas Jefferson in *Notes to the State of Virginia*, in which the Third president of the United States announced with extraordinary preposterousness that "blacks whether originally a distinct race, or made distinct by time and circumstances, are inferior to whites in the endowments both of body and mind" (Jefferson 1999, 6). Sadly, today, reverberations of the same position are visible in the latest account of Richard Herrnstein and Charles Murray's *The Bell Curve: Intelligence and Class Structure in American Life*, according to which "the Gaussian distributions of IQ scores establish a natural distinction of some importance between different races" (Herrnstein and Murray 1994, 106) and position blacks as inferior to whites. From the vantage point of Black Power and the idiom "black is beautiful," other ways of reframing the issue of race go against such conscriptions of blacks' inferiority.

39. See Adam Fitzgerald, "An Interview with Fred Moten" (2015).

40. It is for good reason that Rachel Dolezal (Nkechi Diallo), a white woman who says she is black, creates so much controversy.

41. Brown 2016, 15.

42. Toadvine and Lawlor 2007, 147.

43. The "body without organ" goes against what Achille Mbembe explains and defines as "the politics of viscerality" in a lecture given at Duke University in April 2016.

44. Erni 1998, 169.

45. Mbembe 2017, 13.

46. Mbembe 2017, 32.

47. Foucault 1978, 11.

48. Butler 1993a, 97–98.

49. Butler, 2001, 79.

50. I draw a distinction between the lived experience of blacks and the black experience, which is multifaceted and ambiguous. As Fanon tells us, there is not just one group of blacks.

51. Fanon 1967, 8.

52. *Bad* and *Dangerous* are the titles of Michael Jackson's albums released on August 31, 1987, and November 26, 1991, respectively.

53. Other scholars who have worked within a Fanonian framework on race as epidermalized include: Lewis R. Gordon, "Through the Hellish Zone of Nonbeing" (2007); Richard Wright, "The Ethics of Living in Jim Crow: An Autobiographical Sketch" (2007); George Yancy, "Whiteness and the Return of the

Black Body" (2005); Lou Turner, "Fanon Reading (W)right and (W)right Reading of Fanon: Race, Modernity, and the Fate of Humanism" (2003); Nigel Gibson, "Losing Sight of the Real: Recasting Merleau-Ponty in Fanon's Critique of Mannoni" (2003); Teresa de Lauretis, "Difference Embodied: Reflections on Black Skin" (2002); Jeremy Weate, "Fanon, Merleau-Ponty and Difference of Phenomenology" (2001); Linda Martín Alcoff, "Toward a Phenomenology of Racial Embodiment" (1999); Lewis R. Gordon, "The Black and the Body Politic: Fanon's Existential and Phenomenological Critique of Psychoanalysis" (1996); David Caute, *Frantz Fanon* (1970); and James Baldwin, *The Fire Next Time* (1963).

An opposite view of the epidermalization of race is demonstrated in Paul Gilroy's *Against Race: Imagining Political Culture Beyond the Color Line*. And since, as we will see in chapter 2, Gilroy dismisses how race is lived and instead draws on race as a representation instead of a presentation—that is, how race is presented—he unfortunately misses the non-emancipatory nature of race. In short, given that, to borrow from Walter Benn Michaels in "Autobiography of an Ex-Colored Man," "there is no such thing as race" (1998, 125), we should be "against race" (Gilroy 2000a). And even, according to Gilroy, "if 'race' is to endure, it will be in a new form estranged from the scale respectively associated with political anatomy and epidermalization" (2000a, 47). However, if we take seriously Fanon's argument that race is fixed on the black body and always already positions blacks as the "other," how can we transcend race and its implications? Given that there is considerable violence perpetrated toward the racialized body, we cannot transcend race as a concept. In this sense, one can argue that the racialized body is positioned outside of the human, and Gilroy's proposal to give up the idea of "race" altogether ends up aporetic.

54. Fanon 1967, 109.
55. Yancy 2008, 117. My own emphasis.

Chapter 1

1. Johnson 1984, 156.
2. The fixing of race on the body is one of the hallmarks for racial violence.
3. Cervenak and Carter 2017, 45.
4. Butler 1993b, 97–98.
5. Cervenak and Carter 2017, 45. On the other hand, for blacks—as "overdetermined from the outside," as a manifestation of the disturbing normalization of police surveillance and the cycle of violence in the black "community"—can this enable a psychic bond among blacks? And while I do see the value in Iris Marion Young's use of community to mean homogeneous identification "and the need for social unity and affinity in the communitarian spirit" (Young 1980, 302) that promotes utilitarian goals of survival, I also think that blackness outsideness

makes blacks feel that they are interpenetrated with each other, as "being-in-common," to borrow from Jean-Luc Nancy's *The Inoperative Community*; that is, being duty-bound or obligated together as an interdiction against racial identity as a bodily mark, shaping and upholding their identification process notwithstanding, for example, gender, class, sexuality, and disability differences. In this sense, the psychic bond among blacks, which is "beyond social divisions" (Nancy 1991, 1), is never "lost or broken" (9), and resists and unsettles material conditions and class apartheid in the black community.

    6. Mbembe 2016, 31. Thomas Jefferson, perhaps influenced by the German polygenist Christoph Meiners's *The Outline of History of Mankind*, makes a startling confession in *Notes on the State of Virginia* that skin color "is fixed in nature" (1999, 6). And while it is not a secret that nature as a false determinant is used as a justification for white supremacy, for patriarchy's horrible predispositions, for the non-inclusion of disabled people from jobs that will provide them with resources so they can compete on an equal footing with abled-body people, and to justify the exclusion of the LGBTQ community from heteronormative sexuality, how skin color as natural is a huge part of America's racist history is also not to be ignored. Also, see Nathan Brown's "The Irony of Anatomy: Basquiat's Poetics of Black Positionality," where he writes: "One read in the nineteenth-century *Chambers*['s] *American Encyclopedia*, 'what Strikes the ordinary observer chiefly is, of course, the difference of complexion'" (Brown 2016, 18). Indeed, there is nothing natural about blackness. It is cultural, which means acquired.

    7. Spivak 1998, 45.

    8. See Michel Foucault's *Discipline and Punish: The Birth of the Prison* (1979). Another form of regulatory intension is Black History Month. Meanwhile, blacks congregating together in the public sphere is met with vicious policing and violence.

    9. See Frantz Fanon, *Black Skin, White Masks*, chapter 5, "The Fact of Blackness," which Ronald Judy translates as "The Lived Experience of the Black." See Ronald Judy, "Fanon's Body of Black Experience" (1996).

    10. Moten 2008, 187.

    11. Frankenberg 1993, 1.

    12. Bourdieu 1993, 86.

    13. Judy 1993, 107.

    14. Hannah Arendt, in *The Origins of Totalitarianism*, on the other hand, argues with Sartre's conceptualization that it is the anti-Semite that makes the Jew and calls this a myth, "a myth that has become somewhat fashionable in the intellectual circles after Sartre's 'existentialist' interpretation of the Jew as someone who is regarded and defined as a Jew by others" (1968, xv). Frantz Fanon, on the other hand, in *Black Skin, White Masks*, writes: "At first thought it may seem strange that the anti-Semite's outlook should be related to that of the Negrophobe. It was my philosophy professor, a native of the Antilles, who recalled the

fact to me one day: 'Whenever you hear anyone abuse the Jews, pay attention, because he is talking about you.' And I found that he was universally right—by which I meant that I was answerable in my body and my heart for what was done to my brother. Later I realized that he meant, quite simply, an anti-Semite is inevitably anti-Negro" (1967, 122). In fact, George Yancy, in *Backlash: What Happens When We Talk Honestly About Racism in America*, "speaks to a twisted racist logic emanating from a white racist American imaginary filled with anti-Black racism" (2018, 5).

15. Frye 1983, 114.

16. Foucault 1988, 18.

17. See George Lipsitz, *The Possessive Investment in Whiteness: How White People Profit from Identity Politics* (1998).

18. Mbembe 2016, 31.

19. Mbembe 2016, 31.

20. Morrison 1992, 38.

21. Mills 1998, xiv.

22. Mills, xi. It is Emmanuel Chukwudi Eze, in "The Color of Reason: The Idea of Race in Kant's Anthropology," who first points out that Kant in his geographical and anthropological account of human nature developed the modern concept of race through his structuring of humans, understood differently in terms of their race (1997), in Judith Butler's words, "the legibility of that race, its morphology" (2004, 2) was, for a long time, ignored by philosophers not accepting the essays on race into the twentieth century. However, mainstream philosophy established its racist positioning and naturalized its refusal to inquire into race and race theory. This is what critical race theorists see as the whiteness of philosophy. It is no wonder that, as philosopher Charles W. Mills acknowledges, "the 'whiteness' of academic philosophy has long been a source of wonder and complaint to minorities" (1998, xi) who have examined philosophy from the "outside"—a point to which I will return in order to point out how thoughts from the "outside" unsettle thoughts of the "inside," creating different ways of being and knowing.

23. There is now a journal called *Critical Philosophy of Race*, which was launched in 2013 and is published by Penn State University Press. Also, there is the California Roundtable on Philosophy and Race that started in 2004. For a comprehensive discussion on Kant's theory of race, see Stella Sandford, "Kant, Race, and Natural History" (2018).

24. Mills 2013, 36.

25. Pelbert 2000, 205.

26. Pelbert 2000, 207. Also, see Foucault's work in the first volume of *The History of Sexuality* on the "polymorphous techniques of power" (1978, 11).

27. "The Afro-pessimists," according to Frank B. Wilderson III, "are theorists of Black positionality who share Fanon's insight that though Blacks are indeed

sentient beings, the structure of the entire world's semantic field—regardless of cultural and national discrepancies—'leaving' as Fanon would say 'existence by the way'—is sutured by antiblack solidarity" (Wilderson 2010, 58). For Afro-pessimists, antiblack social dynamics are traceable to slavery, an institution that deemed blacks as fungible, which adds to their inhumane treatment by the masters. For more on Afro-pessimists' thought, see Frank B. Wilderson III, *Afropessimism* (2020).

28. See Frantz Fanon, chapter 5, "The Fact of Blackness," which, as I already noted, Ronald Judy rightfully translates as "The Lived Experience of the Black." And while Fanon engages with several political and philosophical traditions of modernity, another name for European expansion in the later part of the eighteenth century and their critiques, "The Lived Experience of the Black" also points to Fanon's debt to Edmund Husserl's and Maurice Merleau-Ponty's phenomenology in general. See Ronald Judy, "Fanon's Body of Black Experience" (1996).

29. Black resistance takes forms in slave riots, public speeches and lectures, writings, Black Nationalism, the Black Power Movement, riots and demonstrations, and black popular culture. Other forms of black critique include black feminist thought with its emphasis on intersectionality, critical race theory, queer studies, disability studies, and trans discourse.

30. Du Bois 2003, 5.
31. Fields and Fields 2014, 16.
32. Fields and Fields 2014, 16.
33. Indeed, it was a search, "a documentation of his body" (Fuchs 1995, note 1).
34. When Dr. Gates was arrested in 2009, he was the director of the W. E. B. Du Bois Institute for African and African American Research at Harvard University.
35. For more on the police harassing of blacks, see Paul Butler, *Chokehold: Policing Black Men* (2018). The police, Butler writes, "in Ferguson, Missouri, arrested a man named Michael for filing a false report because he told them his name was 'Mike'. Locked up a woman in Ferguson for 'occupancy permit violation' when she called 911 to report that she was being beaten up by her boyfriend and the police learned that the man was not legally entitled to live in the house" (2017, 1).
36. See Michael Jackson's "You Are Not Alone," a song that was released in 2006 on his 1995 album *HIStory, Past, Present and Future Book 1*.
37. Fanon 1967, 14. My own emphasis.
38. Butler 2004, 29.
39. Albrecht 2013, 706.
40. Michael Jackson's body has always been an active spectacle that ricochets between desire and fear and anxiety and fascination. There has always been a fascination with Michael Jackson's body, from the change in the color of his skin, to the numerous reconstructive plastic surgery, to the change of his hairstyle.

41. da Silva 2014, 84.

42. Macaulay Culkin's "lip-synching of 'I'm not going to spend my life being' a color" is tempered, of course, by the fact that he's a blond twelve-year-old billionaire who doesn't have to (Fuchs 1995, 23).

43. Fanon 1967, 109.

44. da Silva 2014, 81. In *West Side Story*, we see how skin color is what determines race. As David Brackett notes, "The relative lightness of the Jets' skin set them apart from the sharks. In other words, the inability of the Sharks to 'pass' as white consolidates what would have then been the newfound whiteness of the Jets" (2012, 173).

45. Vogel 2015, 480.

46. Bhabha 1992, 312.

47. Hartman 1997, 56. We do remember that during the Elizabethan era, the English's first encounter with Africans provided the platform for the English to describe Africans as "blacks," specific categories "of social being that stood in the way of human beings" (Pinder 2012, 6), which would later on be confirmed when the colonists arrived in the United States and were quick to make blacks into slaves, inferior beings, which by the tools of racist reasoning prevailed and continues to do so in the United States. One needs only to look at the police's endless shooting of blacks, which incited the start of the Black Lives Matter movement.

48. Keeling 2003, 96.

49. Fanon 1967, 109. Fanon's analysis of black ontology helps us to see that the world, as well as the categories that we use to describe and explain it, materialize in time; that is, already, even before the ensemble questions of existence and being are contemplated and put forward. Also, see Denise Ferreria da Silva, "Toward a Black Feminist Poethics" (2014, 87). Furthermore, being is always relational—being + something else—as I already pointed out in the body of the text.

50. Fanon 1967, 109.

51. Fanon 1967, 109.

52. This is what Alexander G. Weheliye, in *Habeas Viscus*, says about bare life. Bare life, Weheliye writes, "not only misconstrues how profoundly race and racism shape the modern idea of the human, it also overlooks or perfunctorily writes off theorizations of race, subjection, and humanity found in black and ethnic studies" (2014, 4).

53. Pinder 2018, 66.

54. Fred Moten, for good reason, in "The Case of Blackness," goes against Agamben's "bare life" because a "certain American reception of Agamben" is obsessed with the critical concept of "bare life" that "fetishizes the bareness of life" (2008, 216). However, blacks in the United States are never reduced to bare life. Through laws and policies, the power structure in place keeps blacks "closed in" and exposes them to all forms of discriminatory practice that are truly burdensome.

55. In the United States, then, we are to look at, historically, the political forms that the negation of blacks took on, in that laws, systems, structures, and ideologies upheld and continue to uphold the presumptive hegemony of whiteness. I can point to several examples. But, what, above all, comes to my mind at the moment are laws such as the one-drop rule, which established persons "having any African blood in their veins" (Fields 2003, 1404) as black and, more recently, the colorblind laws that are rooted in racial inequality. For a comprehensive discussion on the colorblind laws, see Michelle Alexander, *The New Jim Crow: Mass Incarceration in the Age of Colorblindness* (2010); Ian F. Haney-Lopéz, "'A Nation of Minorities': Race, Ethnicity and Reactionary Colorblindness" (2007); Jody Armour, "Stereotypes and Prejudices: Helping Legal Decisionmakers Break the Prejudice Habits" (1995); and Paul Finkelman, "The Color of Law" (1993). Other laws that promote the presumptive hegemony of whiteness include the Patriot Act (the United and Strengthening America by Providing Appropriate Tools Required to Intercept and Obstruct Terrorism Act of 2001) and the Arizona Immigration Law (Arizona SB 1070–Support Our Law Enforcement and Safe Neighborhood Act). The former was, immediately after 9/11, implemented by the George W. Bush administration. Even though the Patriot Act, in the minds of those in power, is necessary for America to safeguard itself from future terrorist attacks, a critical analysis of the Patriot Act shows that it, without any remorse, authorizes racial profiling at US borders and airports. The latter is a preemptive measure to address the growing problem of undocumented immigrants in Arizona—even though immigration laws, for the most part, have always been a federal matter—that is at the forefront of racial profiling, which was approved by the Arizona Legislature on April 19, 2010, and was signed into law on April 23 by Governor Jan Brewer. In fact, Governor Brewer defended the law by making claims that the federal government was not doing anything to curtail "illegal immigration." Hence, the state has a right to take measures to control undocumented immigrants. The "show me your papers" rule, one of the most controversial provisions of the Arizona Immigration Law, which was not struck down by the Supreme Court, authorizes the Arizona police to verify the immigration status of persons who have been arrested or stopped. For blacks and other nonwhites, to be stopped by the police is indeed a form of anxiety for them. Two of the other provisions in the Arizona Immigration Law were to make it a crime to violate the federal immigration law by living in Arizona illegally, and the other was to arrest people who the police have probable cause to believe were in violation of the federal immigration law. The Court, for good reasons, struck down both of these provisions.

56. Fanon 1967, 114.
57. Fanon 1967, 150.
58. Fanon 1967, 117.
59. Fanon 1967, 110.

60. Fanon 1967, 110.
61. Sexton 2011, 24.
62. Epstein and Steinberg 2007, 446.
63. Silberman 2007, 437.
64. Butler 1993, 15.

65. What is unnervingly ironic, "the investigation into Michael Jackson's abuse charges was conducted by the Los Angeles Police Department even as its most infamous officers, Stacey Koon and Lawrence Powell (convicted of denying Rodney King his civil rights when they beat him in 1991), were removed from prison in order to shield them from possible inmate violence" (Fuchs 195, 14).

66. A coterie of black scholars from W. E. B. Du Bois to Toni Morrison, the first wave of whiteness studies scholars, took on the task of articulating whiteness invisibility to whites and to undertake a paradigmatic approach looking into the analytics of whiteness sensibility ages before "whiteness studies" surfaced in academia.

67. The emergence of "whiteness studies" was first noted on September 8, 1995, in the *Chronicle of Higher Education* in an article written by Liz McMillen titled "Lifting the Veil from Whiteness: Growing Body of Scholarship Challenges a Racial 'Norm.'" In 1996, David Stone, "Uncolored People," mentioned "whiteness studies." Also, see Alastair Bonnett, "'White Studies': The Problems and Projects of a New Research Agenda" (1996). In disciplines as diverse as history, gender studies, political science, film studies, media studies, humor studies, linguistics, art history, rhetoric and communication, material culture, and dance, scholars focusing on whiteness as a concept for analysis have been lumped together under the opportune label of "whiteness studies" (Fishkin 1995, 442).

68. "The wages of whiteness" can be traced back to W. E. B. Du Bois, *Black Reconstruction in America*, which Du Bois shows is manifested in the social and economic status long established for whites. These advantages, as Du Bois explains, operate as "a sort of public and psychological wages" (1935, 700). Whites, Du Bois writes:

> were given public deference and titles of courtesy because they were white. They were admitted freely with all classes of white people to public functions, public parks, and the best schools. The police were drawn from their ranks, and the courts, dependent upon their votes, treated them with such leniency as to encourage lawlessness. Their votes selected public officials, and while this had small effects upon the economic situation, it had great effects on their personal treatment and the deference shown them. White schoolhouses were the best in the community, and conspicuously placed, and they cost anything from twice to ten times as much per capita as the colored schools. The newspaper specialized on news that flattered the poor

whites and almost utterly exclude the Negroes except in crimes and ridicule. (1935, 701)

Whites are positioned in such a way that they can tap into the economic and social resources. Furthermore, laws and social customs are the mandates that guide and reinforce, perpetuate, and uphold whiteness, which strengthen white privilege and whites' feelings of superiority over blacks and other nonwhites. George Yancy, in *Backlash: What Happens When We Talk Honestly About Racism in America*, reminds us that the social world was created for whites—perhaps never for blacks (2018, 4). This is why Harper Lee, in *Go Set A Watchman*, admits, "For years and years all that man thought he had that made him any better than his black brothers was the color of his skin" (2015, 197). For more on "the wages of whiteness," see David R. Roediger, *The Wages of Whiteness: Race and the Making of the American* (1991).

69. Pinder 2011, xiv.

70. Fine et al. 1997, xi.

71. This is a question that is inspired by Fanon when he asks in *Black Skin, White Masks*, "What the black man wants?" (1967, 8). Freud also posed the question about women: What do women want?

72. According to Keith Byerman, double consciousness did not originate from W. E. B. Du Bois. Byerman notes: "In the psychological theory of the time, including that of Du Bois's mentor William James, 'double consciousness' was a form of mental illness in which the victim experienced self-alienation, an inability to maintain a coherent self-image" (1994, 15).

73. Another way of thinking about desire is put forward by Judith Butler in *Undoing Gender*. She suggests that "the Hegelian tradition links desire with recognition, claiming that desire is always a desire for recognition and it is only through the experience of recognition that any of us becomes constituted as socially viable beings" (2004, 2). Butler recognizes that this might be true. She draws on some important consideration by pointing out, "the terms by which we are recognized as humans are socially articulated and changeable. And sometimes the very terms that confirm 'humanness' on some individuals and those that deprive certain other individuals of the possibility of achieving that status, producing a differential between the human and less human" (2004, 2). For sure, Hegel did not have blacks in mind. A passage from Hegel's *Lectures on Philosophy of World History* refers to blacks/Africans as "an example of animal man in all his savagery and lawlessness, and if we wish to understand him at all, we must abstract from all reverence and morality, and from everything we call feelings. All that is foreign to man in his immediate existence, and nothing consonant with humanity is to be found in his character. For this reason, we cannot properly feel ourselves in his nature, no more than into that of a dog" (1975, 177).

74. Eppert 2017, 92.

75. Mbembe 2017, 13.

76. For more on black positionality as a result of slavery, see Hortense Spillers, *Black, White, and Color: Essays on American Literature and Culture* (2003); David Marriott, *On Black Men* (2000); Achille Mbembe, *On the Postcolony* (2001); Saidiya V. Hartman, *Scenes of Subjection: Terror, Slavery, and Self-Making in Nineteenth-Century America* (1997); Ronald Judy, *DisForming the American Canon: African-Arabic Slave Narratives and the Vernacular* (1993); and Orlando Patterson, *Slavery and Social Death: A Comparative Studies* (1982).

77. Butler 1993b, 18–19.

78. Butler 1993b, 18–19.

79. Epstein and Steinberg 2007, 456.

80. See Hannah Arendt, *The Human Condition* (1958).

81. Fanon helps us see how the Nietzschean ressentiment contributes to black-on-black crimes. In *The Wretched of the Earth*, Fanon writes: "The colonized subject will first train this aggressiveness sedimented in his muscles against his own people. This is the period when black turns on black, and police officers and magistrates don't know which way to turn when faced with the surprising surge of North African criminality" (1963, 15–16).

82. Žižek 2009, 196.

83. David Brackett, "Black or White? Michael Jackson and the Idea of Crossover," points out that black popular culture in terms of its music arises as "a relational construct formed out of a history of black-white interactions and the centrality of race to US public discourse" (2012, 171).

84. Fanon 1967, 109.

85. Fanon 1967, 143.

86. "Remember the Time" is a song written and performed by Michael Jackson. It was released on his *Dangerous* album in 1991.

87. Mercer 1986, 27.

88. See Michael Jackson's song, "Childhood." Some have argued that Michael Jackson's damaged childhood has let him become, in the words of Kobena Mercer, "'a lost boy' whose life is shadowed by morbid obsession and anxieties" (1986, 28). In addition, documentaries such as *Leaving Neverland* and *Michael Jackson's Boys* show Michael Jackson to be a pervert and a child molester.

89. Jackson 1988, 39. When he was in the sixth grade, Michael Jackson attended Gardner Street Elementary School in Los Angeles. In the seventh grade, he attended Emerson Junior High (Taraborrelli 1991, 90).

90. Du Bois 2003, 5.

91. Fanon 1967, 111.

92. Jackson 1988, 162.

93. Harris 1993, 1743.

94. Fine et al. 1997, xi.

NOTES TO CHAPTER 1   143

95. Hartman 1997, 41.
96. Fanon 1967, 110–11.
97. Fanon 1967, 231.
98. Fanon 1967, 114.
99. See Public Enemy's song, "Don't Believe the Hype."
100. Following the Dubosian trail, Stuart Hall on a different topic—the sociopolitical certainties of nonwestern cultures and the part racism as a political and sociocultural force plays in the binary logic of "high" and "low" cultures and "big versus small nations"—declares with certainty, "The capacity to live with difference is, in my view, the coming question of the twenty-first century" (Hall 1993, 361). If we think of the United States, such a declaration would be unusual because, historically, blacks have always lived with difference, which was manufactured, and continues to be so, as a form of indifference bound to the dynamisms of rule, the distinguishing norms of recognition, blackness.
101. Epstein and Steinberg 2007, 449.
102. The 2005 documentary *Michael Jackson's Boys* was directed by Helen Littleboy. Also, see *Leaving Netherland Ranch*, directed and produced by Dan Reed, British filmmaker, in 2019, in which Wade Robson and James Safechuch allege that when they were children Michael Jackson sexually abused them. The film, *Michael Jackson's Face*, was re-aired during the same time the documentary *Michael Jackson's Boys* was aired. The former film focuses on "Michael Jackson's face, skin, and body crossing a range of mediatized genres from newsprint to television, to radio and the internet" (Epstein and Steinberg 2007, footnote 15).
103. Weinraub 1993, A12.
104. Johnson 1984, 156.
105. Epstein and Steinberg 2007, 453.
106. Truth is literally black or white. If you are a black person accused by a white person of a crime, it is terribly hard to prove your innocence.
107. Epstein and Steinberg 2007, 453.
108. Butler 1993b, 15.
109. Blacks continue to be the target of police violence. Some of the well-known fatal cases include George Floyd (2020); Stephon Clark (2018); Philando Castile and Terence Crutcher (2016); Sandra Bland and Freddie Gray (2015); Michael Brown, Eric Garner, Tamir Rice, and Yvette Smith (2014); Oscar Grant (2009); Amadou Diallo (1999); James Byrd (1998); and Garnett Paul Johnson (1997). The list of casualties is too long to cite them all here.
110. Fuchs 1995, 17. For more on Michael Jackson's "penis grabbing" during his performance, see Margo Jefferson, *On Michael Jackson*, where Jefferson writes that Michael Jackson's penis "wasn't real, it was symbolic. Not a penis but a phallus" (2006, 102). When Michael Jackson talked about his "penis grabbing" on stage with Oprah Winfrey, he admitted, "I don't think about it. I just do it."

111. Indeed, Michael Jackson understands this very well when he states, "If I just walked out on stage naked, there's no imagination. I'm letting them imagine what I look like without the clothes" (Johnson 1984, 162).

112. Fuchs 1995, 22.

113. David Marriott, "Bordering on the Black Penis," examines "how the 'real' of lynching, for example, continues to be a trauma, even as, indeed as cultural memory (i.e., whether or not directly witnessed or experienced" (de Lauretis 2002, notes 12, 66). These days, a new form of lynching is embedded in the criminal justice system where black men are sentenced to prison for the alleged raping of white women.

114. According to Freud, "a child fantasizes about another child being beaten because he or she wants parental affection. Freud suggests that this fantasy about another child is actually a fantasy about the child's unconscious masochistic desire to be beaten by his or her father as a punishment for his or her Oedipal desires. This masochistic moment can be read as a sort of nascent superego scripted before Freud theorized the existence of the superego, but similarly marked by guilt and parental judgment" (Musser 2012, 82).

115. Fanon 1967, 179. In fact, Teresa de Lauretis notes that "Fanon's analysis of the fantasy is based not on Freud's famous paper, 'A Child Is Being Beaten,' but rather on Bonaparte's reading of it. Bonaparte much more emphatically than Freud, sees feminine masochism as a reversal of the daughter's phallic and sadistic drives toward the mother, and hence a sign of repressed bisexuality (i.e., homosexuality)" (2002, 63). In addition, Fanon, in the reading of Mayotte Capécia's autobiographical book, extends the rape fantasy to light-skinned Antillean women who wished to be raped by dark-skinned black men. See Fanon, *Black Skin, White Masks*, chapter 2.

116. For more on this, see Angela Y. Davis, "Rape, Racism, and the Myth of the Black Rapist," in *Women, Race & Class* (1983, 172–201).

117. Musser 2012, 83. And while Fanon's treatment of interracial rape is unsettling not due to what he says about white women and black men, but to what he omits to say about black women and white men. Given the complexity of this issue, I rely here on Mary Ann Doane's reading of Fanon's analysis of miscegenation and rape. Doane writes: "Fanon asks (if any) questions about the white man's psycho-sexuality in his violent confrontation with the black woman—fewer still about how one might describe black female subjectivity in the face of such violence. In the historical scenario conjoining rape and lynching, the emotional charge attached to miscegenation, its representational intensity, are channeled onto the figure of the white woman, effectively erasing the black woman's historical role" (1991, 222). This is one reason why Fanon can say, "Those who grant our conclusion on the psychosexuality of the white woman may ask what we have to say about the woman of color. I know nothing about her" (1967, 179–80). Rape itself takes on a certain displacement, "from the white man's prerogative as

master/colonizer to the white woman's fears/desires in relations to the black man" (Doane 1991, 222), which does not enter Fanon's discussion. On another point, in terms of black men's fantasies of raping white woman, this has no "objective value" because the laws are "white." Patrice Douglas and Frank Wilderson make a similar point: "Black fantasies of lynching white people (or, Look a honky!) have no 'objective value' because the law is white." See "The Violence of Presence: Metaphysics in a Blackened World" (2013, 121).

118. Fanon 1967, 192.
119. Musser 2012, 83.
120. Gordon 2002, 21.
121. Gordon 2002, 21. Also, Fanon writes, "The Negro is the genital. Is this the whole story? Unfortunately not. The Negro is something else. . . . The black man is the symbol of Evil and Ugliness" (1967, 180).
122. Fanon 1967, 163.
123. Epstein and Steinberg 2007, 451.
124. For a good overview of the militarization of the police, see the documentary *Do Not Resist*. In the documentary, "Richard Berk, a predictive policing researcher and professor of criminology and statistics at the University of Pennsylvania, who said it would be possible to calculate the likelihood that someone will engage in criminal activity *before they were born*, presumably by analyzing family wealth and support, place of residence, race, and socioeconomic factor. (He explicitly supports the use of race to make crime prediction.)" See Jackie Wang, *Carceral Capitalism* (2017, 43–44). The question, then, is how is crime defined becomes fundamental.
125. Scarry 1985, 4.
126. "Speechless" is a song from Michael Jackson's album *Invisible* released on June 21, 2001, as a promotional single in South Korea.
127. Scarry 1985, 49.
128. Fanon 1967, 138.
129. So, when we do write about black bodily pain, our writings become acts of resistance, an enforced abstraction, always writing against the conservative ways of thinking and writing about the black body as threat to the social body. In this sense, our writings are viewed as inauthentic writing, always writing against the taken-for-granted form of writings. In other words, writing about the black body, in this way, is "an interdiction of the [black], a censorship to be inarticulate, . . . to be without effect, without agency, without thought. The muted body of the [black] is overwritten by the black, and the black that emerges from the ink flow of [blacks'] pen is that which has overwritten itself and so becomes the representation of the very body it sits on" (Wilderson 2010, 38–39). My own emphasis. Also, see Ronald Judy, *(Dis)Forming the American Canon: African-Arabic Slave Narratives and the Vernacular* (1993, 89).
130. These are words from Michael Jackson's song "Speechless."

131. Baldwin 1963, 91.
132. Fanon 1967, 112.
133. Baldwin 1963, 91.
134. Du Bois 2003, 5.
135. Ahmed 2004, 161.
136. Epstein and Steinberg 2007, 441.
137. Fanon 1967, 173. Don King, after the release of the *Victory* album, was hired by the Jackson family to promote the Victory Tour expresses the same sentiments: "What Michael's got to realize is that Michael's a nigger. It doesn't matter how great he can sing and dance. I don't care that he can prance. He's one of the mega stars of the world, but he still going to be a nigger megastar. He must accept that, he's got to accept that, he's got to accept it and demonstrate that he wants to be a nigger. Why? To show that a nigger can do it" (Taraborrelli 1991, 320).
138. de Beauvoir 1976, 76.
139. Yancy 2012, 34.
140. "In the Closet," is a song from Michael Jackson's *Dangerous* album.
141. Fanon 1967, 112.
142. Fanon 1967, 112.
143. Fanon 1967, 109. Louis Althusser, in "Ideology and Ideological State Apparatuses," introduces us to the concept of interpellation to explain and describe the process by which ideology is embedded in political institutions, the Ideological State Apparatuses (ISAs) and the Repressive State Apparatuses (RSAs). The RSAs "function by violence" and the ISAs "function by ideology" (1977, 145). However, in the end both function by ideology and repression. But for the RSAs ideology is secondary, and for the ISAs repression is secondary. "There is no such thing as a purely ideological apparatus. . . . The Schools and Churches use suitable methods of punishment, expulsion, etc. to discipline." The same is true for the Family and other ISAs (1977, 145). And given that the ISAs function merely by ideology (1977, 158), it constitutes the very nature of the individual subject's identity through the process of "hailing" that inserts the individual into social interaction. One thing is certain for Althusser: individuals are subjected to ideology, which functions in such a way that it transforms the individual into a subject. An example of how ideology works that Althusser provides for us, in *On the Reproduction of Capitalism: Ideology and Ideological State Apparatus*, is when a police officer shouts, "hey, you there!" to an individual and the individual turns around and responds to the officer's "hailing." By responding to the "hailing," the individual becomes a subject (2014, 191). As a side note, a question that concerns me: When a black person is hailed by a police officer, and the individual runs away, does it take away from the individual's subjectivity?
144. Fanon 1967, 111–12.
145. Du Bois 2003, 4.

146. Fanon 1967, 110–11.

147. See Michael Jackson's song, "Black or White," released in 1991.

148. Spivak 1998, 45.

149. "Leave Me Alone" is a song by Michael Jackson, which was released on August 31, 1987, by Epic Records around the same time the tabloid was circulating a picture of him lying in a hyperbaric chamber at a hospital he visited.

150. "Gotta have it my way" is taken from Michael Jackson's song, "Speed Demon."

151. Recently, whiteness studies theorists turned their full attention to the notion of whiteness as "a problem" and have now reversed the gaze from blackness (object) to whiteness (subject). It is important to note here the deficiency of whiteness, and the way in which the mechanism of the white gaze is employed by the cultural norm to project whiteness inadequacy onto blacks.

152. After the worldwide debut, on November 14, 1991, of Michael Jackson's *Black or White* video where Michael Jackson, in "a four-minute dance sequence in which the elfin superstar rubs his crouch and violently smashes a car," reports van Rijn of *The Toronto Star*, he is asked to revise his video and eliminate the "violence." And while the final part of the video, now known as the "panther dance," goes against colorblindness in the United States and points to the reality of race in the United States, the media interpreted the "panther dance" as self-indulgent and offensive. Chris Willman of the *Los Angeles Times*, for one, describes the video as a "display of nonsensical violence." What this shows is that the mainstream media is, for the most part, not prepared for or is unwilling to see Michael Jackson to potently assert his identity as a black performer and present his work on his own terms. So, Michael Jackson's *Black or White* video focuses on his chorographical "crotch grabbing" and him smashing cars as destructive behavior (sexual and violent) on his part. It is no wonder Michael Jackson acknowledges, "It upsets me to think that *Black or White* could influence any child or adult to destructive behavior, either sexual or violent" (Silberman 2007, 449). We cannot ignore the fact that many Americans would pay money to go to the movies and enjoy an erroneous amount of violence on screen.

153. Brackett 2012, 177.

154. Keeling 2003, 92.

155. Du Bois 2003, 3–4.

156. Fanon 1967, 111.

157. We do remember how *The Birth of a Nation*, in its racist orientation, draws extensively on the racialized body as deviant and threatening. More recently, in April 2014, the ill-reputed recorded racist slurs submitted by the owner of the Los Angeles Clippers, Donald Sterling, about Magic Johnson is illustrative. This unpleasant incident proves that professional sports like basketball still shrink black men to pure physicality and peddle them as "property" to team owners such as Sterling who perpetuate and uphold the conventional fear and anxiety

according to which black men are an actual danger to the white social body, and to particularly white women. The foundational racist idea returns us to the impeccable account of how race is lived in the United States.

158. Fanon 1967, 14. My own emphasis.

159. See Louis Althusser, "Ideology and Ideological State Apparatuses" (1977).

160. Seshadri-Crooks 1998, 358.

161. Frankenberg 2001, 75.

162. In fact, an autocritique cannot go forward without a consideration of how the persistent "self" comes into being and how it has actually appropriated the norms of whiteness. Self-critique becomes an important component of the autocritique.

163. Moreton-Robinson 2008, 85.

164. Foucault 1980, 59.

165. Du Bois 2003, 3–4.

166. Fanon 1967, 110.

167. Fanon 1967, 111.

168. Foucault 1980, 122.

169. Butler 1997a, 2.

170. Epstein and Steinberg 2007, 444–45. My own emphasis.

171. Foucault 1989, 156.

172. Michael Jackson's pride in his race is expressed in an interview with *Ebony* magazine. "Blacks, as far as artistry, [are] a talented race of people. But when I went to Africa, I was even more convinced" (Johnson 1984, 157).

173. da Silva 2014, 87.

174. Frankenberg 1993, 234.

175. And while the second wave of whiteness studies scholars have focused on making whiteness visible by moving it to the epistemological center, my premise is the illogicality according to which whiteness is only invisible to those for whom it benefits. In this familiar tendency of whiteness to remain invisible to whites, whites unduly hold on to its preeminence, their "property rights of whiteness," while simultaneously whiteness as an ideology and a system with regulatory power in society organizes the lives of blacks within the framework of white supremacy. And while whiteness and white supremacy are not, as some would have, the same, as least for me, the object of analysis should be how whiteness produces white supremacy. In other words, we need to name whiteness as "a problem" which does not fail to signify its preeminence.

176. Foucault 1980, 142.

177. Žižek 1997, 34.

178. Fuchs 1995, 17.

179. Albrecht 2013, 714.

180. Fanon 1967, 8.

181. hooks 1992, 166.
182. Bhabha 1998, 21.

Chapter 2

1. Alcoff 2006, 126.

2. At the same time, I used "identification" instead of "identity" drawing on Judith Butler's analysis of how identification unsettles the "I." Given that the "I" is varied, intertwined, and ambivalent, "they are the sedimentation of the 'we' in the constitution of any 'I,' the structuring presence of alterity in the very formation of the 'I'" (Butler 1993a, 105). And the question of the "we" is one of the crucial questions implicated in any argument for identity politics and the politics of recognition.

3. And while it is true that women can "pass" for men and vice versa, gays can pass for straight, and so on, at the start, when the notion of "passing" was introduced, it was mostly applied to blacks who looked white enough to be able to integrate into the white community. What this meant was a break, either temporary or permanent, from the African American community and an access to resources that were denied to them as blacks. As whites, they could enjoy the privileges of whiteness in the same ways "real whites" did. In James Weldon Johnson's *The Autobiography of an Ex-Colored Man*, Johnson is depicted as a Negro who is "passing." I put "passing" in quotes because in the United States, race is an identity that can never be hidden. It is thus not surprising that Johnson could not do a good job of convincing himself that he is white. Yet, he is unwilling to accept the ill treatment of being black in a blackphobic society. Thus, he constantly moves between racial spaces, *not black, not white*, which translates into "half-lies" and "half-truths." The protagonist becomes not so much an ex-colored man but, in Everett V. Stonequest's words, "the marginal man" who lives and shares "intimately in the cultural life and traditions of two distinct people" (1935, 3). However, he does feel rejected by both cultures. For more on passing, see chapter 9, "Passing; or, Sacrificing a Parvenu," from Werner Sollors, *Neither Black nor White Yet Both: Thematic Explorations of Interracial Literature* (1997); Adrian Piper, "Passing for White: Passing for Black" (1990); and Nella Larsen, *Passing* (1929). For some reasons, these days, many blacks who look white and did "pass" for white are now reclaiming their black identity after, for so long, having lived their lives as whites. One notable example of this change is the story of Gregory Howard Williams. See Williams, *Life on the Colored Line: The True Story of a White Boy Who Discovered That He Was Black* (1996). At the other end of the spectrum, the idea that whites can or want to "pass" for blacks is fascinating.

On the one hand, as George Yancy notes, "'passing for white' can function as a form of resistance. For example, take Walter White, who was from 1931 until his death in 1955 executive secretary of the NAACP. As an effort to gather empirical evidence for the horrible practice of lynching Black bodies so as to more forcefully make a case for creating federal laws against lynching, he would blend in with lynch mobs. Undetected as a Black man, he would use this evidence to strengthen the case for the NAACP's anti-lynching efforts" (2008, 134n8).

4. See Nadine Ehlers, *Performativity and Struggle Against Subjection* (2012, 1–3, chapters 4, 5); and Angela Onwuachi-Willig, "A Beautiful Lie: Exploring *Rhinelander v. Rhinelander* as a formative Lesson on Race, Identity, Marriage, and Family" (2007).

5. Onwuachi-Willig 2007, 2396.

6. Alcoff 2006, 7. We do remember in the movie *Raintree Country*, it is Elizabeth Taylor who explains "havin' a little Negra blood in ya'—just one little teeny drop and a person's all Negra" is the worst thing that could ever happen to a white person (Omi and Winant 2007, 14).

7. Young 2010, 6.

8. Michaels 1998, 128.

9. Michaels 1998, 128.

10. Fanon 1967, 118.

11. Winant 1999, 86.

12. See Frantz Fanon, *Black Skin, White Masks*, 1967.

13. See Hortense Spillers, *Black, White and Color: Essays on American Literature and Culture* (2007).

14. Gilroy 2000a, 47.

15. Gilroy 2000b, 6.

16. West 2001, 155.

17. Yancy 2005, 26.

18. Frankenberg 2001, 75.

19. Frankenberg 2001, 75.

20. Mills 2013, 35.

21. Another racially charged term is the "model minority," which only serves to create conflicts within and among nonwhites and promote the false idea that there is a "declining significance of race" and that "the end of racism" is near. In addition, the "model minority" falls prey to the myth that whites who associate and cooperate with individuals from racialized groups "and give them recognition are not racist" (Hill 2008, 23). In creating this label, there is an additional progression of racism at play that consists in the othering of the "other."

22. Another way of thinking about class in the United States is that while there are class and other social divisions among whites, whites, nonetheless, would come together when, for whatever reasons, they felt threatened by blacks. To put it differently, whites are more mindful of their whiteness when they imagine that

there is some kind of a threat to their "property rights in whiteness." Whiteness has a long history, as David R. Roediger has shown in his writing on the formation the working class in the United States. In fact, the Irish, at the beginning of the formation of the United States, were not considered to be white. Noel Ignatiev's *How the Irish Became White* is certainly important in this regard. However, in terms of skin color, the Irish were already white, a fact which is not properly emphasized. Of course, they had to be culturally whitened—that is, they had to adhere to the actions, attitudes, and values of whiteness. Eventually, the Irish workers defined themselves as white in order to enjoy the privilege and benefits enjoyed by whites, which they could not have obtained by being only Irish. By going against blacks and Chinese, the Irish secured their position by identifying with whites. See Roediger's *The Wages of Whiteness: Race and the Making of the American Working Class* (1991). We cannot deny that white ethnic groups—Irish, Jews, Italians, Polish, and Greeks—at one time in the history of the United States, were referred to as "different races," which were distinct from "the race of Anglo-Saxons." These white ethnic groups had to be culturally whitened in order to gain the "property rights of whiteness" and enjoy their privileges. On the Jews, for example, see Karen Brodkin, *How the Jews Became White Folk and What that Says About Race in America* (1998).

23. See Michael Jackson, "I Can't Help It" from his *Off the Wall* album released on August 10, 1979.

24. For a more comprehensive reading, see Michael Jackson's song, "Black or White," released in 1991.

25. Hall 2004, 261.

26. So, at North Newton Junior-Senior High School, a school comprised of 850 students, (two of the students are black and the rest white), located in Moro, Indiana, several female students calling themselves the "Free to Be Me" group identify with hip-hop culture. In some cases, these students have hair that are dreadlocks and they wear baggy jeans and combat boots. At this school, because of the enforced code of whiteness coupled with maleness, the girls experienced both physical and psychological violence from their peers. The issue, then, is as Charles Mills suggests: that whites who deviate from the norms of whiteness "often carry with it the threat that to persist in subversive behavior would lead one to be treated as blacks" (1998, 63).

27. Marlon Riggs's 1994 documentary *Black Is . . . Black Ain't* remains a fortunate analysis that unsettles any notion of black as an authentic group by drawing on the great diversity of identities among blacks.

28. Besides, "an inauthentic Negro," as Gates writes, quoting Anatole Broyard, "is not only estranged from whites—he is also estranged from his own group and from himself. Since his companions are a mirror in which he sees himself as ugly, he must reject them; and since his own self is merely a tension between an accusation [of being black] and a denial [of being black], he can hardly find

it, must less live it. . . . He is adrift within a role in a world predicated on roles" (Gates 1996).

29. Appiah 1994, 153.

30. Several examples have shown how race is marked on the body and is reduced to anatomy. For instance, the slave woman Sojourner Truth had to bear her breasts in public to confirm her womanhood; Frederick Douglass's aunt Hester was stripped, beaten, and raped by her master, which Douglass recounts in his autobiographic writing; Sarah Baartman was on physical display on a stage in Piccadilly, London; and, as previously mentioned, Michael Jackson's penis and buttocks were photographed by the police as a part of an investigation in an alleged child molestation case.

31. West 1993, 17.

32. hooks 1990, 37.

33. Fanon 1967, 111.

34. Butler 1995, 8.

35. Fanon 1967, 154.

36. Ahmed 2007, 153.

37. Ahmed 2007, 158.

38. Mbembe 2017, 55.

39. The efforts by the state to confront racial inequality through its race-conscious affirmative-action programs, for example, did not result in the demise or alteration of the system of racism in place to benefit whites. In fact, it created a backlash that led many whites to see themselves as the victims of "reverse discrimination" or "preferential treatment." We all remember the 1978 case of the *Regents of the University California v. Bakke*, in which Allan P. Bakke sued the University of California, Davis, on the grounds of "reverse discrimination." And while "reverse discrimination" has little in common with the actual experience of one who is the object of racism, the neoconservatives shamelessly attack affirmative actions with the argument, in its most commonsensical expression, that race should not be one of the determining factors in college admission, employment, and job promotion. In other words, race should not matter. Yet, in the *Bakke* case and in many other affirmative action cases that follow, including *Hopwood v. Texas* (1996) and *Grutter v. Bollinger* (2003), race is openly debated.

40. Fanon 1963, 15. Earlier on, in the same text (*The Wretched of the Earth*), dancing is discussed, which is also actional. Dancing "relaxes their painful contracted muscles." For more on dance as an action, see Fanon 1963, 19–20.

41. Arendt 1958, 7–8.

42. For Hannah Arendt, the other activities of being-in-the-world are labor and work. And while for Arendt each activity is autonomous, each, in its own rights, sustains the human condition. In its simplest formulation, the latter has to do with the conditions of worldliness; that is, its ability to build and sustain a world that humans can make use of. The former is the activity that is tied to the human condition of life. It caters to our biological needs of reproduction and

consumption. For a more comprehensive discussion on labor, work, and action, see Arendt, *The Human Conditions* (1958).

43. Hartman 1997, 8.
44. Fanon 1967, 154.
45. Yancy 2005, 235.
46. Fanon 1967, 194.
47. Bhabha 1994, 61.
48. Foucault 1989, 61.
49. Fanon 1967, 139.
50. Fanon 1967, 120.
51. Braidotti 2013, 2.
52. Braidotti 2013, 2.
53. Fanon 1967, 217. For more on the Hegelian dialectics, see chapter 2, "Independence and Dependence of Self-Consciousness: Lordship and Bondage," in Hegel's *Phenomenology of Sprit* (1977, 111–19).
54. Fanon 1967, 120.
55. Fanon 1967, 114.
56. Morrison 1993, 59.
57. Fanon 1967, 110.
58. Fanon 1967, 110.
59. Fuss 1994, 21.
60. Fuss 1994, 22.
61. Fanon 1967, 211.
62. de Beauvoir 1952, 249.
63. The documentary *Why Can't We Live Together* is a good illustration of "white flight" from neighborhoods that are racially integrated. Indeed, the documentary provides a critical reflection on race and racism, which is illustrative of the data that is gathered in the interviews about whites' motivation to move from a formerly all-white suburb in Chicago to another all-white remote town. For one mother, in no uncertain terms, that an all-white remote town is " 'a good place to raise children [because] life is back to family and playing all day.' Because there are no people of color, particularly African Americans, living nearby, she doesn't have to worry about 'her kids walking into the street and getting shot by gangs' " (Aanerud 2007, 21) is clearly articulated.
64. Brackett 2012, 177.
65. These are words from Michael Jackson's song "Thriller."
66. Rich 1979, 204.
67. Yancy 2002, 227.
68. These are the words from Jackson's song "Black or White" released on November 11, 1991.
69. The Motion Picture Producers and Distributors of America (MPPDA), which in 1946 changed its name to the Motion Picture Association of America (MPAA), did make sure that there was no sex relation between blacks and whites

in movies. On-screen, the first sex scene between a black man and a white woman was Melvin Peebles's 1971 film, *Sweet Sweetback's Baadasssss Song*. In this film, the black male fugitive Sweetback is caught trespassing by a white motorcycle gang. In order to avoid punishment, they challenge him to duel with their leader, Pres, who we later learn in the film is a white woman. In short, Sweetback had to have sex with Pres in order to escape any punishment from the gang. The movie lays the groundwork for sex on-screen between a black man and a white woman.

70. Bonnett 2000, 38.
71. Bonnett 2000, 38.
72. The intersectionality framework was developed by Kimberlé Crenshaw in her 1989 article titled "Demarginalizing the Intersection of Race and Sex: A Black Feminist Critique of Antidiscrimination Doctrine, Feminist Theory and Antiracist Politics." For examples of the prevailing concept of intersectionality, see Bonnie Thornton Dill and Ruth Enid Zambrana, "Critical Thinking about Intersectionality: An Emergence Lens" (2009); Ange-Marie Hancock, "When Multiplication Doesn't Equal Quick Addition: Examining Intersectionality as a Research Paradigm" (2007); Avtar Brah and Ann Phoenix, "Ain't I a Woman? Revisiting Intersectionality" (2004); Angela Y. Davis, *Women, Race and Class* (1983); and bell hooks, *Ain't I a Woman: Black Woman and Feminism* (1981).
73. Fanon 1967, 112.
74. Fanon 1967, 113–14.
75. Ehler 2012, 18.
76. Fanon 1967, 60.
77. To be an authentic black person is to choose to be black and express, with pride, what it means to be black.
78. Yancy 2005, 216.
79. Fanon 1967, 111.
80. Fanon 1967, 189.
81. Fanon 1967, 134.
82. Fanon 1967, 161.
83. This, in some respect, is analogous to Simone de Beauvoir's lucid account of white women as the inessential other of white men in *The Second Sex*.
84. Ahmed 2007, 158.
85. Ahmed 2007, 160.
86. Fanon 1967, 110.
87. Bergson 1991, 9.
88. Fanon 1967, 161.
89. Gates 1996.
90. Ahmed 2007, 161.
91. Fanon 1967, 109.
92. Fanon 1967, 109.

93. Kelly Oliver, *Witnessing Beyond Recognition*, makes good usage of the Sartrean *look*. Oliver writes: "I am imprisoned by the look of the other, yet through the look of the other I am aware of myself as the subject. As an object for another, I become aware of myself as a subject for myself; I become aware of myself as a subject who escapes objectification, even my own attempt at objectifying myself. Yet in spite of what Sartre describes as the totalizing presence of the other, the look of the other always refers back to me" (2001, 41). Fanon, however, problematizes the concept of the Sartrean *look* in his desire to show that the white *look* is always directed at blacks. The look creates an ontological condition for blacks that frames their way of being in the world.

94. Ahmed 2007, 161.
95. Fuss 1994, 21.
96. Fanon 1967, 109.
97. Fanon 1967, 109.
98. Fanon 1967, 112.
99. Fanon 1967, 112.
100. Fanon 1967, 112.
101. Fanon 1967, 94.
102. We can find a good example of Richard Wright's assessment of whiteness in *Black Boy*:

> I learned of [whites'] tawdry dreams, their simple hopes, their home lives, their fears of feeling anything deeply, their sex problems, their husbands. They were an eager, restless, talkative, ignorant bunch. . . . They knew nothing of hate and fear. . . . I often wonder what they were trying to get out of life, but I never stumbled on a clue, and I doubt if they themselves had any notion. They lived on the surface of their days; their smiles were surface smiles; their tears were surface tears. Negroes live a truer and deeper life than they, but I wished Negroes, too, could live as thoughtlessly, serenely as they. . . . How far apart we stood! All my life I had done nothing but feel and cultivate my feelings; all their lives they have done nothing but strive for petty goals, the trivial prizes of American life. We share a common tongue, but my language was a different language from theirs. It was a psychological distance that separated the races that the deeper meaning of the problem of the Negro lay for me. (1937, 319–21)

In this respect, whiteness is exposed for its, in Richard Dwyer's words, "emptiness, absence, denial, or even a kind of death" (1988, 44). Ruth Frankenberg expresses a similar concern when she explains that whiteness represents nothingness, a lack, a cultureless, indistinct existence. See Ruth Frankenberg, *White Women, Race Matters: The Social Construction of Whiteness* (1993). To this list I would have to add Toni Morrison, *Playing in the Dark: Whiteness in Literary Imagination*, where she draws on whiteness parasitism.

103. hooks 1992, 167.

104. Butler 1995, 443.

105. In 2003, Karyn D. McKinney conducted a study on whiteness where she interviewed white students. In the interview, one of the interviewees shamelessly confessed that she was at an amusement park with her parents and, according to the student, no one spoke English. "I have never been so annoyed. . . . I am definitely very ethnocentric in that I think that my culture and my ways are the best," the student admitted. This is a good demonstration of commonsense racism where nationalist is a metonym for racist (2003, 50–51) and the very fact of whiteness as entitlement.

106. If one understands the nature of whiteness in this way, then one would acknowledge that whites are socialized not to be cognizant of their privilege and social positioning. In this regard, naming whiteness as "a problem" is precisely one of the mechanisms for any thoroughgoing analysis of how and why blackness constructivism is made to establish blacks' homogeneity of identity as a bodily mark.

107. Fanon 1967, 136.

108. The Declaration of Independence recognized the rights to life, liberty, and the pursuit of happiness to be bestowed to all men. "All men" meant white men because blacks were slaves, and these rights were granted and upheld by "the rights-granting legal system" so as to preserve rights for white men. I write:

> When the fugitive slave Frederick Douglass on July 5, 1852, gave the speech, "What to the Slave is the Fourth of July?" to the Ladies' Anti-Slavery Society in Rochester, New York, he stated: 'Must I undertake to prove that the slave is a man?' Even though Douglass' question is simply rhetorical, our attention is still drawn to the fact that men who were slaves were not quite men or were not considered as men, but were in the process of becoming rights bearing men subject to the same rights and liberties that white men enjoyed. However, the laws that were in place assumed that the slave was a man, an inferior man, and these laws constantly had to de-(hu)man the slave and undermine his manhood by upholding and reinforcing the unlivablity and ungrievablity of slaves' lives. And while the slave, in the process of becoming 'man,' found in the white man his model of manhood, it transformed the consciousness of the slaves to conform with the white man's consciousness. In short, the behavior of the slave is a prescribed behavior, following, as it does, the guidelines of the white man. . . . Through psychic, physical, ontological, and epistemology

violence, the white man became a man by legally subjugating blacks to his *will*. (Pinder 2018, 122–23)

109. Fyre 1983, 114.

110. Fanon 1967, 139. Fanon starts the discussion by referencing Richard Wright's 1940 novel *Native Son*, where Fanon discusses the main protagonist of the novel, Bigger Thomas, who, in confirming what the white world thinks of black men as murders and rapist, murders two women: Mary, a white woman, and his black girlfriend whom he also rapes. Bigger, on the night he is scheduled to be executed, explains to Mr. Max, his lawyer: "I didn't want to kill. . . . But what I killed for, *I am*! It must've been pretty deep in me to make me kill. I must have felt it awful hard to murder. . . . What I kill for must've been good. . . . When a man kills, it's for something. . . ." In this regard, one sees that for Bigger, killing is the reaction to the effect that characterized his existence. His explosion, in the form of killing, confirms that he was alive, in the present, here and now: "I didn't know I was really alive in this world until I felt things hard enough to kill for them" (1940, 429). This is the "hellish cycle" of blacks' existence. "The Negro," Fanon writes, "is a toy in the white man's hands; so, in order to shatter the hellish cycle, he explodes" (1967, 120). Dehumanization "marks not only those whose humanity has been stolen [blacks], but also (though in a different way) those who have stolen it [whites]" (Freire 2002, 44). Violence expressed by the oppressed is one of the consequences. It is the kind of violence that Fanon speaks of in *The Wretched of the Earth* and Paulo Freire's *Pedagogy of the Oppressed*, where blacks are unprotected, immune to its instillation, which, nonetheless, coincides with whites' thinking of blacks as naturally violent and aggressive.

111. Judy 1993, 94.

112. Mills 2013, 33.

113. Caputo and Yount 1993, 6.

114. Fine et al. 1997, xi.

115. For works that make use of Pierre Bourdieu's concept of *habitus* in order to discuss the racialized body, see Sara Ahmed, "A Phenomenology of Whiteness" (2007); Nirmal Puwar, *Space Invaders: Race, Gender, and Bodies Out of Space* (2004); Ghassan Hage, *White Nation: Fantasy of White Supremacy in a Multicultural Society* (1998); and Hans-Rudolf Wicker, "From Complex Culture to Cultural Complexity" (1997).

116. See Cheryl I. Harris, "Whiteness as Property" (1993).

117. Fred Moten puts this in another way. He writes: "Primordial black is blue. How blue can you? Black." See Moten, chapter 21, "Black and Blue on White. In and And Space," in his book *Black and Blur* (2017, 226).

118. Blackness and whiteness are implicated by each other.

119. Ahmed 2007, 154.

120. Ahmed 2007, 154.

121. Ahmed 2007, 154.

122. Whites are always treated and judged as an individual rather than as a member of a social group. Blacks, on the other hand, are always treated as belonging to a social group, black.

123. Fanon 1967, 111.

124. Fanon 1967, 111.

125. Fanon 1967, 110–111.

126. See Michael Jackson's song, "Man in the Mirror," which was released in 1987.

127. Zack 1997, 104.

128. Michael Jackson is serious about not spending his "life being a color." Listen to his song, "They Don't Care About Us."

129. Mills 1998, 48.

130. On the supposing benignity of whiteness void of racist blemishes, see the feminist Marilyn Frye's *The Politics of Reality: Essays in Feminist Theory*. Frye rightfully asks, "What is this 'being white' that gets me into so much trouble, after so many years of seeming to me to be so benign?" (1983, 113).

131. Fanon 1967, 112.

132. Fuss 1994, 21.

133. Ahmed 2012, 28.

134. Fuss 1994, 21.

135. For a further discussion on blacks being "a problem," see W. E. B. Du Bois, *The Souls of Black Folk*, where he writes: "Between me and the other world there is ever an unasked question: unasked by some through feelings of delicacy; by others through the difficulty of rightly framing it. All, nevertheless, flutter round it. They approach me in a half-hesitant sort of way, eye me curiously or compassionately, and then, instead of saying directly, How does it feel to be a problem? they say, I know an excellent colored man in my town; or, I fought at Mechanicsville; or, Do not these Southern outrages make your blood boil? At these I smile, or am interested, or reduce the boiling to a simmer, as the occasion may require. To the real question, How does it feel to be a problem? I answer seldom a word" (2003, 3–4). In this moment, Du Bois becomes an agentic subject by refusing to oblige to whites' prickly questioning, "How does it feel to be a problem?" (2003, 3–4).

136. For Ralph Ellison, when whites approach blacks, Ellison writes, "they see only my surroundings, themselves or fragments of their imagination—indeed everything and anything except me" (1995, 3). Whites' inability to work through their "blind spots," so to speak, is to also recognize that what is unseen is continuously already "seen," and this has significant social implications. The foundation of the dialectics of the visibility and invisibility of blackness and how it identifies and positions blacks as the "other" is indeed important.

137. Berger 1972, 7. My own emphasis.

138. Gordon 1995, 99.

139. Fuss 1994, 28.
140. Fuss 1994, 28.
141. Vogel 2015, 471. Also, see Stuart Hall, "What Is This 'Black' in Black Popular Culture?" (2004).
142. Touré 2011, xviii.
143. Sexton 2011, 28.
144. Gates 1996.
145. Gates 1996.
146. Mercer 1992, 21.
147. Another word for a white kid "acting black" is wigger, which is a pejorative term. Another word, used for a white person taking on a black persona, is a "White Negro," discussed in Norman Mailer's "The White Negro: Superficial Reflections on the Hipster." Taking my cue from Mailer, the "White Negro" is a form of racial mimicry of black popular culture, especially in hip-hop and rap cultures, which stands for the new discrete variation of African American pop culture. We can certainly recognize white kids "acting black" in the white rapper Eminem's song, "Sing for the Moment," where he says the white kid is "talking black . . . sags his pants, do-rags and a stocking cap." He is "doing black."
148. Mercer 2002, 197.
149. Fuss 1994, 25.
150. These days, there is an emphasis on claiming a multiracial identity (mixed-race identity), the combination of black and white. And even though the one-drop rule does not exist any longer, a person with a multiracial identity where black is one of them sometimes imagines one's self as not "truly black" and in one's imaginative mode believes that one should not be subjected to the same ill treatment as the black person with "unambiguous African ancestry." Is claiming a mixed-race identity a way of moving toward whiteness? Whiteness does matter; it equipped whites with privilege denied to blacks and other nonwhites; whites benefits from what W. E. B. Du Bois explains and describes as the "public and psychological wages" that benefit all whites. And since whiteness is internalized, whiteness does have a damaging impact on the psyche. In the case of blackness, Barbara Fields draws our attention to "the anguish of the Jean Toomer or Anatole Broyard, which rests, ultimately, on a thwarted hope to be excused, on grounds of mixed ancestry, from a fate deemed entirely appropriate for persons of unambiguous African ancestry" (Fields 2003, 1404). For more on Anatole Broyrad, see Henry Louis Gates's article in the *New Yorker*, "White Like Me;" and Gates, *Thirteen Ways of Looking at a Black Man*, "The Passing of Anatole Broyard" (1997).
151. Harris 1993, 1711.
152. See Orlando Patterson, *Slavery and Social Death: A Comparative Study* (1982).
153. Sexton 2011, 15.

154. Mercer 1991, 432–33.

155. It is no wonder that a community of thinkers—scholars, artists (broadly construed to include rappers), musicians, poets, filmmakers, journalists, and activists—draw on the problematics of the United States' version of its own brand of multiculturalism masquerading as a kind of progressive reactionalism to America's history succumbed to cultural homogeneity (cultural oneness) based on a certain brand of nonwhiteness that now cannot resist, de facto, the essentializing of cultures.

156. See David Brackett, "Black or White? Michael Jackson and the Idea of Crossover" (2012, 176).

157. Sechi 1980, 444.

158. Michaels 1992, 683.

159. Pellegrini 1997, 111.

Chapter 3

1. Du Bois 2003, 5.
2. Vigo 2010, 35.
3. Mercer 1986, 26.
4. I suppose, then, an important consideration is whether individuals claiming a mixed-race identity would have anything to do with the way blackness is seen as a lack and to convince themselves that they are not truly "black."
5. Fields 2003, 1404.
6. Butler 1989, 602.
7. Ehler 2012, 3.
8. Ehler 2012, 3.
9. See Michael Jackson's song, "Black or White."
10. Lorde 1984, 116.
11. Revel 2009, 46.
12. Ahmed 2015, 184.
13. Cervenak and Carter 2017, 45.
14. Cervenak and Carter 2017, 47.
15. We do remember how blackface minstrel shows used whites in "blackface" to make fun of black people. For more on this topic, see Eric Lott, *Love and Theft: Blackface Minstrelsy and the American Working Class* (2013).
16. Yancy 2005, 217.
17. Fuss 1994, 22.
18. Broertjes 2013, 690. Also, see Cornel West, *Race Matters* (2001). West writes: "Michael Jackson may rightly wish to be viewed as a person, not a color (neither black nor white), but his facial revisions reveal a self-measurement based on a white yardstick. Hence, despite the fact that he is one of the greatest enter-

tainers who has ever lived, he still views himself, at least in part, through white aesthetics lenses that devalue some of his African characteristics" (2001, 137). See Greg Tate, " 'I'm White!' What's Wrong with Michael Jackson" (1987); and Kobena Mercer, "Monster Metaphors: Notes on Michael Jackson Thriller" (1986, 27–28).

19. Du Bois 2003, 5.

20. For a detailed account of performativity, see J. L. Austin, *How to Do Things with Words* (1963); Judith Butler, *Excitable Speech: A Politics of the Performative* (1997b); and Judith Butler, *Bodies That Matter: On the Discursive Limits of Sex (1993a) and Gender Troubles: Feminism and the Subversion of Identity* (1990).

21. Silberman 2007, 419.

22. Butler 1993a, xii.

23. Foucault 1980, 122.

24. Butler 1997a, 2.

25. Gómez-Barria and Gary 2006, 44.

26. Fuss 1989, xi.

27. Fuss 1989, xi.

28. We can see why Frantz Fanon's *Black Skin, White Masks* focuses on the "whatness" of blackness, in which he asks the brilliant question: "What does the black man want?" In providing an answer, Fanon writes: "The black is not a man; . . . that is, as the result of a series of aberrations of affect, he is rooted at the core of a universe from which he must be extricated. . . . I propose nothing short of the liberation of the man of color from himself" (1967, 8).

29. Michael Jackson's song, "This Is It," was released in 2009.

30. Jackson 1988, 213. Also, quoted in Silberman 2007, 432.

31. Osumare 2018, 5.

32. Jefferson 2006, 10. More negative readings of Michael Jackson's dance moves revealed themselves in the *Village Voice*, in an article written by Gary Dauphin commenting on Michael Jackson's *Black or White* video, in that "Michael's inability to get the visual history of his own body right" is claimed (Silberman 2007, 433). Jon Parles's *New York Times* article, "A Political Song that Casts its Vote for the Money," refers to Michael Jackson's video *Man in the Mirror* as "the most offensive music video clip ever," and Parles states several reasons for his harsh remarks, or as Michele Wallace rightfully asks, "is that finally racism speaking?" (1989, 15). Wallace admits that Parles is right about one thing: when we watch *Man in the Mirror*, "we are snapping our fingers and tapping our feet to world hunger, violence, man's inhumanity to man and woman. But isn't that not what we're doing anyway when we rock 'n' roll? Or when we engage in any cultural activity, which inevitably masks the seriousness and gloom of our global plight? (1989, 15). *Newsweek*, for one, described the lyrics of "Thriller" as "offbeat . . . that hints at Michael's own Secret World of dreams and demons" (1983).

33. On a different note, in *Art Thoughtz* it is Jayson Musson, the artist behind the persona of Hennessy Youngman, who "addresses how to become a

successful black artist, wryly suggesting black people's anger is marketable. He advises black artists to cultivate 'an angry nigger exterior' by watching, among other things, the Rodney King video while working" (Rankine 2014, 23).

34. Lee 2002, 100.

35. When a French Reporter asked Richard Wright about "the Negro problem in the United States," Wright responded, "there is no Negro problem in the United States, there is only a white problem." See George Lipsitz, "The Possessive Investment in Whiteness: Racialized Social Democracy and the 'White' Problem in American Studies" (1995, 369). Whiteness is a problem for blacks.

36. Fanon 1967, 113–14.

37. Warren 2017, 410.

38. Ontological violence was prevalent for race-making in the United States. John Hartigan, in "Culture Against Race: Reworking the Basis for Racial Analysis," writes:

> The middle passage, slavery, and the experience of racial terror produce a race of African Americans out of subjects drawn from different cultures. Genocide, forced removal to reservations, and the experience of racial terror make Native American subjects drawn from different linguistic and tribal affiliations: a race. War relocation camps, legal exclusion, and the experience of discrimination make Asian American subjects drawn from different cultural and linguistic backgrounds: a race. The process of forming the southwestern states of the United States through conquest and subjugation and the continued subordination of Puerto Rico constitutes Chicanos and Puerto Ricans as races." (2005, 547)

This raises important questions about the ontological violence and the creation of an American cultural psyche. For more on this, see Kevin Johnson, "Ontological Violence and American Cultural Psyche: A Psychoanalytic Inquiry of an American Cultural Identity" (2012).

39. Bennett 1975, 73.
40. Fanon 1967, 109.
41. Eppert 2017, 98.
42. de Lauretis 2002, 56.
43. Yancy 2005, 235.
44. Fanon 1967, 194.
45. Butler 2001, 79.
46. Butler 2001, 79.
47. Fanon 1967, 111.
48. Sexton 2008, 2.

49. Shakespeare's play *Hamlet* soliloquy, "To be, or not to be, that is question," is an old question that concerns Plato about being (to be) and not to be (nonbeing). Paul Tillich reminds us, "Plato used the concept of nonbeing because without it the contrast of existence with pure essences is beyond understanding" (Tillich 2000, 32–33).

50. Deleuze and Guattari 1983, 43.

51. Ahmed and Stacey 2001, 16. One of Rosi Braidotti's concerns, in *Nomadic Subjects: Embodiment and Sexual Difference in Contemporary Feminist Theory*, is that of "Organs Without Bodies." She writes:

> I have suggested the formulation "organs without bodies" to refer to this complex strategic field of practices connected to the discursive and normative construction of the subject in modernity. For instance, the whole discourse of biosciences takes the organism as its subject, and therefore takes the body as a mosaic of detachable pieces. In turn, the primacy granted to the discourse of biopower in modernity turns the bioscientist into the very porotype of the instrumental intellectual. In the practice of the "techno dot" the visibility, and intelligibility of the "living body" are the prelude to its manipulation as an available supply of living material. As Haraway points out, in the age of biopower the embodied subject is "cannibalized" by the practice of scientific techno-apparati. (1994, 47)

52. Morrison 1988, 144.

53. Fuchs 1995, 19.

54. *The Wiz* is an American musical adventure fantasy film produced by Universal Pictures and Motown Production starring Michael Jackson and Diana Ross. It is a remake of *The Wizard of Oz* with an all-black cast.

55. Erni 1998, 162.

56. Michael Jackson's various metamorphoses on-screen from human body form to objects provoked some to conclude that he is not quite human. How about, in Michael Jackson's *Black or White* video, he is transformed to a black panther. Indeed, the members of the Black Panther party were constantly dehumanized.

57. Douglas and Wilderson 2013, 121.

58. de Beauvoir 1976, 76.

59. Yancy 2012, 34.

60. Fanon 1967, 173.

61. Jefferson 2006, 81–82.

62. Jefferson 2006, 81.

63. Davis 2003, 85.

64. Davis 2003, 85–86.

65. Pinder 2015, 43.

66. Morris 1994, 6. It is Nietzsche's Zarathustra who reminds us: "Once [humans] were apes, and even now, too, man is more ape than any ape." See *Thus Spoke Zarathustra* (1978, 12).

67. Ahmed 2015, 185.

68. Pinder 2015, 42.

69. Spivak 1995, 4. Professor Spivak's concept of unlearning one's privilege as "one's loss" continues to inform many whiteness studies scholars based on the fact that whites have to unlearn their white privilege as "a loss," which, in itself, creates a recognition that is redoubled—that is, whites acquiring and securing a certain kind of "other knowledge" that they, before the unlearning process, were not equipped to access because of their dominant subject position. To put it differently, given that whites are positioned within cultural norms, they are prevented from accessing a kind of "other knowledge"—not simply information that they have not yet acknowledged or received, but knowledge that they are not prepared to value. See Gayatri C. Spivak, *The Spivak Reader: Selected Works of Gayatri Chakravorty Spivak* (1995, 4). Thus, for Professor Spivak, unlearning dominant systems of knowledge and representation is a "transformation of consciousness—a changing mindset," which intricately encompasses a double recognition (Spivak 1990, 20). This double recognition is certainly significant to disassemble white privilege. I am not sure if African American film maker John Singleton has been schooled in Spivakism, but his movie *Higher Learning*, released on January 11, 1995, encourages one to look back at one's history of discrimination and the many ways one has learned to be discriminatory. These learned forms of discriminations, which are accompanied by both physical and psychological violence on individuals and groups who are different from race, gender, and sexuality norms, for example, must be unlearned if society is to promote justice and equality for all people.

70. Baldwin 1963, 91.

71. Pinder 2015, 9. Even before Obama became the president of the United States, his caricatures were circulated.

72. Pinder 2013, 164.

73. Bosteels 2016, 17.

74. The Naturalization Act of March 26, 1790, states: "All free white persons, who have, or shall migrate into the United States, and shall give satisfactory proof before a magistrate, by oath, that they intend to reside therein, and shall take on oath of allegiance, and shall have resided in the United States for one whole year, shall be entitled to the rights of citizenship." In 1802, the Act of 1790 was revised. It set a five-year residence requirement for immigrants entering the United States after 1802. Like the Act of 1790, the Act of 1802 limited naturalization to an "alien, being free and white."

75. Yancy 2008, 134n11.

76. Thomas F. Gossett, quoting Dr. Charles White, who stated in 1789: "From man down to the smallest reptile. . . . Nature exhibits to our view an immense

chain of beings, endued with various degrees of intelligence and active powers suited to their station in the general system" (1964, 47).

77. See George Lipsitz, *The Possessive Investment in Whiteness: How White People Profit from Identity Politics*, 1998.

78. Pinder 2012, 5.
79. Sartre 1956, 28.
80. Sartre 1956, 242.
81. Bhabha 1984, 125.
82. Davis 2003, 76.
83. Fanon 1967, 139.
84. Fanon 1967., 231.
85. Fanon 1965, 135.
86. Davis 2003, 78.

87. Whiteness has impacted other individuals and groups that assumed that their "whiteness" is questionable and they are viewed as "other." Kathy Davis writes:

> In the US, cosmetic surgery became popular in the wake of large-scale immigration at the begin of the 20th century. John Roe performed the first nose correction for the "pug nose"—a feature that was associated with Irish immigrants and negative qualities of character like slovenliness and dog-like servility (hence the term "pug"). Nose surgery was later performed on European immigrants (Jews, Italians and others of Mediterranean or eastern European descent) as well as on white Americans who were anxious that they "looked Jewish." Following the Second World War, cosmetic surgery to create folded eyelids ("western eyes") became popular among Koreans, Chinese, Japanese, and Asian Americans. (2003, 76)

Also, see Chris Shilling, *The Body: A Very Short Introduction* (2016, 2). Shilling adds, "Breast reduction in Rio de Jeneiro has been linked to a desire to avoid the association of 'pendulous breast' with the black working classes (an image associated with slavery)."

88. Mercer 1990, 247.
89. Lee 2002, 13.
90. Mercer 1990, 252.
91. Mercer 1990, 252.
92. Mercer 1990, 252.
93. Fuchs 1995, 18.
94. Davis 2003, 83.
95. Tate 1987.
96. Taraborrelli 1991, 420.
97. Taraborrelli 1991, 420.

98. Ahmed and Stacey 2001, 10.
99. Ahmed and Stacey 2001, 10.
100. The documentary, *Michael Jackson's Face*, released in 2002 and directed by Liam Humphreys, focuses on Michael Jackson's face, skin, and body.
101. Yancy 2005, 217.
102. Hall 1994, 395.
103. Awkward 1996, 179.
104. Johnson 1984, 156.
105. Lee 2002, 33.
106. Mercer 1986, 29.
107. Eagleton 2005.
108. Mercer 1986, 29.
109. Davis 2003, 81.
110. Mercer 1986, 29.
111. Davis 2003, 81.
112. Gómez-Barris and Gary 2006, 44.
113. Gómez-Barris and Gary 2006, 49.
114. Fanon 1967, 111.
115. Ahmed and Stacey 2001, 9.
116. Gómez-Barris and Gary 2006, 44.
117. Gates 1997, 190.
118. Gómez-Barris and Gary 2006, 44. In *Living with Michael Jackson*, Michael Jackson comments that whites are always tanning so that they can have a dark complexion. He encourages us to ask the underlying question: Is this because whites want to be black? What about whites who are sporting a Rastafarian hairstyle? We do remember John Howard Griffin, who changed from "white" to "black." His experimentation was not to be black, but to experience firsthand what it meant to be black and living in a racist society such as the United States. See Griffin, *Black Like Me* (1977).
119. Davis 2003, 82.
120. Mills 1997, 7.
121. Fanon 1967, 10. As W. E. B. Du Bois notes, "whiteness is the ownership of the earth, forever and ever Amen." See Du Bois, *Darkwater: Voices from Within the Veil* (1969, 18).
122. Davis 2003, 89. Jay Prosser, in *Second Skin: The Body Narrative of Transsexuality*, comments on the artist Orlan's surgical performance. He writes: "Orlan's image for the superficiality of her face only raises anxious questions about the meaning of bodily matter for identity" (1998, 61). Prosser goes on to say: "I asked Orlan about the relation of body and identity in her work. Did she feel any sense of identity transformation, of an internal shifting, as her face underwent its successive alterations? Was the transformation only really skin deep? (I wondered what it was like to wake up to a different face every morning. I wondered how

she sustained herself in the face—literally—of such change.) Skimming over the substance of my question (there were problems in translation) but picking up my reference to transsexuality, Olan replied simply that she felt like 'une transsexuelle femme-à-femme'" (1998, 62).

Also, see the performance artist Stelarc whose works focus on extending the human capabilities; in one of his performances, a cell-cultivated ear was surgically fastened to his left arm as reported by BBC news on October 11, 2007.

123. Davis 2003, 83–84.
124. Mercer 1990, 247.
125. Awkward 1995, 177.
126. Fanon 1967, 111.
127. de Lauretis 2002, 58.
128. Toadvine and Lawlor 2007, 147.
129. For a more comprehensive discussion of the normativity of the corporeal schema, see Iris Marion Young, "A Phenomenology of Feminine Body Comportment, Motility, and Spatiality" (1980).
130. Fanon 1967, 111.
131. Fanon 1967, 110–11.
132. See Jared Sexton, "The Social Life of Social Death: On Afro-Pessimism and Black Optimism, 2011; Fred B. Wilderson III, *Red, White and Black: Cinema and the Structure of US Antagonisms* (2010); Fred Moten, "The Case of Blackness" (2008); George Yancy, "Whiteness and the Return of the Black Body" (2005); and Saidiya Hartman, *Scenes of Subjection: Terror, Slavery, and Self-Making in Nineteenth-Century America* (1997).
133. Warren 2017, 407. Also, quoted in Eppert 2017, 87.
134. Fanon 1967, 110.
135. Fanon 1967, 116.
136. See Michael Jackson's "I Can't Help It" from his *Off the Wall* album released on August 10, 1979.
137. Alcoff 1998, 17.
138. Cox 1948, 336.
139. Dyson 1999, 220.
140. Gates 1996.
141. We remember the story of the *Ex-Colored Man* who rejects his racial identity by concealing it.
142. *The flesh of my flesh, the blood of my blood* is the second studio album of DMX released on December 22, 1998.
143. Cixous 2009, 1.
144. hooks 1994, 179.
145. Noliwe M. Rooks traces the history of hair straightening by drawing on the discourse of "racial uplift" and "self-hate" in the black community. The latter is tied to "racial inferiority" and the former focuses on generating a community

of women and their possibilities for upward mobility. See Rooks, *Hair Raising: Beauty, Culture, and African American Women* (1996).

146. "In the Closet" is the title of Michael Jackson's eighth song on his *Dangerous* album.

147. Sexton 2011, 15.

148. Michael Jackson visited the White House when Ronald Reagan was the president to receive "an award for his efforts to prevent drunk driving" (Vogel 2015, 474).

149. Broertjes 2013, 684.

150. Fanon 1967, 116.

151. See Andrew Broertjes, "He's Sending His People Message out of His Pain: Michael Jackson and the Black Community" (2013).

152. Broertjes 2013, 680.

153. Broertjes 2013, 682.

154. "Vitiligo," writes Jay Prosser, "incarnates the transgression of the colour boundary. Consisting of the death of Melanin cells in the epidermis, though it can strike any race, vitiligo threatens greater loss for those with dark skin because the loss of colour is greater and more noticeable" (2001, 57).

155. Prosser 2001, 57.

156. Awkward 1990, 179.

157. Angelou 1993.

158. Awkward 1990, 178.

159. In postcolonial Britain, in the 1980s, there was a redefinition of a black identity, which was a construction of "an identity made out of differences." In fact, "when various peoples—of Asian, African, and Caribbean descent—interpellated themselves and each other as / black / they invoked a collective identity predicated on political and not biological similarities. In other words, the naturalized connotations of the term / black / were disarticulated out of the dominant codes of racial discourse, and rearticulated as signs of alliance and solidarity among dispersed groups of people sharing common historical experiences of British racism" (Mercer 1991, 426–427).

160. See Henry Louis Gates Jr., "White Like Me" (1996); and Angela Onwuachi-Willig, "A Beautiful Lie: Exploring *Rhinelander v. Rhinelander* as a formative Lesson on Race, Identity, Marriage, and Family" (2007).

161. Stuever 2002, C1.

162. Wallace 2015.

163. de Lauretis 2002, 57.

164. Fanon 1967, 109.

165. Fanon 1967, 111.

166. de Beauvoir 1976, 100.

167. Silberman 2007, 431.

168. In a word, to borrow from Halifu Osumare, "black dance across time and space—from West Africa to the United States" (2018, 2).
169. Mercer 1986, 32.
170. Mercer 1986, 27.
171. Mercer 1986, 27.
172. Barthes 1977, 188. Also, quoted in Mercer 1986, 27.
173. Barthes 1977, 188. About "grain," Roland Barthes writes that his "discussion has been limited to 'classical music.' It goes without saying, however, that the simple consideration, of 'grain' in music could lead to a different history of music from the one we know now (which is purely pheno-textual). Were we to succeed in refining a certain 'aesthetics' of musical pleasures, then doubtless we would attach less importance to the formidable break in tonality accomplished by modernity" (1977, 189).
174. Mercer 1986, 27.
175. Johnson 1984, 158.
176. Mercer 1986, 32.
177. Johnson 1984, 158. Frantz Fanon, in *The Wretched of the Earth*, discusses "the ecstasy of dance" in colonized Algeria (1963, 19–20).
178. Spillers 2003, 206.
179. Fanon 1967, 45.
180. Fanon 1967, 135.
181. A person, in "Slave to the Rhythm" (my own emphasis):

Works to the rhythm
Lives to the rhythm
Loves to the rhythm
Is a slave to the rhythm

In fact, you cannot fight with the rhythm, as Michael Jackson says in his song "Rock with You": "Girl, close your eyes/Let that rhythm get into you/Don't try to fight it." And on May 2014, Michael Jackson's black feminist version of "Slave to the Rhythm" was posthumously released.
182. Fuchs 1995, 18.
183. Gómez-Barris and Gray 2006, 45.
184. To illustrate her point, Thelma Pinto makes use of John Maxwell Coetzee's novel *Disgrace*. In the novel, "David Lurie [is] a White, middle-aged, twice divorced professor of foreign languages at the University of Cape Town. . . . Melanie Isaacs is a Black student who is a drama major and attend[s] his Romantic poetry class." The sexual encounter of the white professor and the black student is discussed. "The girl is lying beneath him, her eyes closed, her hands slack above her head, slight frown on her face. . . . Not rape, not quite that, but undesired

nevertheless, undesired to the core. As though she decided to go slack, die within herself for the duration, like a rabbit when the jaws of the fox close on his neck" (Pinto 152–153). "So that everything done to her might be done, as it were, far away," Coetzee continues in *Disgrace* (2000, 25). Pinto writes, "It is not difficult to link this [scene] to the Sarah Baartman [syndrome], for here as well, the black female character is mute and experienced as a desirable body that should be available for the taking." After the encounter, Isaacs "asks Lurie, whether he often does 'this kind of thing.'" See Thelma Pinto, "Claiming Sarah Baartman: Black Womanhood in the Global Imaginary" (2012, 152–53).

185. Joice Heth, an African American slave who was almost crippled, was, for the first time, exhibited by Phineas T. Barnum on August 10 1835, at Niblo's Garden, a Broadway theater in New York City. According to Margo Jefferson, "the showman saw promise in those gnarled limbs and stooped shoulders. Barnum put her in a clean gown and a fresh white cap, and sat her down" (2006, 5).

186. Mercer 1986, 27.

187. Gates 1996.

188. Nelson 2015, 3.

189. Warren 2017, 398.

190. Ahmed and Stacey 2001, 15.

191. In the United States, these days, there is an emphasis on having a mixed-race identity. And while the rules for racial designation, in many ways, might be vague, there are many scholarly articles and books on mixed-race identity. For a comprehensive reading, see Habiba Ibrahim, *Troubling the Family: The Promise of Personhood and the Rise of Multiracialism* (2012); Tru Leverette, "Speaking of Mixed Race Identity in the Black Community" (2009); Kevin R. Johnson, ed., *Mixed-Race Identity and the Law: A Reader* (2003); David Parker and Miri Song, *Rethinking 'Mixed Race'* (2001); G. Reginald Daniel, *More Than Black? Multiracial Identity and the New Racial Order* (2001); Jon M. Spencer, *The New Colored People: The Mixed-Race Movement in America* (1997); Naomi Zack, *American Mixed Race: The Culture of Microdiversity* (1995); Julie C. Lythcott-Haims, "Note: Where Do Mixed Babies Belong? Racial Classification in America and Its Implications for Transracial Adoption" (1994); and Naomi Zack, *Race and Mixed Race* (1993).

192. See Michael Jackson's song, "Childhood," released in 1995.

193. Fuchs 1995, 17.

194. Revel 2009, 46.

195. Fuchs 1995, 17.

196. *Man in the Mirror: The Michael Jackson Story* is a movie that was aired on August 6, 2004. This "staged performance" presents Michael Jackson in a negative and harmful manner.

197. Warren 2017, 395.

198. Wilderson 2010, 84.

199. Fuss 1994, 24.
200. de Lauretis 2002, 54.
201. We remember that the election of the first black president Barack Obama triggered false hopes and assumptions that there was "a declining significance of race" and even "the end to racism" in the United States. With the election of Donald Trump, the post-racialist enthusiasts have to work through the pathology of racism and reckon with the fact that the United States has not yet transcended race and racism. Rather, racism is alive and well.
202. Sexton 2011, 27.
203. Ahmed and Stacey 2001, 9.
204. Johnson 1984, 155.
205. See Michael Jackson's "I Can't Help It" from his *Off the Wall* album released on August 10, 1979.
206. Silberman 2007, 423.
207. Fanon 1967, 134.
208. Eagleton 2005.
209. Vigo 2010, 38.
210. Haraway 1991, 1.
211. Haraway 1991, 150. Also, quoted in Miller 2012, 127. And if Donna Haraway is correct that "the cyborg is a creature in a post-gender world," the cyborg knows what goes on; the cyborg is postreproductive and does not need, for example, the phallus. As Harraway puts it, "the cyborg does not dream of community on the model of the [nuclear] family" (1991, 151).
212. The Elephant Man was born Joseph Carey Merrick on August 5, 1862, in Leicester, England. Because of Merrick's severe face and body deformities, he was first exhibited at a freak show as the Elephant Man. After his encounter with the prominent British surgeon Sir Frederick Treves, Merrick was moved to the London hospital where he lived until his death on April 11, 1890. His skeleton "became the ultimate in static curiosities when it was put on display in a glass case at the London Hospital" (Yuan 1996, 371). For more on the Elephant Man, see Michael Howell and Peter Ford, *The True History of the Elephant Man: The Definitive Account of the Tragic and Extraordinary Life of Joseph Carey Merrick* (2010).
213. See Robert Johnson, "The Michael Jackson Nobody Knows" (1984).
214. Cervenak and Carter 2017, 53.
215. Fanon 1967, 112. However, it was Friedrich Nietzsche in *Ecco Homo*, who declares, "I am not a man. I am dynamite," giving humanity the greatest gift it has received.
216. See Michael Jackson's song, "I Can't Help It," from his *Off the Wall* album released by Epic Records on August 10, 1979.
217. Du Bois 2003, 5–6.
218. Fanon 1967, 114.

219. These words are from Michael Jackson's "Man in the Mirror," which was released in 1987.

220. Ahmed 2015, 184.

Chapter 4

1. This is a song on Prince and the Revolution's *Purple Rain* album released in 1984 by Warner Bros. Records. Also, quoted in Vogel 2015, 477. "With *Purple Rain* Prince became the first artist since the Beatles to have the # 1 film album" (Vogel 2015, 484, footnote 14).

2. Baldwin 1998, 814.

3. Baldwin 1998, 828.

4. Baldwin 1998, 828.

5. Vogel 2015, 475.

6. Margo Jefferson's *On Michael Jackson* is focused on oppositional binaries in her discussion of Michael Jackson in which she asks: "Is it the brown-skinned self we can no longer see except in old photo and video? Is he a good man or a predator? Child protector or pedophile? A damaged genius or scheming celebrity trying to hold on to his fame at any cost? A child star afraid of aging, or a psychotic freak/pervert/sociopath? What if the 'or' is an 'and'? What if he is all these things?" (2006, 18). To start thinking through these questions, it is true, for example, that some see Michael Jackson as a freak while other extol him for his refusal to be "normal." And given that society promotes binary oppositional thinking, Michael Jackson's refusal to be positioned as either black or white, for example, unsettles and constructs him as not normal.

7. "Will You Be There" is a song from Michael Jackson's 1991 *Dangerous* album. The song was released in 1993.

8. Baldwin 1998, 829.

9. I am using metric with some skepticism because one cannot calculate weirdness/freakiness, and Michael Jackson is subject to so many metrics that it is not always mathematical.

10. This shows that Michael Jackson refuses to draw the rigid boundary between culture and nature because, as Donna J. Haraway explains, human beings "exist in the realm of culture, buffered, if not exempted, from the physiologist's gonadectomies and injections" (1991, 29) to maintain the boundary between culture and nature that was already imposed by man, the human animal. "But society," Fanon warns, "unlike biochemical processes, cannot escape human influences. Man is what brings society into being" (1967, 11). Michael Jackson's "sole fidelity is to his conception of universal harmony" (Miller 2012, 129) among beings, living beings. His companion specie, Bubbles the chimp, is a perfect example. He is not

rejecting culture per se (but who can, given that nurture is always there ready to overwhelm us), but he embraces nature in its fullest and is prepared to treat it as an unquestionable master over culture. To put it differently, nature thus remains, in all its majesty, an overwhelming reality for Michael Jackson compared to what he appears to be viewed by his critics as freaky or weird.

11. In *Michael Jackson: The Magic and the Madness*, Taraborrelli explains why Michael Jackson wears the surgical mask: "It's not always because he is attempting to hide his identity or even avoid germs. Sometimes, it's simply because he was not inclined to wear the latex appliance, a prosthetic nose-tip (prosthesis). If nothing else, the prosthesis must be a painful and daily reminder to Michael of his past choices where plastic surgery is concerned, and the impact they have on his life" (1991, 435).

12. Jefferson 2006, 26.

13. Vogel 2012.

14. See Michael Jackson's song, "Childhood," released in 1995.

15. Fast 2012, 282.

16. Vogel 2015, 471.

17. Butler 1993a, 2.

18. Alter 1993. I am aware that Little Richard's performance was considered as "over the top." In one of his songs, he declares: "You're going to make me scream like a white lady." In fact, Little Richard's performance (the screaming part) was stereotypically viewed as a part of "black masculinity." See Julian Vigo, "Metaphor of Hybridity: The Body of Michael Jackson" (2010, 33). Little Richard identified himself as gay even though he had sexual relations with older women. For more autobiographic notes on Little Richard, see Charles White, *The Life and Time of Little Richard* (2003). Michael Jackson's persona, in some ways, goes against the stereotype of black masculinity as macho, as is clearly expressed in his *Thriller* video when he says, "I am not like other guys."

In terms of androgynous sexuality, the remaking of Michael Jackson's identity follows the pattern of white male singers such as David Bowie, Boy George, and Mick Jagger. It "refuses a bellicose model of manliness" (Mercer 1986, 42). It was Little Richard, long before white singers, who used " 'camp,' in the sense that Susan Sontag calls 'the love of the unnatural: of artificial and exaggeration, . . . began to exploit its 'shocking value' " (Mercer 1986, 42). For more on camp, see Susan Sontag, *Notes on 'Camp'* (2018, 4–33). Notwithstanding Susan Sontag's recognition that "to talk about Camp is therefore to betray it" (2018, 1–2), critics of "camp" argue that "camp is a solely male gay practice, where gay reads white." Eventually, with the introduction of the intersectionality framework and whiteness studies, camp critics "start speaking of a racially informed camp aesthetic, which was mostly informed by an African American culture. Progressively the emergence of camp with pop culture and cultural studies scholarship has invigorated queer-of-color critiques that seek to historicize an existent non-white camp past"; see Constantine Chatzipapatheodoridis, "Beyoncé's Slay Trick: The Performance of Black Camp and its Intersectional Politics" (2017, 406).

19. Fast 2012, 282.
20. Entman and Rojecki 2000, xi.
21. Entman and Rojecki 2000, 5.
22. Entman and Rojecki 2000, 11.
23. Entman and Rojecki, 2000, 13.
24. That whites, individually and collectively, can be openly racist is just a fact. Certainly, it is comprehensible that many whites think of themselves as not racist and may very well cite as evidence the fact that they voted for a black president. However, take the case of the infamous recorded racist slurs submitted by the owner of the Los Angeles Clippers, Donald Sterling, in April 2014; the disreputable "nappy-headed hos" comment by Don Imus on April 5, 2007, when he was discussing members of the women's basketball team at Rutgers University; and the incident at a comedy club in Los Angeles, The Laugh Factory, on November 18, 2006, when actor Michael Richards, who is celebrated for portraying the character Kramer on the Television show *Seinfeld*, on numerous occasions shouted the word "nigger" at blacks who were present in the audience. The usage of the N-word, in this context, is extremely derogatory and should not be defended. In fact, many films from a multiplicity of genres offer no apologies for using racist language and portraying the racialized "other" as savage, uncivilized, and nonhuman. Some movies that come to mind are *Ace Ventura: When Nature Calls* (1996); *Pulp Fiction* (1995); and *Just Cause* (1995). In fact, with the Donald Trump administration in power, many Americans do not need to be "blind" to differences any longer. Like their president, Americans can now be openly racist, sexist, homophobic, classicist, xenophobic, and so on.
25. Joseph Vogel's "How Michael Jackson Made 'Bad' " explains the racist genealogy of the term "Wacko Jacko." Vogel writes: "It was a term first applied to the pop star by the British tabloid, *The Sun*, in 1985, but its etymology goes back further. 'Jacko Macacco' was the name of a famous monkey used in monkey-baiting matches at the Westminster Pit in London in the early 1820s. Subsequently, the term 'Jacko' or 'Jacko Macacco' was Cockney slang to refer to monkeys in general. The term persisted into the 20th century as 'Jacko Monkeys' became popular children's toys in Great Britain in the 1950s. They remained common in British households into the 1980s (and can still be found on eBay today)." Quoted in Vogel 2015, 485, note 16. In a word, "Wacko Jacko" is a term used to denigrate Michael Jackson.
26. Silberman 2007, 417.
27. An article written by Joan Kron, "Michael Jackson's Dermatologist and Former Plastic Surgeon Talks," suggests that Michael Jackson suffered from "body dysmorphic disorder"; that is, "a loathing of one's body no surgery can cure,"

which, accordingly, propels him to have multiple plastic surgeries in order to change his appearance. Such a diagnosis raises the question of Michael Jackson's mental state. In short, Michael Jackson's behavior stems from a psychological rather than physical explanation. And even though the psychological explanation for his surgeries is not explained very well, the bottom line is: "Jackson was not immune to the often harsh criticism of the changes he made to his appearance" (Kron, 2009).

28. Woolf 1995, 152.
29. Fanon 1967, 14.
30. Butler 1993a, 97–98.
31. See Frantz Fanon, *Black Skin, White Masks* (1967).
32. Ehlers 2012, 17.
33. Ehlers 2012, 17.
34. Corliss 2009, 57. Also, quoted in Miller 2012, 117.
35. Vigo 2010, 38.
36. Newsweek Staff 1983.
37. Haraway 1991, 151. Also, quoted in Miller 2012, 127.
38. Spivak 1988, 280.
39. See Michael Jackson's song, "Childhood." This song was released on June 16, 1995.
40. Copeland 2005.
41. Silberman 2007, 419.
42. For example, on November 19, 2002, Michael Jackson dangles his baby from the fourth-floor balcony of the Hotel Adlon.
43. Ahmed 2007, 149. My own emphasis.
44. Agamben 2013.
45. And if, as Charles Gallagher suggested, a "transformation of whiteness" is occurring, whiteness is indeed in some kind of "crisis." For more on this, see Charles Gallagher, "White Reconstruction in the University" (2003). What suggests a "crisis," in the first place, is the commonsensical idea that white entitlement is currently challenged and hindered.
46. Fanon 1967, 116.
47. Yancy 2012, 34.
48. Fanon 1967, 116.
49. For a good discussion on racialization, see Herbert J. Gans, "Racialization and Racialization Research" (2017); Steve Martinot, *The Machinery of Whiteness: Studies in the Structure of Racialization* (2010); Karim Murji and John Solomos, *Racialization: Studies in Theory and Practice* (2005); and David Theo Goldberg, *The Racial State* (2001).
50. Miles 1989, 74. Another definition of racialization comes from Herbert J. Gans: "racialization is best understood as a process, beginning with a temporal process" (2017, 342); that is, "the extension of racial meaning to a previously racially

unclassified social relation, social practice or group" (2017, 341–342). Also, see Michael Omi and Howard Winant, *Racial Formation in the United States: From the 1960s to the 1990s* (1994).

51. Lott 2013, 81.

52. Fuss 1994, 22.

53. For a more comprehensive view of the terrifying nature of whiteness, see Richard Wright, "The Ethics of Living Jim Crow: An Autobiographical Sketch" (2007); W. E. B. Du Bois, *The Souls of Black Folk* (2003); Ralph Ellison, *Invisible Man* (1995); bell hooks, *Black Looks: Race and Representation* (1992); Ida B. Wells, *Southern Horrors: Lynch Laws in All Its Phases* (1992); John Howard Griffin, *Black Like Me* (1977); James Baldwin, *The Fire Next Time* (1963); and Richard Wright, *Black Boy* (1937).

54. Deleuze and Guattari 1983, 43.

55. Revel 2009, 51.

56. Hall 1994, 395.

57. Butler 2015, 5.

58. I am using self-fashioning as the construction of one's identity that unsettles and disturbs the socially accepted standards of the either/or racial category.

59. Miller 2012, 118.

60. This is taken from Al Sharpton's eulogy on July 7, 2009, at the memorial service held for Michael Jackson. Sharpton (2009) added: Michael Jackson "created a comfort level . . . later it wasn't strange [for] us to watch Oprah on television. It wasn't strange to watch Tiger Woods golf. Those young kids grew up from teenage, comfortable fans of Michael to being 40 years old and being comfortable to vote for a person of color to be the president of the United States of America. Michael did that. Michael made us love each other."

61. Yuan 1996, 368.

62. Yuan 1996, 368.

63. *Captain EO*, Carl Miller describes for us, is seventeen minutes long. It "would run continually until being discontinued at EPCOT in July 1994 and at Disneyland in April 1997—in each case being replaced by another sci-fi attraction, *Honey, I Shrunk the Audience*, which was by that time judged less controversial (and, consequently, more family friendly) than its predecessor" (2012, 118). Nonetheless, Miller goes on to say, *Captain EO* "offers a prime test case of what Lyotard calls 'the relationship of scientific knowledge to 'popular' knowledge" (2012, 129).

64. Miller 2012, 129.

65. Miller 2012, 118.

66. Miller 2012, 118.

67. Miller 2012, 129.

68. Gates 1992, 109.

69. In the documentary *Living With Michael Jackson*, Michael Jackson did say, "I am Peter Pan in my heart," which many view as a "bizarre revelation" (Gómez-Barris and Gray 2006, 40). Margo Jefferson, in *On Michael Jackson*, notes

that in Michael Jackson's fun house at his Neverland Ranch, he has a picture of Peter Pan. She provides us with an account of the fictional character Peter Pan's life (2006, 21–22); she lets us know how much Michael Jackson identities with Peter Pan. She writes: "When Jane Fonda told Michael that she wanted to produce Peter Pan for him, he began to tremble. He identified so much with Peter Pan, he told her; he had read everything written about him. Did he know that the book's original title was *The Boy Who Hated His Mother*? As Michael wrote in his autobiography: 'I don't trust anybody except Katherine. And sometime I'm not so sure about her'" (2006, 22).

70. Newsweek Staff 1983.
71. Graham-Smith 2008, 279.
72. Silberman 2007, 429.
73. Miller 2012, 129.
74. Foucault 1979, 17.
75. Foucault 1979, 178.
76. Knight 2004, 143.
77. Jefferson 2006, 82.
78. Hackett's anxiety of Michael Jackson's "will to power," of course a negative form of power, or a "shifting disposition of power," in Stuart Hall's words 2004), an eventual descension from the "high" to the "low" is important. That is to say, a brief "triumph of the will." The *Triumph of the Will* is a Nazi propaganda film, which was cowritten and produced by Leni Riefenstahl in 1935. It examines the 1934 Nazi Party Congress in Nuremberg attended by 700,000 Nazi supporters. See Richard Meran Barsam, *Filmguide to Triumph of the Will* (1975, 21). Some of the speeches in the book are drawn from speeches by Nazi leaders such as Adolph Hitler, Julius Streicher, and Rudolph Hess.

79. Silberman 2007, 426.
80. Silberman 2007, 418.
81. This was on the BBC news on Wednesday, November 20, 2000, at 8:17 GMT.
82. Most recently, on May 10, 2018, Donna Pendergast (Bob Marley's granddaughter) and her friends (Komi-Oluwa Olafimihan and Kelly Fyffe-Marshall) were staying at an Airbnb in a white neighborhood and were detained by the police after a white woman called the police.
83. Silberman 2007, 418.
84. Silberman 2007, 423.
85. Vogel 2015, 480.
86. Vogel 2015, 479.
87. Baldwin 1998, 828. My own emphasis.
88. Baldwin 1998, 828.
89. Baldwin 1999, 828. Also, this observation is not sugarcoated by Don King, the promoter for the Jacksons' Victory Tour, a concert tour of Canada and the United States, which started in July 1984. See Taraborrelli 1991, 320. Joseph

Vogel, quoting Dave Marsh, expresses the same realization: "Michael Jackson played a dangerous game. He imagined himself capable of receiving an exemption from the visits of the horrible ghosts of American racism. This is an exceedingly dangerous illusion, for in the end, the ghosts will always come to call, all you've done is condemn yourself to a role of a villain or fool. There is no exemption, not only because of what such fame as Michael Jackson's stirs among such spirits of the past but because of what it awakens among the livings" (2015, 484n18).

90. Copeland 2005.
91. Jefferson 2006, 27.
92. Fuss 1989, 53. The body, as site of its inevitable demise, it is believed, at least in Western cultures, that a strict diet, daily exercises, cosmetics, treatments, and plastic surgeries can somewhat slowdown the aging process.
93. Jefferson 2006, 8.
94. Jefferson 2006, 12.
95. Vigo 2012, 28.
96. Vigo 2012, 28.
97. Butler 1993a, 2.
98. Eagleton 2005.
99. Virgo 2012, 26. Also, see Margo Jefferson, "Freaks," a chapter from *On Michael Jackson*" (2012, 3–27). In addition, Michael Jackson, in his music video "They Don't Care About Us," dances "with an animator's fantastic rendition of the Elephant Man's bones: a skeletal human figure on which is superimposed a genuine elephant's massive skull and tusks. No textual reference to the Elephant Man appears in Jackson's autobiography, but an arresting black-and-white photograph of Jackson dressed in dancing regalia (fedora and glove) does appear to be a reference to the Elephant Man. Graham and Oehlschlaeger describe the parallels: 'His hat, curls, and contorted profile with puffed-out upper lip suggest Merrick's large, lumpy head. The twist of the torso and partial bend to the legs give an impression of spinal curvature and hip misalignment. . . . [One] hand has a blurred, flipperlike quality" (Yuan 1996, 376).
100. Kristeva 1997, 372.
101. Fanon 1967, 189.
102. Foucault 1978, 11.
103. Butler 1993a, 237.
104. *Michael Jackson's Boys* is a sixty-minute TV movie, directed by Helen Littleboy, that was released on January 25, 2005, in the United Kingdom. This movie attempts to convey a negative and disturbing view of Michael Jackson's relations with young boys by extracting from interviews with Michael Jackson's family, friends, and others who are a part of his life, both private and public.
105. *Michael Jackson and the Boy He Paid Off* was released on March 7, 2004.
106. Epstein and Steinberg 2007, 449.

107. The British journalist Martin Bashir's claim to fame was in 2003 after he interviewed Princess Diana in 1995 about her failed marriage. *Living With Michael Jackson* was based on Bashir's eight-month interaction with Michael Jackson in which Bashir portrays Michael Jackson in a negative light. He says mean things about Michael Jackson and refers to him as a strange guy. Bashir commented in the documentary, "Jackson's behavior was beginning to alarm me." In his negative assessment of Michael Jackson's limitations, Bashir refers to Michael Jackson as "bizarre." Trying to correct this, *The Michael Jackson Interview: The Footage You Were Never Meant to See* was shown on Fox News. Nonetheless, the harm done to Michael Jackson with *Living With Michael Jackson*, in Michael Jackson's words, is "here to stay" (see Michael Jackson's song, "You Are Not Alone") and can never be unswayable.

108. Hill 2007, 462.

109. *Wacko About Jacko* was broadcasted on January 4, 2005, in the United Kingdom on Channel 4. It is produced and directed by Lucy Leveugle.

110. Fanon 1967, 18. For more on the view of Michael Jackson's UK fans, see Matt Hill, "Michael Jackson's Fans on Trial? Documenting Emotivism and Fandom in *Wacko About Jacko*" (2007).

111. See Dana Kennedy, "Michael Jackson's Career Woes" (2009). Also, quoted in Fuchs 1995, 27.

112. Hill 2007, 462.

113. Vigo 2012, 26–27.

114. Vigo 2012, 32.

115. These are the words from the song by The Jackson 5, "I'll Be There," released on August 28, 1970.

116. Silberman 2007, 429.

117. See the documentary, *Living With Michael Jackson* (2003).

118. Jackson 2010, 7. Michael Jackson's lecture at Oxford University was presented on March 6, 2001. It was published in a special series dedicated to Michael Jackson in *The Journal of Pan African Studies* in March 2010.

119. Flett 2003.

120. We remember how energized Michael Jackson was climbing on top of his favorite tree when he was being interviewed by Martin Bashir in the documentary *Living With Michael Jackson*. With uncontrollable enthusiasm, he even invited Bashir to climb the tree with him.

121. Martin Heidegger and Bernd Magnus in "Who Is Nietzsche's Zarathustra?" explain what *everyone and no one* means. They write: "*For Everyone* does not, of course, mean for just anybody. *For Everyone* means for each man as man, in so far as his essential nature becomes at any given time an object worthy of [Michael Jackson's] thought. *And No One* means for none of the idle curious who come drifting in from everywhere, who merely intoxicate themselves with isolated

fragments and particular aphorisms from [his lyrics]; who won't proceed along the path of thought that here seeks its expression, but blindly stumble about in its half-lyrical, half-shrill, now deliberate, now stormy often lofty and sometimes trite language" (1967, 411). For those people, Michael Jackson acknowledges in *Moonwalk* that he wants to make them "see pictures, make them cry and laugh, take them anywhere emotionally with something as deceptively simple as words. I'd like to tell tales to move their souls and transform them. Imagine how the great writers must feel, knowing they have that power. I sometimes feel I could do it" (Jackson 1988, 5).

122. See Michael Jackson's song, "You Are Not Alone," from his album *HIStory; Past, Present and Future Book 1*, released in 1995.

123. Before "Man in the Mirror" was released in 1987, 'We Are the World' was released on March 27, 1985, and the two are not indistinguishable. The latter was written by Michael Jackson and Lionel Richie and takes into consideration the suffering of children and how we can all help to improve their condition. See, "We are the World" (1985). Some of Michael Jackson's other songs about general suffering include "Heal the World" (1991) and "Earth Song" (1995).

124. Heidegger and Magus 1967, 412.

125. Michael Jackson pointing out that nobody says anything about single-mother households is not exactly accurate. How race, gender, and class play into family values is significant here. See Dawn Marie Dow, "Negotiating the 'Welfare Queen' and 'the Strong Black Woman' " (2015); Michele Estrin Gilman, "The Return of the Welfare Queen" (2014); Stephen Pimpare, "The Welfare Queen and the Great White Hope" (2010); "Ange-Marie Hancock, *The Politics of Disgust: The Public Identity of the Welfare Queen* (2004); and Bonnie Thornton Dill et al., "Valuing Families Differently: Race, Poverty, and Welfare Reform" (1998).

126. Silberman 2007, 426.

127. Silberman 2007, 426.

128. Silberman 2007, 426. Another one of Michael Jackson's hoaxes was to get his manager Frank Dileo to announce "that Jackson, impressed by 'the ethical, medical, and historical significance of the elephant Man,' had offered the London Hospital Medical College half a million dollars for his skeleton. In fact, Jackson had made no such offer to the medical college at the time" (Yuan 1996, 376).

129. Yuan 1996, 371.

130. Copeland 2005.

131. In *Living With Michael Jackson*, Michael Jackson discusses with Bashir how some of his most creative works manifest themselves when he sits at the top of his favorite tree.

132. These are the words from Michael Jackson's song "Human Nature" from his *Thriller* album released in 1982.

133. Caputo and Yount 1993, 6.

134. Foucault 1979, 217.

135. Ehlers 2012, 3.
136. Ehlers 2012, 3.
137. Butler 1990, 45.
138. Foucault 1978, 65.
139. Vogel 2015, 475.
140. Butler 2000b, 5.
141. Nancy 1991, 1.
142. Foucault 1979, 170.
143. Ehlers 2012, 18–19.
144. Butler 1993a, xi.

145. In 1619, when the first Africans arrived in Virginia, according to English colonial customs at that time, these Africans were to be considered as indentured servants. For the next several years, no differences were made between European and African indentured servants. However, European indentured servants were freed persons who were either convicts sentenced to labor for a term of years; the poor who, in order to pay their fare from Europe to the colonies, were contracted for a term of years; and sometimes persons who had been kidnapped. Eventually, while the conditions for white servants improved, the opposite held true for black servants. Maryland in 1639, and Virginia in 1643, "enacted laws fixing limits to the terms of servants who entered without written contract, Negroes were not included in such protective provision." As early as 1640, Maryland law, for instance, "provided that 'all masters' should try to furnish arms to themselves and 'all those of their families which shall be capable of arms—which would include servants—('excepting Negroes')." See Carl N. Degler, "Slavery and the Genesis of American Race Prejudice," which provides a comprehensive account of this (1959, 57).

146. In the United States, the lynching of blacks was a social event that was well attended by whites who came with picnic baskets. In addition, postcards were replicated from the pictures that were taken during lynchings to send to relatives and friends.

147. In terms of the biopolitical, Foucault tells us biopower is that sphere of life where power has taken over to regulate who lives and who dies. For a more comprehensive reading on biopower, see Michel Foucault, "*Society Must be Defended*" (2002). Certainly, race figures prominently into biopower, which targeted the entire black population through racism as a mechanism of control through which racial discipline—relying on the surveillance of blackness, for example, what Foucault described as the panoptic power of persistent observation—is sustained. With the emergence of disciplinary power, the body of the individual becomes the target. Through various forms of knowledge, technologies, and techniques, and through organizing, surveying, separating, and hierarchizing, the individual body is disciplined into the values and norms, products of the disciplinary power of society, until one becomes self-disciplined in line with these values and norms.

This is a good example of how a body is made into a docile "normal" body trained to adhere to its race assignment; it a disciplinary practice that shapes and modifies identity by targeting the body (Ehlers 2012, 4).

148. Erni 1998, 158.

149. Epstein and Steinberg 2007, 446.

150. Yuan 1996, 380.

151. Yuan 1996, 381. Michael Jackson further told the LAPD, "If I am guilty of anything, it is of believing what God said about children: 'suffer little children to come unto me and forbid them not, for such is the kingdom of heaven.' In no way do I think that I am God, but I do try to be Godlike in heart." See Michael Jackson, "Neverland Statement 1993" (1993). From a Christian viewpoint, indeed, Michael Jackson's acknowledgment makes sense. In the King James version of the Bible, 1 John 4: 8 tells us, "God is love" and 1 John 4: 8 notes, "He that loveth not knoweth not God; For God is love."

152. Fanon 1967, 17.

153. Onwuachi-Willig 2017, 1116.

154. Erni 1998, 169.

155. Wilderson 2014, 7.

156. Alcoff 2006, 7.

157. Wilderson 2014, 7.

158. For more on "commonsense racism," see Angela Onwuachi-Willig, "Policing the Boundaries of Whiteness: The Tragedy of Being 'Out of Place' from Emmett Till to Trayvon Martin" (2017); Michael Tonry, *Punishing Race: A Continuing American Dilemma* (2012); Rose Capdevila and Jane E. Callaghan, " 'It's not Racist. It's Common Sense' " (2008); Ian F. Haney-Lopéz, *Racism on Trial: The Chicago Fight for Justice* (2003); and John D. Brewer, "Competing Understandings of Commonsense Understanding: A Brief Comment on 'Commonsense Racism' " (1984).

159. Wilderson 2014, 7.

160. Eppert 2017, 94.

161. Judy 1993, 89.

162. Yuan 1996, 381. Also, quoted in Michael Jackson's "Neverland Statement 1993."

163. In the end, one can only imagine Michael Jackson recalling the speech of Iago in Shakespeare's *Othello*:

> Good name in man and woman, dear my Lord,
> Is the immediate jewel of their souls:
> Who steal my purse steals trash; 'Tis something, nothing;
> 'Twas mine, 'tis his, and has been a slave to thousands;
> But he who flinches from me my good name
> Robs me of that which not enriches him
> And make me poor indeed. (Shakespeare 2019, 64)

164. Arendt 1966, 157.

165. According to George M. Fredrickson, the word *racism* first appeared in the 1930s to describe the Nazi's persecution of the Jews (2002, 4).

166. The laws and customs that were in place were indicative of the broader system of racism as a multifaceted interdiscursive activity where the nature of "difference" fascinated and appealed to a concealed racist description of blacks, First Nations, Chinese, and other racialized ethnic groups as physically different. In Europe, up until the eighteenth century, there were several explanations for the physical differences of people, which drew from the Bible. Alden T. Vaughan, for one, points to how the English equated Africans with the biblical "curse of Ham" in Geneses 9: 20–27, which describes how Noah cursed Ham's son, Canaan, to a life of perpetual servitude to his brothers Shem and Japheth. The English identified Ham as the ancestor of black Africans and themselves as the descendants of Japheth. In the United States, Sylvester A. Johnson, in *The Myth of Ham in Nineteenth-Century American Christianity*, shows how the "curse of Ham" was also used by slave owners in the southern states to justify slavery. In other words, the Bible is often used to establish and maintain certain groups as the "other." When indentured servitude ultimately legalized racism through laws and practices that determined the unequal treatment of blacks, First Nations, Chinese, and other racialized ethnic groups, it founded the racial model that would govern the new colonies. The unequal treatment of blacks, especially, would reemerge and extend itself into legalized slavery, the unique designation for the definitive racism in the United States, which provided a template for the unequal treatment of all racialized ethnic groups. In other words, *black* became the signifier for *nonwhite*.

167. Fanon 1967, 116.

168. Yancy 2012, 34.

169. Butler 2000a, 56.

170. In its oddity, the United States is now supposed to be colorblind. This is wearily illustrated in statements such as "I don't see race," and it is announced to declare that "race does not matter." This attitude, among other things, returns blacks to a state of "not to be" (nonbeing). The questions that Judith Butler poses in "Appearances Aside" become important here: "How do we consider such a person without taking into consideration what we see, or are we being asked to look at a person without actually seeing what we see, engaging in a practice of disavowal? Are either of these strategies of compliance practicable?" (Butler 2000a, 56). To answer the last question, no, they are not. Charles Mills, in *The Racial Contract*, is correct that American society is structured in such a way as "to bring in race" (1997, 7) always. Also, see Cornel West, *Race Matters* (2001).

171. In fact, in a class I teach on race and ethnicity in the United States, we were discussing colorblindness. To my amazement, a white student was explaining the inappropriateness of colorblindness not to "see" race. He announced, "When I am taking to a person on the phone, I can tell just from talking to that person that he or she is black. I don't have to see the person."

172. Yuan 1996, 382.
173. Ahmed 2007, 161.
174. Sexton 2011, 28.
175. Eubanks 2017, 5.
176. Pinder 2018, x.
177. For a more comprehensive reading on the "North African Syndrome," see Frantz Fanon's "The 'North African Syndrome,'" chapter one in *Toward the African Revolution: Political Essays* (1964, 1–16).
178. Wilderson 2009, 7.
179. Indeed, in 1995, Michael Jackson was crowned a "King" of Ghana regions by King Amon Ndoufou IV of Sanwi. For more on this, see Adrian Grant, *Michael Jackson: The Visual Documentary* (2001).
180. Yancy 2004, 111.
181. Fanon 1967, 169. Also, quoted in Lewis Gordon, "A Questioning Body of Laughter and Tears: Reading *Black Skin, White Masks* Through the Cat and Mouse of Reason and a Misguided Theodicy" (2002, 21).
182. Fanon 1967, 170.
183. Albrecht 2013, 718.
184. Ehler 2012, 18.
185. Gómez-Barris and Gray 2006, 44.
186. Gordon 2002, 10.
187. Du Bois also understands the souls of white folk. In "The Souls of White Folk," he admits that the souls of white folk intrigue him enormously. He writes: "I know many souls that toss and whirl pass, but none there are that intrigue me than the Souls of White Folk. Of them I am singularly clairvoyant. I see in and through them. . . . I see these souls undressed from the back and the side. I see the working of their entrails. I know their thoughts and they know that I know. This knowledge now makes them embarrassed, now Furious." See Du Bois's *Darkwater: Voices from the Veil* (1969, 29).

Epilogue

1. For blacks, there is a struggle around a black identity. George Yancy, in "The Agential Black Body: Resisting the Black Imago in White Imaginary" in *Black Bodies White Gazes*, writes: "Black identity-talk [in the United States] must begin from below, that is, one must begin with the existential terror of whiteness faced by Black people, and realize that Black people continue to define and redefine themselves through the deployment of conceptual and affective resources that are themselves historical" (2008, 110).
2. Cervenak and Carter 2017, 45.
3. Spillers 1984, 88.

4. See Hortense Spillers, "Interstices: A Small Drama of Words" (1984).

5. Fanon writes: "There is a quest for the Negro, the Negro is in demand, one cannot get along without him, he is needed, but only if he is made palatable in a certain way" (1967, 176).

6. Fanon 1967, 112. My own emphasis.

7. Fanon 1967, 110–11.

8. Spillers 1984, 74.

9. In Harper Lee, *Go Set A Watchman*, Lee writes: "For thus hath the Lord said unto me, Go set a watchman, let him declare what he seeth" (2015, 95).

10. Weheliye 2014, 1.

11. Gordon 1997, 57.

12. Collins 1989, 758.

13. Yancy 2008, 110.

14. Albrecht 2013, 707.

15. Albrecht 2013, 710.

16. Albrecht 2013, 710.

17. Fanon 1967, 111.

18. For more on to "dance in blackness," see Halifu Osumare, *Dancing in Blackness: A Memoir* (2018).

19. Rankine 2014, 69.

20. Fanon 1967, 8.

21. Fanon 1967, 110.

22. Fanon 1967, 111.

23. Fanon 1967, 225.

24. Marriott 2000, 15.

25. Du Bois 2003, 5.

26. Collins 1989, 749.

27. *Things Fall Apart* is the title of Chinua Achebe's 2010 book.

28. Moten 2008, 187.

29. Du Bois 2003, 3–4.

30. Chandler 2014, 9.

31. Chandler 2014, 1.

32. Chandler 2014, 1.

33. Chandler 2008, 351.

34. Butler 2015, 5.

35. Butler 2015, 5. In an additional sense, whiteness as the norm forces a black person to confess their own blackness. At the heart of this practice, the confession is thus structured as a verbal act by which the subject is affirming the "truth": I am black.

36. See Toni Morrison, *The Bluest Eyes* (2007). Also, see George Yancy, "Desiring Bluest Eyes, Desiring Whiteness: The Black Body as Torn Asunder," chapter 6 in *Black Bodies, White Gazes: The Continuing Significance of Race* (2008).

37. Du Bois 1969, 24.

38. See Michael Jackson's song, "They Don't Really Care About Us" (1995).

39. Pope 2003, 50. This is taken from Alexander Pope's major poem, "An Essay of Cultural Criticism," originally published in 1711.

40. See Michael Jackson's song, "Childhood" (1995).

41. Alcoff 2000, 320.

42. When we see negative images of Michael Jackson presented in the media as concrete evidence, in light of the idiom "Seeing Is Believing,"—that is to say, only concrete evidence is compelling—we tend to forgo, for the most part, any form of meaningful critique. I am using critique, here, in the Foucauldian sense. In "What Is a Critique?" in *The Politics of Truth*, Michel Foucault lets us know that "critique only exists in relation to something other than itself: it is an instrument, a means for a future or a truth that it will not know or happen to be, it oversees a domain it would want to police and it unable to regulate. All this means that it is a function which is subordinated in relation to what philosophy, science, politics, ethics, law, literature, etc. positively constitute" (1997, 42). In this case, the media's depiction of Michael Jackson, for the most part, receives the "dominant" reading by Michael Jackson's critics. A dominant reading accepts the content of the media's presentation of him without question and critique. See Jacqueline Bobo, "The Color Purple: Black Women as Cultural Readers" (2004, 181). And while "seeing is believing" is merely "false seeing" because of the objective way of understanding what we see, a second way of seeing that "resees"—that is, seeing again differently—here, is essential.

43. Fanon 1967, 173.

44. Fanon 1967, 112.

45. Fanon 1967, 112.

46. Walker 2020, 25.

47. Walker 2020, 25.

48. Cox 1948, 336.

49. Fanon 1967, 81.

50. Frankenberg 1993, 87.

51. Lee 2002, 232.

52. Hammonds 2004, 301.

53. Aretha Franklin released "You Make Me Feel Like a Natural Woman" on her 1967 album, *Lady Soul*. This song was cowritten by Carl King and Gerry Goffin.

54. Fanon 1967, 49.

55. Before the case of *Loving v. Virginia*, it was a criminal offense for a black and a white person to be legally married. And while the Court declared that the Virginia statute criminalizing marriage between a colored person and a white person violated the Fourteenth Amendment privacy protection clause, the anti-miscegenation laws were to prevent the corruption of white blood so

as to maintain white supremacy. In other words, black-white relations point to America's historicity.

56. Fanon 1967, 63.
57. Fanon 1967, 63.
58. See Michael Jackson, "Black or White" (1991).
59. Simone de Beauvoir, in *The Second Sex*, demonstrates that white women are the inessential "other" of white men. Woman, she writes, "is defined and differentiated with reference to a man and not he in reference to her; she is the incidental, as opposed to the essential. He is the Subject, he is the Absolute—she is the Other" (1952, 16). For Fanon, in *Black Skin, White Masks*, the inessential "other" for a white man is the black man (1967, 161).
60. Epstein and Steinberg 2007, 448. In some cases, Michael Jackson is viewed as asexual. And given that black masculinity is perceived as a threat to the white social body, his asexuality, then, should not be a threat to whites. However, the either/or (gay/straight) plays on the anxiety for the social body.
61. Alcoff 2000, 341.
62. Bhabha 1994, 5.
63. Ross 2004, 163.
64. Squires 2004, 194.
65. See William Julius Wilson, *The Declining Significance of Race* (1980).
66. See Dinesh D'Souza, *The End of Racism: Principles for a Multiracial Society* (1995).
67. Sartre 1953, 48.
68. Jean-Paul Sartre, in *Being and Nothingness*, makes a distinction between lying to oneself and lying to others, which is "lying in general." For Sartre, "the liar actually is in complete possession of the truth which he is hiding" (1953, 48).
69. Mills 1997, 18.
70. Fields and Fields 2014, 10.
71. Yancy 2018, 5.
72. Other scholars point to the escalation of racism in the United States of America. See *Backlash: What Happens When We Talk Honestly About Racism in America* (2018); Ibram X. Kendi, *Stamped From the Beginning: The Definitive History of Racist Ideas in America* (2017); Sherrow O. Pinder, *Colorblindness, Post-Raciality, and Whiteness in the United States* (2015); Ta-Nehisi Coates, *Between the World and Me* (2015); Claudia Rankine, *Citizen: An American Lyric* (2014); Cornel West, *Race Matters* (2001); Charles W. Mills, *The Racial Contract* (1997); and James Baldwin, *The Fire Next Time* (1963).
73. Trey 1989, 233.
74. West 2001, xxv. Later on, West lets us know that he was stopped by the police "while driving from New York to teach at Williams College." He writes: "I was stopped on fake charges of trafficking cocaine. When I told the police

officer I was a professor of religion, he replied, 'Yeh, and I'm the Flying Nun. Let's go, nigger!" (2001, xxv). These moments are indeed habitual; that is to say, they have happened all the time, *before*. The *before* is indeed a part of the *now*, an ever-present now.

75. Chandler 2014, 18.
76. Carlye 2015, 71.
77. Morrison 2007, 4.
78. de Beauvoir 1976, 100.
79. Fanon 1967, 111.
80. McLaren 1997, 6.
81. Kendi 2017, 2. According to Ibram X. Kendi, "*stamped from the beginning* comes from a speech that Mississippi senator Jefferson Davis gave on the floor of the US Senate in 1860. The future president of the Confederacy objected to a bill funding black education in Washington, DC. 'This government was not founded by negroes for negroes, but 'by white men for white men,' Davis lectured his colleague. 'The bill was based on a false notion of racial equality,' he declared. The 'inequality of the white and black race was stamped from the beginning'" (2017, 2).
82. *Stembein* means to misuse, to trample.
83. Césaire 2002, 63. This is the situation of blacks in the United States of America, "who have been skillfully injected with fear, inferiority complexes, trepidation, servility, despair, abasement." See the opening of Frantz Fanon, *Black Skin, White Masks* (1967, 7), which is taken from Aimé Césaire's *Discours sur le Colonialisme (Discourse on Colonialism)*.
84. Césaire 2000, 43.
85. Césaire 2000, 20.
86. Fanon 1967, 112.
87. Fanon 1967, 112.
88. Nietzsche 1978, 108.
89. Sartre 1953, 48.
90. de Lauretis 2002, 56.
91. Fanon 1967, 111.
92. de Lauretis 2002, 56.
93. Fanon 1967, 138.
94. de Lauretis 2002, 61.
95. Touré 2011, 20. In truth, there is no "authentic" blackness. I think that this is what Marlon Riggs's 1994 documentary *Black Is . . . Black Ain't* is getting at.
96. See Ralph Ellison, *The Invisible Man* (1952).
97. Fanon 1967, 10. My own emphasis. For James Baldwin, the destiny that Fanon describes, "the price of the ticket" (2010, 136) was, in his words, "becoming white" (2010, 136). See "On being 'White' . . . and Other Lies," in *James Baldwin: The Cross of Redemption Uncollected Writings* (2010).

98. Mercer 1987, 33.

99. Mercer 1987, 33.

100. Freire 2000, 47. In discussing the oppressor and oppressed dichotomy, this is how Paulo Freire, *The Pedagogy of the Oppressed*, explains it: "The oppressed, having internalized the image of the oppressor and adopted his guidelines, are fearful of freedom. Freedom would require them to eject this image and replace it with autonomy and responsibility. Freedom is acquired by conquest, not by gift. It must be pursued constantly and responsibly. Freedom is not an ideal located outside of man; nor is it an idea which becomes myth. It is rather the indispensable condition for the quest for human completion" (2000, 47). Fanon, in *Black Skin, White Masks*, goes on to say: "But the Negro knows nothing of the cost of freedom, for he has not fought for it. From time to time he has fought for Liberty and Justice: that is, values secreted by his masters. The former slave, who can find in his memory no trace of the struggle for liberty or of that anguish of liberty of which Kierkegaard speaks, sits unmoved before the young white man singing and dancing on the tightrope of existence" (1967, 221).

101. Yancy 2008, 118.

102. Mercer 1987, 33.

103. Trey Ellis describes the "new black aesthetic" as having its roots "from a few seventies pioneers that shamelessly borrows and reassembles across both race and class lines. This muscly combination of zeal, *Glasnost*, and talent is daily commanding the ever-larger chunks of the American art worlds" (1989, 234).

104. Tate 1997.

105. Hall 2004, 258.

106. Hall 2004, 259.

107. Collins 1989, 746.

108. Chandler 2008, 351.

109. Fanon 1967, 111.

110. The Du Bosian double consciousness is reworked in George Yancy's chapter, "Desiring Bluest Eyes, Desiring Whiteness: The Black Body as Torn Asunder," in *Black Bodies, White Gazes: The Continuing Significance of Race*, where Yancy writes, "As did W. E. B. Du Bois, Morrison also engages the process of exposing whiteness and its impact on Black embodiment" (2008, 183).

111. Johnson 2012, 71.

112. Fanon 1967, 211.

113. Ellis 1989, 235.

114. Morrison 2007, 46. Unlike Pecola Breedlove who prayed for blue eyes, Janie, in Zora Neale Hurston's *Their Eyes Were Watching God*, thought that if everyone is white, then she is also white. See Thelma Pinto, "Claiming Sarah Baartman" (2013, 159).

115. Fanon 1967, 45.

116. Pinder 2012, xiv.

117. Fanon 1967, 218. In the Hegelian dialectics of recognition, when race and racism are introduced, it forecloses any form of recognition between the masters (whites) and the slaves (blacks). The master does not seek recognition from the slaves. His interest is only the labor that the slaves provide.

118. Fuss 1994, 22.

119. Morrison 1992, 52.

120. Morrison 1992, 52.

121. Paul Waldman, in "The Privilege of Whiteness," writes: "As a white person, I am myself, nothing more or less. That's privilege" (2013). My own emphasis. Also, quoted in George Yancy, *Backlash* (2018, 11). Yancy acknowledges, "As a white person, you are a part of a system that allows you to walk into the stores where you are not followed, where you go for a bank loan and your skin color does not count against you, where you don't need to engage in 'the talk' that Black people and people of color must engage in with their children so that they might live for another day" (2018, 11).

122. See El Greco's 1557 painting, "Healing the Man Born Blind." The blind man is healed with Christ's touch and love. The painting is housed in the Gemäldegalerie Alte Meister in Dresden, Germany.

123. Fanon 1967, 231.

124. Fanon 1967, 117.

125. Freire 2002, 47.

126. Fanon 1967, 139.

127. Fanon 1967, 139.

128. Fanon 1967, 139.

129. Broertjes 2013, 688.

130. Césaire 2002, xv.

131. Lorde 1984, 115.

132. Césaire 2002, 18.

References

Aanerud, Rebecca. 2007. "The Legacy of White Supremacy and the Challenge of White Antiracist Mothering." *Hypatia* 22, no. 2: 20–38.
Achebe, Chinua. 2010. *Things Fall Apart*. New York: Bloom's Literary Criticism.
Agamben, Giorgio. 2013. *The Endless Crisis as an Instrument of Power: In Conversation with Giorgio Agamben*. London: Verso Books. http://www.versobooks.com/blogs/1318-the-endless-crisis-as-an-instrument-of-power-in-conversation-with-giorgio-agamben.
Ahmed, Sara. 2004. "The Politics of Good Feelings." *Critical Race and Whiteness Studies* 10, no. 2: 1–19.
———. 2007. "A Phenomenology of Whiteness." *Feminist Theory* 8, no. 2: 149–68.
———. 2012. *On Being Included: Racism and Diversity in Institutional Life*. Durham, NC: Duke University Press.
———. 2015. "Being in Trouble: In the Company of Judith Butler." *Lambda Nordica* 20, nos. 2–3: 179–89.
Ahmed, Sara, and Jackie Stacey. 2001. "Introduction: Dermographies." In *Thinking Through the Skin*, edited by Sara Ahmed and Jackie Stacey, 1–17. New York: Routledge.
Albrecht, Michael Mario. 2013. "Dead Man in the Mirror: The Performative Aspects of Michael Jackson's Posthuman Body." *The Journal of Popular Culture* 46, no. 4: 705–34.
Alcoff, Linda Martín. 1998. "What Should White People Do?" *Hypatia* 7, no. 13: 6–26.
———. 1999. "Toward a Phenomenology of Racial Embodiment." *Radical Philosophy* 95: 15–25.
———. 2000. "Who's Afraid of Identity Politics?" In *Reclaiming Identity: Realist Theory and the Predicament of Postmodernism*, edited by Paula M. L. Moya and Michael Hames-Garcí, 312–42. Berkeley: University of California Press.
———. 2006. *Visible Identities: Race, Gender, and the Self*. New York: Oxford University Press.

Alexander, Michelle. 2010. *The New Jim Crow: Mass Incarceration in the Age of Colorblindness*. New York: New Press.

Alter, Jonathan. 1993. "The Shield of Vulnerability." *Newsweek*, September 5, 1993. https://www.newsweek.com/shield-vulnerability-193110.

Althusser, Louis. 1977. "Ideology and Ideological State Apparatuses." In *Lenin and Philosophy and Other Essays*, translated by Ben Brewster, 127–86. New York: New Left Books.

———. 2014. *On the Reproduction of Capitalism: Ideology and Ideological State Apparatus*. Translated by G. M. Goshgarian. New York: Verso.

Angelou, Maya. 1993. *On the Pulse of Morning: The Inaugural Poem*. New York: Random House.

Appiah, Anthony K. 1994. "Identity, Authenticity, Survival: Multicultural Societies and Social Reproduction." In *Multiculturalism: Examining the Politics of Recognition*, edited by Amy Gutmann, 149–64. Princeton, NJ: Princeton University Press.

Arendt, Hannah. 1958. *The Human Condition*. Chicago: University of Chicago Press.

———. 1964. "Understanding and Politics." In *Essays in Understanding, 1930–1954: Formation, Exile, and Totalitarianism*, 307–27. New York: Schocken Books.

———. 1966. *The Origins of Totalitarianism*. New York: Harcourt Brace and Company.

Armour, Jody. 1995. "Stereotypes and Prejudices: Helping Legal Decisionmakers Break the Prejudice Habits." *California Law Review* 83, no. 3: 733–72.

Austin, J. L. 1963. *How to Do Things with Words*. Oxford: Oxford University Press.

Awkward, Michael. 1995. *Negotiating Difference: Race, Gender, and the Politics of Positionality*. Chicago: University of Chicago Press.

Baldwin, James. 1963. *The Fire Next Time*. New York: Dell.

———. 1985. *The Price of the Ticket: Collected Nonfiction, 1948–1985*. New York: St Martin's Press.

———. 1998. "Freaks and the American Ideal of Manhood." In *Baldwin: Collected Essays*, edited by Toni Morrison, 814–29. New York: The Library of America.

———. 2010. *The Cross of Redemption: Uncollected Writings*. Edited by Randall Kenan. New York: Pantheon Books.

Barsam, Richard Meran. 1975. *Filmguide to* Triumph of the Will. Bloomington: Indiana University Press.

Barthes, Roland. 1977. *Image-Music Text*. Translated by Stephen Heath. New York: Hill and Wang.

de Beauvoir, Simone. 1952. *The Second Sex*. Translated by H. M. Parshley. New York: Bantam.

———. 1974. *The Ethics of Ambiguity*. Translated by Bernard Frechtman. New York: Citadel Press.

Bennett, Lerone. 1975. *The Shaping of Black American Thought: The Struggles and Triumphs of African-Americans, 1619–1990s*. Chicago: Johnson.
Berger, John. 1972. *Ways of Seeing*. London: BBC and Penguin.
Bergson, Henri. 1991. *Matter and Memory*. Translated by Nancy Margret Paul and W. Scott Palmer. New York: Zone Books.
Bhabha, Homi K. 1984. "Of Mimicry and Man: The Ambivalence of Colonial Discourse." *Discipleship: A Special Issue on Psychoanalysis* 28: 125–23.
———. 1992. "The Other Question: The Stereotype and Colonial Discourse." In *The Sexual Subject: A Screen Reader in Sexuality*, edited by Mandy Merck, 312–31. New York: Routledge.
———. 1994. *The Location of Culture*. New York: Routledge Press.
———. 1998. "The White Stuff." *Artforum* 36, no. 9: 21–24.
Bobo, Jacqueline. 2004. "*The Color Purple*: Black Women as Cultural Readers." In *The Black Studies Reader*, edited by Jacqueline Bobo, Cynthia Hudley, and Claudine Michel, 177–92. New York: Routledge.
Bonnett, Alastair. 1996. "'White Studies': The Problems and Projects of a New Research Agenda." *Theory, Culture & Society* 13, no. 2: 145–55.
———. 2000. "Whiteness in Crisis." *History Today* 50, no. 12: 38–40.
Bosteels, Bruno. "Introduction: The People Which Is Not One." In *What Is a People?* by Alain Badiou, Pierre Bourdieu, Judith Butler, George Didi-Huberman, Sadri Khiari, and Jacques Rancière, and translated by Jody Gladding, 1–20. New York: Columbia University Press, 2016.
Bourdieu, Pierre. 1993. *Sociology in Question*. Translated by Richard Nice. London: SAGE.
Brackett, David. 2012. "Black or White? Michael Jackson and the Idea of Crossover." *Popular Music and Society* 35, no. 2: 169–85.
Brah, Avtar, and Ann Phoenix. 2004. "Ain't I a Woman? Revisiting Intersectionality." *Journal of International Women's Studies* 5, no. 3: 75–86.
Braidotti, Rosi. 1994. *Nomadic Subjects: Embodiment and Sexual Difference in Contemporary Feminist Theory*. New York: Columbia University Press.
———. 2013. *The Posthuman*. Malden, MA: Polity Press.
Brewer, John D. 1984. "Competing Understandings of Commonsense Understanding: A Brief Comment on 'Commonsense Racism.'" *The British Journal of Sociology* 35, no. 1: 66–74.
Brodkin, Karen. 1998. *How Jews Became White Folk and What That Says About Race in America*. New Brunswick, NJ: Rutgers University Press.
Broertjes, Andrew. 2013. "'He's Sending His People Messages Out of His Pain': Michael Jackson and the Black Community." *Popular Music and Society* 36, no. 5: 677–98.
Brown, Nathan. 2016. "The Irony of Anatomy: Basquiat's Poetics of Black Positionality." *Radical Philosophy* 195: 11–24.

Buchhart, Dieter, ed. 2015. *Jean-Michel Basquiat: Now's the Time*. Toronto: Art Gallery of Ontario and DelMonico Books.
Butler, Judith. 1989. "Foucault and the Paradox of Bodily Inscriptions." *The Journal of Philosophy* 86, no. 11: 601–7.
———. 1990. *Gender Troubles: Feminism and the Subversion of Identity*. New York: Routledge.
———. 1991. "Imitation and Gender Insubordination." In *Inside/Out: Lesbian Theories, Gay Theories*, edited by Diana Fuss, 13–31. New York: Routledge.
———. 1993a. *Bodies That Matter: On the Discursive Limits of Sex*. New York: Routledge.
———. 1993b. "Endangered/Endangering: Schematic Racism and White Paranoia." In *Reading Rodney King/Reading Urban Uprising*, edited by Robert Gooding-Williams, 15–22. New York: Routledge.
———. 1995. "Collected and Fractured: Responses to Identities." In *Identities*, edited by Kwame Anthony Appiah and Henry Louis Gates Jr., 439–47. Chicago: University of Chicago Press.
———. 1997a. *The Psychic Life of Power: Theories of Subjection*. Stanford, CA: Stanford University Press.
———. 1997b. *Excitable Speech: A Politics of the Performative*. New York: Routledge.
———. 2000a. "Appearances Aside." *California Law Review* 88, no. 1: 55–63.
———. 2000b. *Antigone's Claim*. New York. University of Columbia Press.
———. 2001. "Appearances Aside." In *Prejudicial Appearances: The Logic of American Antidiscrimination Law*, edited by Robert C. Post, Judith Butler, Thomas C. Grey, and Reva B. Siegel, 73–83. Durham, NC: Duke University Press.
———. 2004. *Undoing Gender*. New York: Routledge.
———. 2009. *Frames of War: When Is Life Grievable?* New York: Verso Books.
———. 2015. *Senses of the Subject*. New York: Fordham University Press.
Butler, Paul. 2017. *Chokehold: Policing Black Men*. New York: New Press.
Byerman, Keith. 1994. *Seizing the World: History, Art, and Self in the Work of W. E. B. Du Bois*. Athens: University of Georgia Press.
Capdevila, Rose, and Jane E. Callaghan. 2008. " 'It's Not Racist. It's Common Sense': A Critical Analysis of Political Discourse Around Asylum and Immigration in the UK." *Journal of Applied Social Psychology* 18, no. 1: 1–16.
Caputo, John, and Mark Yount. 1993. "Institutions, Normalizations, and Power." In *Foucault and the Critique of Institutions*, edited by John Caputo and Mark Yount, 3–23. University Park: Pennsylvania State University Press.
Carlyle, Thomas. 2015. *Sartor Resartus: The Life and Opinions of Herr Teufelsdrockh*. Scotts Valley, CA: CreateSpace Independent Publishing.
Caute, David. 1970. *Frantz Fanon*. London, UK: Penguin.
Cervenak, Sara Jane, and J. Cameron Carter. 2017. "Untitled and Outdoors: Thinking with Saidiya Hartman." *Women & Performance: A Journal of Feminist Theory* 27, no. 1: 45–55.

Césaire, Aimé. 2000. *Discourse on Colonialism*. Translated by Joan Pinkham. New York: Monthly Press.
———. 2002. *A Tempest*. Translated by Richard Miller. New York: Theatre Communications Group, Inc.
Chandler, Nahum D. 2008. "Of Exorbitance: The Problem of the Negro as a Problem for Thought." *Criticism* 50, no. 3: 345–410.
———. 2014. *X—The Problem for the Negro as a Problem for Thought*. New York: Fordham University Press.
Chatzipapatheodoridis, Constantine. 2017. "Beyoncé's Slay Trick: The Performance of Black Camp and Its Intersectional Politics." *Open Cultural Studies* 1, no. 1: 406–16.
Cixous, Hélène. 2009. *The Third Body*. Evanston, IL: Northwestern University Press.
Coates, Ta-Nehisi. 2015. *Between the World and Me*. New York: Spiegel & Grau.
Coetzee, J. M. 2000. *Disgrace*. London: Vintage Books.
Collins, Patricia Hill. 1989. "The Social Construction of Black Feminist Thought." *Signs: Journal of Women in Culture and Society* 14, no. 4: 745–73.
Copeland, Libby. 2005. "One Strange Case." *Washington Post*, June 13, 2005. http://www.washingtonpost.com/wpdyn/content/article/2005/06/13/AR2005061301718_2.html.
Corliss, Richard. 2009. "Michael Jackson's *This Is It* Review: He's Still a Thriller." *Time*, November 9, 2009. http://content.time.com/time/magazine/article/0,9171,1933215,00.html.
Cox, Oliver C. 1948. *Caste, Class & Race: A Study in Social Dynamics*. New York: Doubleday.
Crenshaw, Kimberlé. 1989. "Demarginalizing the Intersection of Race and Sex: A Black Feminist Critique of Antidiscrimination Doctrine, Feminist Theory, and Antiracist Politics." *University of Chicago Legal Forum*, no. 1: 139–67.
Daniel, G. Reginald. 2001. *More Than Black? Multiracial Identity and the New Racial Order*. Philadelphia: Temple University Press.
da Silva, Denise Ferreria. 2014. "Toward a Black Feminist Poethics: The Quest(ion) of Blackness Toward the End of the World." *The Black Scholar* 41, no. 2: 81–97.
Davis, Angela Y. 1983. "Rape, Racism, and the Myth of the Black Rapist." In *Women, Race & Class* (172–201). New York: Vintage Book
———. 1983. *Women, Race & Class*. New York: Vintage Books.
Davis, Kathy. 2003. "Surgical Passing: Or Why Michael Jackson's Nose Makes 'Us' Uneasy." *Feminist Theory* 4, no. 1: 73–92.Degler, Carl N. "Slavery and the Genesis of American Race Prejudice." *Comparative Studies in Society and History* 2, no. 1: 49–66.
de Lauretis, Teresa. 2002. "Difference Embodied: Reflections on *Black Skin, White Masks*." *Parallax* 8, no. 2: 54–68.
Deleuze, Gilles, and Félix Guattari. 1983. *Anti-Oedipus Capitalism and Schizophrenia*. Minneapolis: University of Minnesota Press.

Dill, Bonnie Thornton, and Ruth Enid Zambrana. 2009. "Critical Thinking About Intersectionality: An Emergence Lens." In *Emerging Intersections: Race, Class, and Gender in Theory and Practice*, edited by Bonnie Thornton Dill and Ruth Enid Zambrana, 1–21. New Brunswick, NJ: Rutgers University Press.

Dill, Bonnie Thornton, M. Baca Zinn, and Sandra Patton. 1998. "Valuing Families Differently: Race, Poverty, and Welfare Reform." *Sage Race Relations Abstract* 23, no. 3: 4–30.

Doane, Mary Ann. 1991. *Femmes Fatales: Feminism, Film Theory, Psychoanalysis*. New York: Routledge.

Douglas, Patrice, and Frank Wilderson. 2013. "The Violence of Presence: Metaphysics in a Blackened World." *The Black Scholar* 43, no. 4: 117–23.

Dow, Dawn Marie. 2015. "Negotiating the 'Welfare Queen' and 'the Strong Black Woman': African American Middle-Class Mothers' Work and Family Perspectives." *Sociological Perspective* 58, no. 1: 36–55.

D'Souza, Dinesh. 1995. *The End of Racism: Principles for a Multiracial Society*. New York: Free Press.

Du Bois, W. E. B. 1935. *Black Reconstruction in America: An Essay Toward a History of the Part Black Folk Played in the Attempt to Reconstruct Democracy in America, 1860–1880*. New York: Harcourt, Brace and Company.

———. 1969. *Darkwater: Voices from Within the Veil*. New York: Schocken Books.

———. 2003. *The Souls of Black Folk*. Introduction by David Levering Lewis. New York: Modern Library.

Dyer, Richard. 1988. "White." *Screen* 29, no. 4: 44–64.

———. 1997. *White*. London: Routledge.

Dyson, Eric M. 1999. "The Labor of Whiteness, the Whiteness of Labor, and the Perils of Whitewashing." In *Race, Identity, and Citizenship: A Reader*, edited by Rodolfo D. Torres, Louis F. Miron, and Johnathan Xaver Inda, 219–24. Malden, MA: Blackwell Publishing.

Eagleton, Terry. 2005. "The Ultimate Postmodern Spectacle: Michael Jackson and His Trial Hold a Mirror to Modern Western Civilisation and Its Blurring of Fact and Fiction." *Guardian*, May 25, 2005. https://www.theguardian.com/comment/story/0,3604,1491420,00.html.

Ehlers, Nadine. 2012. *Performativity and Struggle Against Subjection*. Bloomington: Indiana University Press.

Ellis, Trey. 1989. "The New Black Aesthetics." *Callaloo*, no. 38: 233–243.

Ellison, Ralph. 1995. *Invisible Man*. New York: Vintage Books.

Entman, Robert, and Andrew Rojecki. 2000. *The Black Image in the White Mind: Media and Race in America*. Chicago: University of Chicago Press.

Eppert, Nicholas. 2017. "(Black) Non-Analysis: From the Restrained Unconscious to the Generalized Unconscious." *Labyrinth* 19, no. 2: 86–101.

Epstein, Debbie, and Deborah Lynn Steinberg. 2007. "The Face of Ruin: Evidentiary Spectacle and the Trial of Michael Jackson." *Social Semiotics* 17, no. 4: 441–58.

Erni, John Nguyet. 1998. "Queer Figuration in the Media: Critical Reflections on Michael Jackson's Sex Scandal." *Critical Studies in Mass Communication* 15, no. 2: 158–80.
Eubanks, Kevin P. 2017. "After Blackness, Then Blackness: Afro-Pessimism, Black Life, and Classical Hip Hop as Counter-Performance." *Journal of Hip Hop Studies* 4, no. 1: 5–22.
Eze, Emmanuel Chukwudi. 1997. "The Color of Reason: The Idea of Race in Kant's Anthropology." In *Postcolonial African Philosophy: A Critical Reader*, edited by Emmanuel Chukwudi Eze, 104–31. Cambridge, MA: Blackwell.
Fanon, Frantz. 1963. *The Wretched of the Earth*. Commentary by Jean-Paul Sartre and Homi K. Bhabha. Translated by Richard Philcox. New York: Grove.
———. 1964. *Toward the African Revolution: Political Essays*. Translated by Haakon Chevalier. New York: Grove Press.
———. 1967. *Black Skin, White Masks*. Translated by Charles Lam Markmann. New York: Grove.
Fast, Susan. 2012. "Michael Jackson's Queer Musical Belongings." *Popular Music and Society* 55, no. 2: 281–300.
Fields, Barbara. 2001. "Whiteness, Racism, and Identity." *International Labor and Working Class History* 60: 48–56.
———. 2003. "Of Rouges and Geldings." *American Historical Review* 180, no. 5: 1397–405.
Fields, Barbara, and Karen Fields. 2014. *Racecraft: The Soul of Inequality in American Life*. New York: Verso Books.
Fine, Michele, Linda Powell, Louis Weis, and L. Mun Wong, eds. 1997. *Off White: Readings on Race, Power, and Society*. New York: Routledge.
Finkelman, Paul. 1993. "The Color of Law." *Northwestern University Law Review* 87, no. 3: 937–91.
Fishkin, Shelley Fisher. 1995. "Interrogating 'Whiteness,' Complicating 'Blackness': Remapping American Culture." *American Quarterly* 47, no. 3: 428–66.
Fitzgerald, Adam. 2015. "An Interview with Fred Moten, Part 1; In Praise of Harold Bloom, Collaboration and Book Fetish." *Literary Hub*, August 5, 2015. https://lithub.com/an-interview-with-fred-moten-pt-i.
Flett, Kathryn. 2003. "Bashir'd, but Not Beaten." *The Guardian*, February 9, 2003. https://www.theguardian.com/theobserver/2003/feb/09/features.review137.
Foucault, Michel. 1978. *The History of Sexuality, Vol. 1*. Translated by Robert Hurley. New York: Pantheon.
———. 1979. *Discipline and Punish: The Birth of the Prison*. Translated by Alan Sheridan. New York: Vintage Book.
———. 1980. *Power/Knowledge: Selected Writings and Interviews, 1972–1977*. Edited and translated by Colin Gordon. New York: Pantheon.
———. 1981. "The Order of Discourse." In *Untying the Text: A Post-Structuralist Reader*, edited by Robert J. C. Young, 48–78. Boston: Routledge and Kegan Paul.

———. 1988. *Technologies of Self: A Seminar with Michel Foucault*. Edited by Luther H. Martin, Huck Gutman, and Patrick H. Hutton. Boston: University of Massachusetts Press.

———. 1989. *The Order of Things: An Archaeology of the Human Science*. New York: Routledge.

———. 1997. *The Politics of Truth*. Edited by Sylvère Lotringer. Translated by Lysa Hochroth and Catherine Porter. Los Angeles: Semiotext(e).

Frankenberg, Ruth, ed. 1993. *White Women, Race Matters: The Social Construction of Whiteness*. Minneapolis: University of Minnesota Press.

———. 1997. *Displacing Whiteness: Essays in Social and Cultural Criticism*. Durham, NC: Duke University Press.

———. 2001. "Mirage of an Unmarked Whiteness." In *The Making and Unmaking of Whiteness*, edited by Birgit Brander Rasmussen, Erik Klineberg, Irene Nexica, and Matt Wray, 72–96. Durham, NC: Duke University Press.

Frazier, E. Franklin. 1968. *The Negro Family in the United States*. Chicago: University of Chicago.

Fredrickson, George M. 2002. *Racism: A Short History*. Princeton, NJ: Princeton University Press.

Freire, Paulo. 2000. *The Pedagogy of the Oppressed*. Translated by Myra Bergman Ramos. New York: Continuum.

Frye, Marilyn. 1983. *The Politics of Reality: Essays in Feminist Theory*. Trumansburg, NY: Grove Press.

Fuchs, Cynthia J. 1995. "Michael Jackson's Penis." In *Crushing the Performative: Interventions into Representation of Ethnicity, Nationality, and Sexuality*, edited by Sue-Helen Case, Philip Brent and Susan Leigh Foster, 13–33. Bloomington: Indiana University Press.

Fuss, Diana. 1989. *Essentially Speaking: Feminism, Nature, and Difference*. New York: Routledge.

———. 1994. "Interior Colonies: Frantz Fanon and the Politics of Identification." *Diacritics* 24, nos. 2–3: 19–42.

Gallagher, Charles. 2003. "White Reconstruction in the University." In *Privilege: A Reader*, edited by Michael Kimmel and Abby Ferber, 299–318. Boulder, CO: Westview.

Gans, Herbert J. 2007. "Deconstructing the Underclass." In *Race, Class, and Gender in the United States*, 7th ed., edited by by Paula S. Rothenberg, 102–8. New York: Worth.

———. 2017. "Racialization and Racialization Research." *Ethnic and Racial Studies* 40, no. 3: 341–52.

Garber, Marjorie. 1997. *Vested Interests: Cross Dressing and Cultural Anxiety*. New York: Routledge.

Gates, Henry Louis Jr. 1992. *Loose Cannons: Notes on the Culture War*. New York: Oxford University Press.

———. 1996. "White Like Me." *The New Yorker*, June 17, 1996. https://www.newyorker.com/magazine/1996/06/17/white-like-me.

———.1997. *Thirteen Ways of Looking at a Black Man*. New York: Vintage Books.

Gibson, Nigel. 2003. "Losing Sight of the Real: Recasting Merleau-Ponty in Fanon's Critique of Mannoni." In *Race and Racism in Continental Philosophy*, edited by Robert Bernasconi and Sybol Cook, 129–50. Bloomington: Indiana University Press.

Gilman, Michele Estrin. 2014. "The Return of the Welfare Queen." *The American Journal of Gender, Social Policy & the Law* 22, no. 2: 247–79.

Gilroy, Paul. 2000a. *Against Race: Imaging Political Culture Beyond the Color Line*. Cambridge, MA: Harvard University Press.

———. 2000b. *Between Camps: Nature, Culture, and the Allure of Race*. London: Allen Lane.

Goldberg, David Theo. 2001. *The Racial State*. Malden, MA: Wiley-Blackwell.

Gómez-Barris, Macarena, and Herman Gray. 2006. "Michael Jackson, Television, and Post-Op Disaster." *Television & News Media* 7, no. 1: 40–51.

Gordon, Lewis R. 1995. *Bad Faith and Antiblack Racism*. Atlantic Highlands, NJ: Humanity Press.

———. 1996. "The Black and the Body Politic: Fanon's Existential and Phenomenological Critique of Psychoanalysis." In *Fanon: A Critical Reader*, edited by Lewis R. Gordon, T. Denean Sharpley-Whiting, and Renee T. White, 74–84. Malden, MA: Blackwell.

———. 1997. *Her Majesty's Other Children: Sketches of Racism from a Neocolonial Age*. Lanham, MD: Rowman & Littlefield.

———. 2002. "A Questioning Body of Laughter and Tears: Reading *Black Skin, White Masks* Through the Cat and Mouse of Reason and a Misguided Theodicy." *Parallax* 8, no. 2: 10–29.

———. 2007. "Through the Hellish Zone of Nonbeing: Thinking Through Fanon, Disaster, and the Damned of the Earth." *Human Architecture: Journal of the Sociology of Self Knowledge* 5, no. 3: 5–12.

Gossett, Thomas F. 1967. *Race: The History of an Idea in America*. Dallas: Southern Methodist University Press.

Graham-Smith, Greg. 2008. "Habeas Corpus: Bodies of Evidence and Performed Litigiousness—The Spectacle of Michael Jackson's Trial." *Comunicatio* 34, no. 2: 278–89.

Grant, Adrian. 2001. *Michael Jackson: The Visual Documentary*. London: Omnibus.

Griffin, John Howard. 1977. *Black Like Me*. Boston: Houghton Mifflin.

Hage, Ghassan. 1998. *White Nation: Fantasy of White Supremacy in a Multicultural Society*. Annandale, PA: Pluto.

Hall, Stuart. 1993. "Culture, Community, Nation." *Cultural Studies* 7, no. 3: 349–63.

———. 1994. "Cultural Identity and Diaspora." In *Colonial Discourse and Postcolonial Theory: A Reader*, edited by Patricia Williams and Laura Chrisman, 392–403. New York: Columbia University Press.

———. 1997. *Race, the Floating Signifier*. Northampton, MA: Media Education Foundation.

———. 2004. "What Is This 'Black' in Black Popular Culture?" In *The Black Studies Reader*, edited by Jacqueline Bobo, Cynthia Hudley, and Claudine Michel, 255–63. New York: Routledge.

Hammonds, Evelynn. 2004. "Black (W)holes and the Geometry of Black Female Sexuality." In *The Black Studies Reader*, edited by Jacqueline Bobo, Cynthia Hudley, and Claudine Michel, 301–14. New York: Routledge.

Hancock, Ange-Marie. 2004. *The Politics of Disgust: The Public Identity of the Welfare Queen*. New York: New York University Press.

———. 2007. "When Multiplication Doesn't Equal Quick Addition: Examining Intersectionality as a Research Paradigm." *Perspectives on Politics* 5, no. 1: 63–79.

Haney-López, Ian F. 2003. *Racism on Trial: The Chicago Fight for Justice*. Cambridge, MA: Belknap Press of Harvard University Press.

———. Feb. 2007. "'A Nation of Minorities': Race, Ethnicity, and Reactionary Colorblindness." *Stanford Law Review* 57, no. 4: 985–1063.

Haraway, Donna J. 1991. *Simians, Cyborgs, and Women: The Reinvention of Nature*. New York: Routledge.

Harris, Cheryl I. June 1993. "Whiteness as Property." *Harvard Law Review* 106, no. 8: 1707–791.

Hartigan, John. 2005. "Culture Against Race: Reworking the Basis for Racial Analysis." In *Race Identity, and Citizenship: A Reader*, edited by Rodolfo D. Torres, Louis F. Miron, and Johnathan Xaver Inda, 183–99. Malden, MA: Blackwell.

Hartman, Saidiya V. 1997. *Scenes of Subjection: Terror, Slavery, and Self-Making in Nineteenth-Century America*. New York: Oxford University Press.

Hegel, Georg Wilhelm Friedrich. 1975. *Lectures on the Philosophy of World History*. Translated by Huge Barr Nisbet. Introduction by Duncan Forbes. Cambridge: Cambridge University Press.

———. 1977. *Phenomenology of Spirit*. Translated by A.V. Miller. Foreword by J. N. Findlay. New York: Oxford University Press.

Heidegger, Martin, and Bernd Magnus. 1967. "Who Is Nietzsche's Zarathustra?" *The Review of Metaphysics* 20, no. 3: 411–31.

Herrnstein, Richard J., and Charles Murray. 1994. *The Bell Curve: Intelligence and Class Structure in America*. New York: Free Press.

Hill, Jane H. 2008. *The Everyday Language of White Racism*. Malden, MA: Wiley-Blackwell.

Hill, Matt. 2007. "Michael Jackson's Fans on Trial? Documenting Emotivism and Fandom in *Wacko About Jacko*." *Social Semiotics* 17, no. 14: 460–77.

hooks, bell. 1981. *Ain't I a Woman: Black Woman and Feminism*. Boston: South End Press.

———. 1990. *Yearning: Race, Gender, and Cultural Politics*. Boston: South End Press.

———. 1992. *Black Looks: Race and Representation*. Boston: South End Press.

———. 1994. *Outlaw Culture: Resisting Representation*. New York: Routledge.

Howell, Michael, and Peter Ford. 2010. *The True History of the Elephant Man: The Definitive Account of the Tragic and Extraordinary Life of Joseph Carey Merrick*. New York: Skyhorse Publishing.

Ibrahim, Habiba. 2012. *Troubling the Family: The Promise of Personhood and the Rise of Multiracialism*. Minneapolis: University of Minnesota Press.

Ignatiev, Noel. 1995. *How the Irish Became White*. New York: Routledge.

Jackson, Michael. 1988. *Moonwalk*. New York: Doubleday.

———. 1993. "Neverland Statement 1993." True Michael Jackson. https://www.truemichaeljackson.com/speeches/neverland-statement-1993.

———. 2010. "Love: The Human Family Most Precious Legacy." *The Journal of Pan African Studies* 3, no. 7: 4–13.

Jefferson, Margo. 2006. *On Michael Jackson*. New York: Pantheon Books.

Jefferson, Thomas. 1999. "Notes on the State of Virginia." In *Documents of American Prejudice: An Anthology of Writings from Thomas Jefferson to David Duke*, edited by S. T. Joshi, 3–11. New York: Basic Books.

Johnson, James Weldon. 1990. *The Autobiography of an Ex-Colored Man*. New York: Penguin.

Johnson, Kevin. 2012. "Ontological Violence and American Cultural Psyche: A Psychoanalytic Inquiry of an American Cultural Identity." In *American Multicultural Studies: Diversity of Race, Ethnicity, Gender and Sexuality*, edited by Sherrow O. Pinder, 69–82. Thousand Oaks, CA: SAGE.

Johnson, Kevin R., ed. 2003. *Mixed-Race Identity and the Law: A Reader*. New York: New York University Press.

Johnson, Robert E. 1984. "The Michael Jackson Nobody Knows." *Ebony* 40, no. 2: 155–58, 160–62.

Johnson, Sylvester A. 2004. *The Myth of Ham in Nineteenth-Century American Christianity: Race, Heathens, and the People of God*. New York: Palgrave Macmillan.

Judy, Ronald A. T. 1993. *DisForming the American Canon: African-Arabic Slave Narratives and the Vernacular*. Minneapolis: University of Minnesota Press.

———. 1994. "On the Question of Nigga Authenticity." *boundary 2* 21, no. 3: 211–30.

———. 1996. "Fanon's Body of Black Experience." In *Fanon: A Critical Reader*, edited by Lewis R. Gordon, T. Denean Sharpley-Whiting, and Renee T. White, 53–73. Malden, MA: Blackwell.

Keeling, Kara. 2003. "'In the Intervals': Frantz Fanon and the 'Problems' of Visual Representation." *Qui Parle* 13, no. 2: 91–117.

Kendi, Ibram X. 2017. *Stamped from the Beginning: The Definitive History of Racist Idea in America*. New York: Bold Type Books.

Kennedy, Dana. 2009. "Michael Jackson's Career Woes: The King of Pop Fights Allegations of Child Abuse." *Entertainment Weekly*, June 25, 2009. https://ew.com/article/2009/06/25/michael-jacksons-career-woes.

Knight, Frederick. 2004. "Justifiable Homicide, Police Brutality, Or Governmental Repression? The 1962 Los Angeles Police Shooting of Seven Members of the Nations of Islam." In *The Black Studies Reader*, edited by Jacqueline Bobo, Cynthia Hudley, and Claudine Michel, 139–52. New York: Routledge.

Kristeva, Julia. 1997. *The Portable Kristeva*. Edited by Kelly Oliver. New York: Columbia University Press.

Kron, Joan. 2009. "Michael Jackson's Dermatologist and Former Plastic Surgeon Talks." *Allure*, August 12, 2009. https://www.allure.com/gallery/michael-jackson.

Larsen, Nella. 1929. *Passing*. New York: Knopf.

Lazarre, Jane. *Beyond the Whiteness of Whiteness: Memoir of a White Mother of Black Sons*. Durham, NC: Duke University Press.

Lee, Harper. 2002. *To Kill A Mocking Bird*. New York: Harper Perennial Modern Classics.

———. 2015. *Go Set a Watchman: A Novel*. New York: HarperCollins Publisher.

Leverette, Tru. 2009. "Speaking Up: Mixed Race Identity in the Black Community." *Journal of Black Studies* 39, no. 3: 434–45.

Lévinas, Emmanuel. 1979. *Totality and Infinity: An Essay on Exteriority*. Translated by Alphonso Lingis. Boston: Martinus Nijhoff Publishers.

———. 1985. *Ethics and Infinity: Conversations with Philippe Nemo*. Translated by Richard A. Cohen. Pittsburgh: Duquesne University Press.

Lipsitz, George. 1995. "The Possessive Investment in Whiteness: Racialized Social Democracy and the 'White' Problem in American Studies." *American Quarterly* 47, no. 3: 369–87.

———. 1998. *The Possessive Investment in Whiteness: How White People Profit from Identity Politics*. Philadelphia: Temple University Press.

Lorde, Audre. 1984. *Sister Outsider: Essays and Speeches*. Freedom, CA: Crossing Press.

Lott, Eric. 2013. *Love and Theft: Blackface Minstrelsy and the American Working Class*. New York: Oxford University Press.

Lythcott-Haims, Julie C. 1994. "Where Do Mixed Babies Belong? Racial Classification in America and Its Implications for Transracial Adoption." *Harvard Civil Rights-Civil Liberties Law Review* 29, no. 531: 1–27.

Mailer, Norman. 1957. "The White Negro: Superficial Reflections on the Hipster." *Dissent* 4, no. 3: 276–93.

Marriott, David. 2000. *On Black Men*. New York: Columbia University Press.

Martinot, Steve. 2010. *The Machinery of Whiteness: Studies in the Structure of Racialization*. Philadelphia: Temple University Press.

Martinot, Steve, and Jared Saxon. 2003. "The Avant-Garde of White Supremacy." *Social Identities* 9, no. 2: 169–81.

Mbembe, Achille. 2001. *On the Postcolony*. Berkeley: University of California Press.

———. 2016. "The Society of Enmity." *Radical Philosophy* 200: 23–35.

———. 2017. *Critique of Black Reason*. Translated by Laurent Dubois. Durham, NC: Duke University Press.

McKinney, Karyn D. 2003. "I Feel 'Whiteness' When I Hear People Blaming Whites: Whiteness as Cultural Victimization." *Race and Society* 6, no. 1: 39–55.

McLaren, Peter. 1997. "Unthinking Whiteness, Rethinking Democracy: Or Farewell to the Blonde Beast; Towards a Revolutionary Multiculturalism." *Educational Foundations* 11, no. 2: 5–39.

McMillen, Liz. 1995. "Lifting the Veil from Whiteness: Growing Body of Scholarship Challenges a 'Racial' Norm." *Chronicle of Higher Education*, September 8, 1995.

Mercer, Korbena. 1986. "Monster Metaphors: Notes on Michael Jackson's Thriller." *Screen* 27, no. 1: 26–43.

———. 1987. "Black Hair/Style Politics." *New Formations*, no. 3: 33–54.

———. 1990. "Black Hair/Style Politics." In *Out There: Marginalization and Contemporary Cultures*, edited by Russell Ferguson, Martha Gever, Trinh T. Minh-ha, and Cornel West, 257–65. Cambridge, MA: MIT Press.

———. 1991. "'1968': Periodizing Postmodern Politics and Identity." In *Cultural Studies*, edited by Lawrence Grossberg, Cary Nelson, and Paula Treichler, 424–29. New York: Routledge.

———. 1992. "Skin Head Sex Thing: Racial Difference and the Homoerotic Imaginary." *New Formations*, no. 16: 1–23.

———.2002. "Skin Head Sex Thing: Racial Difference and the Homoerotic Imaginary." In *The Masculinity Studies Reader*, edited by Rachel Adams and David Savran, 188–200. Malden, MA: Wiley-Blackwell.

Merleau-Ponty, Maurice. 1962. *Phenomenology of Perception*. Translated by Colin Smith. New York: Humanities.

Michaels, Walter Benn. 1992. "Race into Culture: A Critical Genealogy of Cultural Identity." *Critical Inquiry* 18, no. 4: 655–58.

———. 1998. "Autobiography of an Ex-Colored Man." *Transitions* 73, no. 1: 122–43.

Miles, Robert. 1989. *Racism*. London: Routledge.

Miller, Carl. 2012. "We Are Here to Change the World": *Captain EO* and the Future of Utopia." In *Michael Jackson: Grasping the Spectacle*, edited by Christopher R. Smit, 117–29. Burlington, VT: Ashgate.

Mills, Charles W. 1997. *The Racial Contract*. Ithaca, NY: Cornell University Press.

———. 1998. *Blackness Visible: Essays on the Philosophy of Race*. Ithaca, NY: Cornell University Press.

———. 2013. "An Illuminating Blackness." *The Black Scholar* 43, no. 4: 32–37.
Moreton-Robinson, Aileen. 2008. "Writing Off Treaties: White Possession in the United States Critical Whiteness Studies Literature." In *Transnational Whiteness Matters*, edited by Aileen Moreton-Robinson, Maryrose Casey, and Fiona Nicoll, 81–96. Lanham, MD: Lexington.
Morris, Desmond John. 1994. *The Human Animal: A Personal View of the Human Species*. London: BCA.
Morrison, Toni. 1987. *Beloved*. New York: Penguin.
———. 1988. "Unspeakable Things Unspoken: The Afro-American Presence in Literature." Presented at the Turner Lecture on Human Values on October 7, 1988, at the University of Michigan.
———. 1992. *Playing in the Dark: Whiteness in Literary Imagination*. Cambridge, MA: Harvard University Press.
———. 2007. *The Bluest Eyes*. New York: Vintage Books.
Moten, Fred. 2003. *In the Break: The Aesthetics of Black Traditions*. Minneapolis: University of Minnesota Press.
———. 2008. "The Case of Blackness." *Criticism* 50, no. 2: 177–218.
———. 2017. *Black and Blur*. Durham, NC: Duke University Press.
Moynihan, Daniel P. 1965. *The Negro Family: The Case for National Action*. Washington, DC: United States Department of Labor.
Murji, Karim, and John Solomos, eds. 2005. *Racialization: Studies in Theory and Practice*. New York: Oxford University Press.
Musser, Amber Jammila. 2012. "Anti-Oedipus, Kinship, and the Subject of Affect: Reading Fanon with Deleuze and Guattari." *Social Text 112* 30, no. 3: 77–95.
Nancy, Jean-Luc. 1991. *The Inoperative Community*. Translated by Peter Conner, Lisa Garbus, Michael Holland, and Simona Sawhney. Minneapolis: University of Minnesota Press.
Nelson, Maggie. 2015. *The Argonauts*. Minneapolis, MN: Graywolf Press.
Newsweek Staff. 1983. "Michael Jackson: The Peter Pan of Pop." *Newsweek*, January 9, 1983. https://www.newsweek.com/michael-jackson-peter-pan-pop-207034.
Nietzsche, Friedrich. 1978. *Thus Spoke Zarathustra: A Book for All and None*. Translated by Walter Kaufmann. New York: Penguin.
Obasogie, Osagie K. 2013. *Blinded by Sight: Seeing Race through the Eyes of the Blind*. Stanford, CA: Stanford Law Books.
Oliver, Kelly. 2001. *Witnessing Beyond Recognition*. Minneapolis: University of Minnesota Press.
Omi, Michael, and Howard Winant. 2007. "Racial Formations." In *Race, Class, and Gender in the United States: An Integrated Study*, edited by Paula S. Rothenberg, 12–21. New York: Worth.
———. 1994. *Racial Formation in the United States: From the 1960s to the 1990s*. New York: Routledge.

Onwuachi-Willig, Angela. 2007. "A Beautiful Lie: Exploring *Rhinelander v. Rhinelander* as a formative Lesson on Race, Identity, Marriage, and Family." *California Law Review* 95, no. 6: 2393–458.

———. 2017. "Policing the Boundaries of Whiteness: The Tragedy of Being 'Out of Place' from Emmett Till to Trayvon Martin." *Iowa Law Review* 102, no. 3: 1113–185.

Osumare, Halifu. 2018. *Dancing in Blackness: A Memoir*. Gainesville: University Press of Florida.

Parker, David, and Miri Song. 2001. *Rethinking 'Mixed Race.'* Sterling, VA: Pluto.

Patterson, Orlando. 1982. *Slavery and Social Death: A Comparative Study*. Cambridge, MA: Harvard University Press.

Pelbart, Peter Pál. 2000. "The Thought of the Outside: The Outside of Thought." Translated by Constantin V. Boundas and Susan Dyrkton. *Journal of the Theoretical Humanities* 5, no. 2: 201–9.

Pellegrini, Ann. 1997. *Performance Anxieties: Staging Psychoanalysis, Staging Race*. New York: Routledge.

Pimpare, Stephen. 2010. "The Welfare Queen and the Great White Hope." *New Political Science* 32, no. 3: 453–57.

Pinder, Sherrow O. 2010. *The Politics of Race in the United States: Americanization and De-Americanization of Racialized Ethnic Groups*. New York: Palgrave Macmillan.

———. 2012. *Whiteness and Racialized Ethnic Groups in the United States*. Boulder, CO: Lexington Books.

———. 2015. *Colorblindness, Post-Raciality, and Whiteness in the United States*. New York: Palgrave Macmillan.

———. 2018. *Black Women, Work, and Welfare in the Age of Globalization*. Boulder, CO: Lexington Books.

———, ed. 2020. *Black Political Thought: From David Walker to the Present*. New York: Cambridge University Press.

Pinto, Thelma. 2013. "Claiming Sarah Baartman: Black Womanhood in the Global Imaginary." In *American Multicultural Studies: Diversity of Race, Ethnicity, Gender and Sexuality*, edited by Sherrow O. Pinder, 149–64. Los Angeles: SAGE.

Piper, Adrian. 1990. "Passing for White, Passing for Black." *Transition*, no. 58: 14–32.

Pope, Alexander. 2003. "An Essay on Criticism." In *Alexander Pope: Selected Poetry and Prose*, edited by Robin Sowerby, 36–54. New York: Routledge.

Prosser, Jay. 1998. *Second Skin: The Body Narratives of Transsexuality*. New York: Columbia University Press.

———. 2001. "Skin Memories." In *Thinking Through the Skin*, edited by Sara Ahmed and Jackie Stacey, 52–68. New York: Routledge.

Puwar, Nirmal. 2004. *Space Invaders: Race, Gender, and Bodies out of Space*. Oxford: Berg.

Rankine, Claudia. 2014. *Citizen: An American Lyric*. Minneapolis, MN: Graywolf Press.

Revel, Judith. 2009. "Identity, Nature, Life: Three Biopolitical Deconstructions." *Theory, Culture & Society* 26, no. 6: 45–54.

Rich, Adrienne. 1979. *On Lies, Secrets, and Silence: Selected Prose 1966–1978*. New York: W. W. Norton.

Ross, Marlon B. 2004. "Some Glances at the Black Fag: Race, Same-Sex Desire, and Cultural Belonging." In *The Black Studies Reader*, edited by Jacqueline Bobo, Cynthia Hudley, and Claudine Michel, 153–73. New York: Routledge.

Roediger, David R. 1991. *The Wages of Whiteness: Race and the Making of the American Working Class*. New York: Verso Books.

Rooks, Noliwe M. 1996. *Hair Raising: Beauty, Culture, and African American Women*. New Brunswick, NJ: Rutgers University Press.

Sandford, Stella. 2018. "Kant, Race, and Natural History." *Philosophy and Social Criticism* xx, no. x: 1–28.

Sartre, Jean-Paul. 1956. *Being and Nothingness: An Essay on Phenomenological Ontology*. Translated by Hazel E. Burns. New York: Philosophical Library.

Scarry, Elaine. 1985. *The Body in Pain: The Making and Unmaking of the World*. New York: Oxford University Press.

Sechi, Joanne Harumi. 1980. "Being Japanese-American Doesn't Mean 'Made in Japan.'" In *The Third Woman: Minority Women Writers of the United States*, edited by Dexter Fisher, 442–49. Boston: Houghton Mifflin.

Seshadri-Crooks, Kalpana. 1998. "The Comedy of Domination: Psychoanalysis and the Conceit of Whiteness." In *The Psychoanalysis of Race: An Introduction*, edited by Christopher Lane, 353–79. New York: Knopf.

Sexton, Jared. 2008. *Amalgamation Schemes: Antiblackness and the Critique of Multiracialism*. Minneapolis: University of Minnesota Press.

———. 2011. "The Social Life of Social Death: On Afro-Pessimism and Black Optimism." *InTensions*, no. 5: 1–47.

Sharpton, Al. 2009. "Eulogy for Michael Jackson." *American Rhetoric*, July 7, 2009. https://www.americanrhetoric.com/speeches/alsharptoneulogyformichaeljackson.htm.

Shakespeare, William. 2019. *Othello*. Orinda, CA: SeaWolf Press.

Shilling, Chris. 2016. *The Body: A Very Short Introduction*. Oxford: Oxford University Press.

Silberman, Seth Clark. 2007. "Presenting Michael Jackson." *Social Semiotics* 17, no. 4: 417–40.

Sollors, Werner. 1997. *Neither Black Nor White Yet Both: Thematic Explorations of Interracial Literature*. New York: Oxford University Press.

Spencer, Jon M. 1997. *The New Colored People: The Mixed-Race Movement in America*. New York: New York University Press.

Spillers, Hortense J. 1984. "Interstices: A Small Drama of Words." In *Pleasure and Dangers: Exploring Female Sexuality*, edited by Carole Vance, 73–100. Boston: Routledge & Kegan Paul.

———. 2003. *Black, White, and Color: Essays on American Literature and Culture*. Chicago: University of Chicago Press.

Spivak, Gayatri C. 1988. "Can the Subaltern Speak?" In *Marxism and the Interpretation of Culture*, edited by Cary Nelson and Lawrence Grossberg, 271–13. Urbana: University of Illinois Press.

———. 1990. *The Post-Colonial Critic: Interviews, Strategies, Dialogues*. Edited by Sarah Harasym. New York: Routledge.

———. 1995. *The Spivak Reader: Selected Works of Gayatri Chakravorty Spivak*. Edited by Donna Landry and Gerald Maclean. New York: Routledge.

———. 1998. "Race Before Racism: The Disappearance of the American." *boundary 2* 213, no. 2: 35–53.

Squires, Catherine R. 2004. "Black Talk Radio: Defining Community Needs and Identity." In *The Black Studies Reader*, edited by Jacqueline Bobo, Cynthia Hudley, and Claudine Michel, 193–10. New York: Routledge.

Stuever, Hank. 2002. "Moonwalk in Neverland." *Washington Post*, December 11, 2002. https://www.washingtonpost.com/archive/lifestyle/2002/12/11/moonwalker-in-neverland/25dd5a06-1441-49e5-89ce-30e9a52e5593.

Stone, David W. 1996. "Uncolored People." *Lingua Franca* 6, no. 6: 68–77.

Stonequest, Everett V. 1935. "The Problem of the Marginal Man." *American Journal of Sociology* 41, no. 1: 1–12.

Taraborrelli, J. Randy. 1991. *Michael Jackson: The Magic and the Madness*. New York: Birch Lane.

Tate, Greg. 1987. "'I'm White!' What's Wrong with Michael Jackson." *The Village Voice*, September 22, 1987, 15–17.

Tillich, Paul. 2000. *The Courage to Be*. New Haven, CT: Yale University Press.

Toadvine, Ted, and Leonard Lawlor, eds. 2007. *The Merleau-Ponty Reader*. Evanston, IL: Northwestern University Press.

Tonry, Michael. 2012. *Punishing Race: A Continuing American Dilemma*. New York: Oxford University Press.

Touré. 2011. *Who's Afraid of Post-Blackness: What It Means to Be Black Now*. New York: Atria.

Turner, Lou. 2003. "Fanon Reading (W)right and (W)right Reading of Fanon: Race, Modernity, and the Fate of Humanism." In *Race and Racism in Continental Philosophy*, ed. Robert Bernasconi and Sybol Cook, 157–79. Bloomington: Indiana University Press.

Vigo, Julian. 2012. "Michael Jackson and the Myth of Race and Gender." In *Michael Jackson: Grasping the Spectacle*, edited by Christopher R. Smit, 23–37. Burlington, VT: Ashgate.

———. 2010. "Metaphor of Hybridity: The Body of Michael Jackson." *The Journal of Pan African Studies* 3, no. 7: 29–41.

Vogel, Joseph. 2012. "How Michael Jackson Made 'Bad.'" *The Atlantic*, September 10, 2012. https://www.theatlantic.com/entertainment/archive/2012/09/how-michael-jackson-made-bad/262162.

———. 2015. "Freaks in the Regan Era: James Baldwin, the New Pop Cinema, and the American Ideal of Manhood." *The Journal of Popular Culture* 48, no. 3: 464–86.

Waldman, Paul. 2013. "The Privilege of Whiteness." *The American Prospect*, July 22, 2013. https://prospect.org/article/privilege-whiteness.

Walker, David. 2020. "Our Wretchedness in Consequence of Slavery." In *Black Political Thought: From David Walker to Present*, edited by Sherrow O. Pinder, 24–32. New York: Cambridge University Press.

Wallace, Carvell. 2015. "The Two Lives of Michael Jackson." *New Yorker*, November 25, 2015. https://www.newyorker.com/books/page-turner/the-two-lives-of-michael-jackson.

Wallace, Michele. 1989. "Michael Jackson, Black Modernisms, and the 'Ecstasy of Communication.'" *Third Text* 3, no. 7: 11–22.

Wang, Jackie. 2018. *Carceral Capitalism*. Los Angeles: Semiotext (e).

Warren, Calvin L. 2017. "Onticide: Afro-Pessimism, Gay Nigger #1, and Surplus Violence." *GLQ: A Journal of Lesbian and Gay Studies* 23, no. 3: 391–18.

Weate, Jeremy. 2001. "Fanon, Merleau-Ponty and Difference of Phenomenology." In *Race*, edited by Robert Bernasconi, 169–83. Oxford: Blackwell.

Weheliye, Alexander G. 2014. *Habeas Viscus: Racializing Assemblages, Biopolitics, and Black Feminist Theory of the Human*. Durham, NC: Duke University Press.

Wells, Ida B. 1992. *Southern Horrors: Lynch Laws in All Its Phases*. New York: New York Age Print.

West, Cornel. 1993. *Keeping Faith: Philosophy and Race in America*. New York: Routledge.

———. 2001. *Race Matters*. New York: Vintage Books.

White, Charles. 2003. *The Life and Times of Little Richard*. London: Omnibus Press.

Wicker, Hans-Rudolf. 1997. "From Complex Culture to Cultural Complexity." In *Debating Cultural Hybridity: Multicultural Identities and the Politics of Anti-Racism*, edited by Pnina Werbner and Tariq Modood, 29–45. London: Zed Books.

Wilderson, Fred B. III. 2010. *Red, White and Black: Cinema and the Structure of US Antagonisms*. Durham, NC: Duke University Press.

———. 2014. "'We're Trying to Destroy the World': Antiblackness and Police Violence After Ferguson. An Interview with Fred B. Wilderson III." Interview by Jared Ball, Todd Steven Buroughs and Dr. Hate. *Ill Will Edition*, November 14, 5–23. https://illwilleditions.noblogs.org/files/2015/09/Wilderson-We-Are-Trying-to-Destroy-the-World-READ.pdf.

———. 2020. *Afropessimism*. New York: Liveright.
Williams, Gregory Howard. 1996. *Life on the Colored Line: The Truth Story of a White Boy Who Discovered That He Was Black*. New York: Plume.
Willman, Chris. 1991. "Michael Video Takes Beating; 4 Minutes Cut: Review: Jackson Crams So Much into His 'Black or White' Video That It Is an Unfocused Mess, but It Has Some Incredible Spots." *Los Angeles Times*, November 16, 1992. https://www.latimes.com/archives/la-xpm-1991-11-16-ca-1629-story.html.
Wilson, William Julius. 1980. *The Declining Significance of Race*. Chicago: University of Chicago Press.
Winant, Howard. 1994. *Racial Conditions: Politics, Theory, Comparisons*. Minneapolis: University of Minnesota Press.
Weinraub, Bernard. 1993. "Jackson Calls Sexual Abuse Charges 'Totally False.' " *New York Times*, December 23, 1993. https://www.nytimes.com/1993/12/23/us/jackson-calls-sexual-abuse-charges-totally-false.html.
Woolf, Virginia. 1995. *Orlando*. Hertfordshire, UK: Wordsworth.
Wright, Richard. 1937. *Black Boy*. New York: Harper and Row.
———. 1940. *Native Son*. New York: Harper.
———. 2007. "The Ethics of Living Jim Crow: An Autobiographical Sketch." In *Race, Class, and Gender in the United States: An Integrated Study*, edited by Paula S. Rothenberg, 22–31. New York: Worth.
Yancy, George. 2005. "Whiteness and the Return of the Black Body." *Journal of Speculative Philosophy* 19, no. 4: 215–41.
———. 2008. *Black Bodies, White Gazes: The Continuing Significance of Race*. Lanham, MD: Rowman and Littlefield.
———. 2012. *Look, a White!: Philosophical Essays on Whiteness*. Philadelphia: Temple University Press.
———. 2018. *Backlash: What Happens When We Talk Honestly About Racism in America*. Lanham, MD: Rowan and Littlefield.
Young, Harvey. 2010. *Embodying Black Experience: Stillness, Critical Memory, and the Black Body*. Ann Arbor: University of Michigan Press.
Young, Iris Marion. 1980. "A Phenomenology of Feminine Body Comportment, Motility, and Spatiality." *Human Studies* 3, no. 2: 137–56.
———. 1990. *Justice and the Politics of Difference*. Princeton, NJ: Princeton University Press.
Yuan, David D. 1996. "The Celebrity Freak: Michael Jackson's 'Grotesque Glory.' " In *Freakery: Cultural Spectacles of the Extraordinary Body*, edited by Rosemari Garland Thomson, 368–84. New York: New York University Press.
Zack, Naomi. 1993. *Race and Mixed Race*. Philadelphia: Temple University Press.
———, ed. 1995. *American Mixed Race: The Culture of Microdiversity*. New York: Rowan and Littlefield.

———. 1997. "Race, Life, Death, Identity, Tragedy, and Good Faith." In *Existence in Black: An Anthology of Black Existential Philosophy*, edited by Lewis R Gordon, 99–109. New York: Routledge.

Žižek, Slavoj. 1997. "Multiculturalism, or, the Cultural Logic of Multinational Capitalism." *New Left Review* 1, no. 225: 28–55.

———. 2009. *In Defense of Lost Causes*. New York: Verso.

Index

action, 42
Afro-pessimism, 15–16, 136n27
Against Race (Gilroy), 38, 133n53
Agamben, Giorgio, 18
Ahmed, Sara, 29
   on black body, 70, 75–76, 89
   on blackness, 53
   on self, 41
   on whiteness, 48–49, 96
Albrecht, Michael Mario, 117
Alcoff, Linda Martín, 80
Alexander, Michelle, 139n55
Althusser, Louis, 32, 146n143
Angelou, Maya, 83
Appiah, Anthony, 40
appropriation, 59, 151n26, 159n147
The Archeology of Knowledge (Foucault), 2
Arendt, Hannah, 21, 110, 135n14, 152n42
The Argonauts (Nelson), 86
Armstrong, Louis, 4, 53
assimilation, 8
Astaire, Fred, 67
authenticity, 40
The Autobiography of an Ex-Colored Man (Johnson, J.), 57
   on passing, 59
   racial ambiguity in, 149n3

Awkward, Michael, 3–4

Backlash (Yancy), 135n14
Baldwin, James, 28–29
   on Jackson, 100
   on racial ambiguity, 91
bare life, 138n52, 138n54
Bashir, Martin
   on Jackson, 105, 179n107, 179n120
   weirdness exploited by, 103
Basquiat, Jean-Michel, 1, 131n1
de Beauvoir, Simone, 29, 45
   on blackness, 84
   on other, 71
   on white women, 187n 59
Berger, John, 56
Beyond the Whiteness of Whiteness (Lazarre), 59–60
Bhabha, Homi K., 17–18, 35, 74
Bible, 183n166
biopower, 181n147
The Birth of a Nation (film), 27, 147n157
Black and White, 30, 54–55, 85, 163n56
black body. *See also* black penis
   Ahmed on, 70, 75–76, 89
   Appiah on, 40
   authenticity of, 40

black body *(continued)*
  in *Birth of the Nation*, 147n157
  black identity and, 34–35
  as blackness, 28
  Braidotti on, 163n51
  Butler on, 22
  in child molestation case, 27
  as dangerous, 21
  as deterministic, 3, 5, 6
  Fanon on, 31, 38, 50, 94, 125, 144n117
  Gordon on, 27
  hair straightening and, 167n145
  of Jackson, 77, 78, 84–85, 137n40, 161n32
  knowledge about, 41, 79
  likeness of, 83
  Mbembe on, 80
  Michaels on, 37–38
  normativity against, 108
  plastic surgery on, 62, 66, 70, 74–78, 165n87
  plasticity of, 88
  without protection, 50
  race defined by, 152n30
  racialization of, 117
  on Rhinelander, 109
  Scarry on, 28
  self influenced by, 54, 117–118
  Shilling on, 165n87
  skin bleaching on, 81
  Stacey on, 70, 75–76
  white fear of, 47
  white gaze on, 24, 72, 79, 111–112
  whiteness and, 64, 96
  writing and, 145n129
Black Boy (Wright), 155n102
black dreams, 42
black experience, 51
black gaze, 51
Black History Month, 138n8

black identity. *See also* self
  Afro-pessimism in, 15–16, 136n27
  black body and, 34–35
  blackness and, 37–62, 51
  Césaire on, 124
  Du Bois on, 29
  Fanon on, 17, 29–30, 137n28
  Fyre on, 14
  implication of, 45–54
  of Jackson, 2, 3, 10–11, 59, 147n152
  King, R., exemplifying, 19
  media framing informing, 116
  Mills on, 39
  name-calling in, 4
  one-drop rule impacting, 93
  as other, 41, 102–103
  racial binary of, 9
  third space and, 18, 48
  Touré on, 125
  white gaze influencing, 96
  whiteness defining, 7, 31, 39, 43, 127
  Yancy on, 184n1
Black Like Me (Griffin), 32
Black Lives Matter, 124–125
black men
  white women and, 27, 46, 120–121, 147n157
  whiteness threatened by, 113
black ontology
  black experience influencing, 51
  Butler on, 111
  death of, 112
  Fanon on, 138n49
  other in, 55
  violence in, 162n38
  Wilderson on, 87
Black or White, 45, 147n152
black penis, 27
  in *Black or White*, 147n152
  castration of, 46

Fanon on, 113
of Jackson, 26, 108–109, 112–113, 143n110
Marriott on, 144n113
black people. *See also* black body; black identity; black men
Jackson on, 148n172
police brutality killing, 143n109
self-determination of, 51
sexualization of, 25–26
stakes for, 57–62
as underclass, 49
in white space, 49
whiteness imitated by, 50, 74
Black Power Movement, 75
black rape fantasy
Fanon on, 144n115
of white women, 26–27
Black Skin, White Masks (Fanon), 1–3, 24, 132n32, 135n9, 135n14, 161n28
on racism, 11, 16, 29–30, 52
on self, 52, 57
on white fear, 47
black talk radio, 122
blackface, 160n15
blackness, 52
Ahmed on, 53
appropriation of, 59, 151n26, 159n147
Arendt on, 110
de Beauvoir on, 84
black body as, 28
black identity and, 37–62, 51
camp informed by, 173n18
construction of, 45–54
danger of, 101
Ellis on, 189n103
Fanon on, 7, 71, 74, 82, 129, 161n28
Hall on, 126

Hartman on, 42
as honorary, 60
of Jackson, 12, 40, 146n137
knowledge through, 5
one-drop rule on, 64
opposing normativity, 44
as other, 2, 6, 10, 13, 44, 68–69, 115, 121–122, 124, 183n166
as outdoors, 65–66
as performative, 43
policing of, 109, 177n82
post, 58
as problem, 30–31, 54–57, 158n135
racial ambiguity contrasted with, 160n4
racial identification influencing, 161n33
racial transcendence blocked by, 15
racialization of, 25, 49, 96, 116, 175n50
racism and, 61, 116
redefinition of, 168n159
Rock on, 120
self through, 130
as simple, 87
as social determinism, 1–2
stereotypes of, 49
weirdness with, 99
white gaze policing, 68
whiteness and, 14, 57, 110, 119, 130, 185n35
Winant on, 38
black-on-black crimes, 142n81
Blinded by Sight (Obasogie), 111
The Bluest Eye (Morrison), 128
Bodies That Matter (Butler), 33
The Body in Pain (Scarry), 28
"Bordering on the Black Penis" (Marriott), 144n113
Bosteels, Bruno, 73
Bourdieu, Pierre, 14

Brackett, David, 61
Braidotti, Rosi
  on black body, 163n51
  on racial binary, 43
Brown, Nathan, 135n6
Broyard, Anatole, 59
Butler, Judith, 5–6, 10, 17, 21, 33, 149n2
  on black body, 22
  on black ontology, 111
  on colorblindness, 183n170
  on inhumanity of, 41, 141n73
  on media framing, 92, 95
  on name-calling, 102
  on normativity, 107
  on race, 119
  on race performed, 9, 66, 131n7, 136n22
  on racial identification, 149n2
  on racism, 55, 73
  on whiteness, 69

camp, 173n18
Captain EO (film)
  Jackson in, 98
  Miller on, 176n63
Carter, J. Cameron, 65, 89
censorship, 34
Cervenak, Sara Jane, 65, 89
Césaire, Aimé, 124, 129–130
Champley, Henry, 45
Chandler, Nahum, 119
child molestation case, alleged
  black body in, 27
  against Jackson, 9–10, 25–26, 65, 100, 108, 110, 122, 182n151
  in *Michael Jackson's Boys*, 178n104
childhood, 142n88
class, 49
Collins, Patricia Hill, 126
colonists, of US, 138n47
colorblindness
  Butler on, 183n170

  Mills on, 123
  Obasogie on, 111
  in *Plessy v. Ferguson*, 38
construction, of blackness, 45–54
Corliss, Richard, 98
corporeal schema, 167n129
  Fanon on, 115–116
  self in, 79
Cox, Oliver C., 80–81
Crenshaw, Kimberlé, 154n72
cultural norm, 147n151
"Culture Against Race" (Hartigan), 162n38

danger, of blackness, 101
Davis, Kathy, 72, 74
  on Jackson, 76
  on other, 165n87
death. *See also* lynching
  of black ontology, 112
  of Jackson, 116–117
Declaration of Independence, 156n108
Deleuze, Gilles, 70
"Demarginalizing the Intersection of Race and Sex" (Crenshaw), 154n72
Discipline and Punish (Foucault), 23, 99, 135n8
discrimination
  Fanon experiencing, 45
  of Naturalization Act, 164n74
  reverse, 152n39
  Singleton on, 164n69
Disgrace (Pinto), 169n184
Do Not Resist (documentary), 145n124
Doane, Mary Ann, 144n117
double consciousness, 5
  by Du Bois, 16, 57, 63, 97, 141n72
  white privilege and, 164n69
  whiteness creating, 44, 127, 141n72
Douglass, Frederick, 156n108
Du Bois, W. E. B., 1, 3, 5
  on black identity, 29

double consciousness by, 16, 57, 63, 97, 141n72
    on other, 66
    on racism, 143n100, 158n135
    on self, 119
    on white gaze, 30
    on whiteness, 140n68, 184n187
Dwyer, Richard, 155n102

Eagleton, Terry, 102
Ecce Homo (Nietzsche), 106
Ellis, Trey, 189n103
Ellison, Ralph, 158n136
Endangered/Endangering (Butler), 21

Fanon, Frantz, 1–2, 11, 14–16, 132n32, 135n9, 135n14
    on black body, 31, 38, 50, 94, 113, 125, 144n117
    on black dreams, 42
    on black identity, 17, 29–30, 137n28
    on black ontology, 138n49
    on black rape fantasy, 144n115
    on blackness, 7, 71, 74, 82, 129, 161n28
    on black-on-black crimes, 142n81
    on corporeal schema, 115–116
    on discrimination, 45
    Doane on, 144n117
    on interracial rape, 144n117
    on knowledge, 20, 24, 63
    on other, 3, 18, 31, 109
    on racism, 52
    on self, 48, 57
    on slavery, 189n100, 190n117
    on violence, 27, 68, 157n110
    on white fear, 47
fans, 103–104
Farrakhan, Louis, 82
Fast, Susan, 93
Fields, Barbara, 16
Fields, Karen, 16
film, interracial sex in, 153n69

The Fire Next Time (Baldwin), 28–29
Flett, Kathryn, 104
Foucault, Michel, 2, 33, 135n8
    on biopower, 181n147
    on normativity, 23, 99, 106–107
    on violence, 68
    on white gaze, 21
    on whiteness, 14–15
Frames of War (Butler), 55
Frankenberg, Ruth, 32, 155n102
    on other, 39
    on whiteness, 14
Frantz Fanon (documentary), 45
freakiness. *See* weirdness
Fredrickson, George M., 110, 183n165
Freire, Paulo, 189n100
Freud, Sigmund, 26, 144n114, 144n115
Frye, Marilyn, 51, 52
Fuchs, Cynthia J., 87
Fuss, Diane
    on racial ambiguity, 58
    on whiteness, 44
Fyre, Marilyn, 14

Gates, Henry Louis, Jr., 59, 151n28
    arrest of, 100
    on Jackson, 81
    on knowledge, 98
Gilroy, Paul, 38, 133n53
Gordon, Lewis, 27
Griffin, John Howard, 32
Guatteri, Félix, 70

hair straightening, 167n145
Hall, Stuart, 97, 126
Haraway, Donna J., 95
Haring, Keith, 71
Harris, Cheryl I., 23–24, 53
Hartigan, John, 162n38
Hartman, Saidiya, 42
Hegel, Georg, 141n73
hegemony, of whiteness, 49–50, 54, 78, 123, 139n55

Heidegger, Martin, 179n121
Heth, Joice, 170n185
homogenization, 38, 40
humanity, 16

ideology, 146n143
"Ideology and Ideological State Apparatuses" (Althusser), 146n143
immigration, 139n55
inhumanity, 41, 141n73
The Inoperative Community (Nancy), 134n5
interracial marriage, 121, 186n55
interracial rape
  in *Disgrace*, 169n184
  Fanon on, 144n117
interracial sex, 153n69
intersectionality
  Crenshaw on, 154n72
  other in, 46–47
Irish people, 150n22
"The Irony of Anatomy" (Brown), 135n6
Irony of Negro Policeman (1981), 1

Jackson, Michael
  Albrecht on, 117
  Baldwin on, 100
  Bashir on, 105, 179n107, 179n120
  black body of, 77, 78, 84–85, 137n40, 161n32
  black identity of, 2, 3, 10–11, 59, 147n152
  black penis of, 26, 108–109, 112–113, 143n110
  on black people, 148n172
  blackness of, 12, 40, 146n137
  in *Captain EO*, 98
  child molestation case against, 9–10, 25–26, 65, 100, 108, 110, 122, 182n151
  childhood of, 142n88
  Davis on, 76
  death of, 116–117
  disciplining of, 106–113
  Eagleton on, 102
  fans of, 103–104
  Fast on, 93
  Fuchs on, 87
  Gates on, 81
  interracial marriage of, 121
  Jefferson, M., on, 143n110, 172n6
  Judy on, 110
  King, D., on, 146n137
  Little Richard contrasted with, 173n18
  maleness challenged by, 173n18
  "Man in the Mirror" by, 105, 180n123
  Marsh on, 97
  media framing of, 95, 99–100, 103, 108, 186n42
  Miles on, 96
  monkey compared with, 72
  name-calling experienced by, 45–46, 58, 91, 93, 95–96, 101, 120
  at Neverland Ranch, 104–105, 176n69
  nonconformity of, 91–113
  normalizing of, 106–113
  nose job of, 75
  Orlan contrasted with, 78
  as other, 8–9, 29, 65, 66, 87–89
  passing by, 64, 81
  plastic surgery of, 126, 174n27
  racial ambiguity of, 30–31, 62, 63–64, 77, 82, 88, 107
  racial identification of, 63–89
  on self, 87
  self-fashioning of, 70–86
  Sharpton eulogizing, 82, 176n60
  Silberman on, 19
  "Slave to the Rhythm" by, 169n181
  Taylor on, 71
  Tucker on, 98

Vigo on, 104
violence portrayed by, 147n152
Vogel on, 177n89
weirdness of, 64, 86, 92, 99–106, 172n10, 178n99, 180n128
West on, 160n18
white gaze defining, 17
at White House, 82
whiteness excluding, 81, 83–84
women and, 104
Jay-Z, 112
Jefferson, Margo, 67, 71
on Jackson, 143n110, 172n6
on transsexuality, 101
Vigo on, 101–102
Jefferson, Thomas, 133n38, 135n6
Johnson, James Weldon, 57, 59
on passing, 149n3
on racial ambiguity, 89
Johnson, Magic, 147n157
Jones, Billie T., 127–128
Jones, Grace, 85–86
Judy, Ronald, 14, 110, 137n28

Kendi, Ibram X., 188n81
King, Don, 146n137
King, Rodney
black identity exemplified by, 19
Musson on, 161n33
police brutality against, 26
kinship, 107
knowledge, 41, 79
through blackness, 5
Fanon on, 20, 24, 63
Gates on, 98
Hall on, 97
Kristeva, Julia, 102
Kron, Joan, 174n27

Lazarre, Jane, 59–60
Leaving Neverland Ranch (documentary), 143n102

Lee, Harper, 67, 74–75, 116
Lewis, Emmanuel, 25–26
Little Richard, 173n18
Living with Michael Jackson (documentary), 77, 104, 166n118
Lorde, Audre, 64–65
lynching
as discipline, 108
White against, 149n3
white women in, 144n113
whiteness minimizing, 181n146

Magnus, Bernd, 179n121
maleness. *See also* black men
Jackson challenging, 173n18
white gaze of, 86
whiteness compared with, 52, 151n26
"Man in the Mirror," 105, 180n123
marginalization, 32
Marriott, David, 144n113
Marsh, Dave, 97
Mbembe, Achille, 4, 10
on black body, 80
on nanoracism, 13, 15
on racism, 13
on violence, 58
McKinney, Karyn D., 156n105
McMillen, Liz, 19–20
media framing
black identity informed by, 116
black talk radio ignored by, 122
Butler on, 92, 95
of Jackson, 95, 99–100, 103, 108, 186n42
Vogel on, 100
Mercer, Kobena, 22–23
Merleau-Ponty, Maurice, 79
Merrick, Joseph Carey, 171n212
Michael Jackson and The Boy He Paid Off (film), 25
Michael Jackson's Boys (documentary), 25, 143n102, 178n104

Michael Jackson's Face (film), 143n102
Michaels, Walter Benn, 37–38
Miles, Robert, 96
Miller, Carl, 98, 176n63
Mills, Charles, 15, 77, 136n22
  on black identity, 39
  on colorblindness, 123
  on white supremacy, 52–53
mixed-race people, 64, 76, 170n191
model minority, 150n21
monkey, 72–73
Morrison, Toni, 2, 15, 43, 128
Moten, Fred, 8, 18, 118
Motion Picture Association of America (MPAA), 153n69
Mottola, Tommy, 85
MPAA. *See* Motion Picture Association of America
multiculturalism, 61, 160n155
multiracial identity, 159n150
Musson, Jayson, 161n33

name-calling
  in black identity, 4
  Butler on, 102
  Jackson experiencing, 45–46, 58, 91, 93, 95–96, 101, 120
  racial ambiguity influencing, 11, 58
  Rich on, 46
  Vogel on, 174n25
  of weirdness, 122
Nancy, Jean-Luc, 107, 134n5
nanoracism, 13, 15
Native Son (Wright), 157n110
Naturalization Act (1790)
  discrimination of, 164n74
  whiteness determined by, 73
Nelson, Maggie, 86
Neverland Ranch, 104–105, 176n69
The New Jim Crow (Alexander), 139n55
Nguyet Erni, John, 10

Nietzsche, Friedrich Wilhelm, 104, 106, 118, 128, 164n66
Nomadic Subjects (Braidotti), 163n51
nonconformity, 91–113
normativity
  against black body, 108
  blackness opposing, 44
  Butler on, 107
  as disciplinary, 99
  Foucault on, 23, 99, 106–107
  racial ambiguity contrasting, 172n6
  Rankine on, 117
  Spillers on, 115
  white privilege benefiting from, 129
nose job, 75
Notes on the State of Virginia (Jefferson, T.), 133n38, 135n6

Obama, Barack, 72–73, 171n201
Obasogie, Osagie K., 111
Oliver, Kelly, 155n93
On Michael Jackson (Jefferson, M.), 71, 143n110
On the Reproduction of Capitalism (Althusser), 146n143
one-drop rule
  black identity impacted by, 93
  on blackness, 64
  Onwuachi-Willig on, 37
  passing under, 83
  racial ambiguity and, 158n150
  racial identification by, 118
Onwuachi-Willig, Angela, 37
The Origins of Totalitarianism (Arendt), 135n14
Orlan
  Jackson contrasted with, 78
  Prosser on, 166n122, 168n54
Othello (Shakespeare), 182n163
the other
  de Beauvoir on, 71
  black identity as, 41, 102–103

in black ontology, 55
blackness as, 2, 6, 10, 13, 44, 68–69, 115, 121–122, 124, 183n166
Davis on, 165n87
doubling of, 69
Du Bois on, 66
Ellison on, 158n136
Fanon on, 3, 18, 31, 109
Frankenberg on, 39
in intersectionality, 46–47
Jackson as, 8–9, 29, 65, 66, 87–89
model minority as, 150n21
multiculturalism demonstrated by, 61
racial ambiguity as, 70, 84, 86, 101
racism creating, 111
as self, 42–43
Spivak on, 95
as threat, 55–56
weirdness of, 97
white gaze on, 82

passing, as white. *See also* hair straightening; mixed-race people; plastic surgery; racial ambiguity
The Autobiography of an Ex-Colored Man on, 59
by Jackson, 64, 81
Johnson, J., on, 59, 149n3
Lazarre on, 59–60
under one-drop rule, 83
in *Plessy v. Ferguson*, 80
as resistance, 149n3
reversal of, 149n3, 166n118
through skin bleaching, 126
Pelbart, Peter Pál, 15
Pinto, Thelma, 169n184
plastic surgery
on black body, 62, 66, 70, 74–78, 165n87
of Jackson, 126, 174n27
Kron on, 174n27

Taraborrelli on, 173n11
whiteness through, 165n87
Plato, 163n49
Plessy v. Ferguson
colorblindness in, 38
passing in, 80
police brutality, 137n35
Black Lives Matter against, 124–125
black people killed by, 143n109
in *Do Not Resist*, 145n124
against King, R., 26
policing blackness
whiteness as, 177n82
Wilderson on, 109
The Politics of Reality (Frye), 52
postblackness, 58
The Posthuman (Braidotti), 43
Power/Knowledge (Foucault), 33
Prince, 172n1
Prosser, Jay, 166n122, 168n54
protection, black body without, 50
The Psychic Life of Power (Butler), 33
Purple Rain, 172n1

race
black body defining, 152n30
Butler on, 66, 119
as performative, 66
racism producing, 54
in *Rhinelander v. Rhinelander*, 37
as social concept, 7
Race Matters (West), 160n18
race performed
Butler on, 9, 66, 131n7, 136n22
as kinship, 107
racial ambiguity
in *The Autobiography of an Ex-Colored Man*, 149n3
Baldwin on, 91
blackness contrasted with, 160n4
Fuss on, 58

racial ambiguity *(continued)*
   of Jackson, 30–31, 62, 63–64, 77, 82, 88, 107
   Johnson, J. on, 89
   of mixed-race people, 64, 76, 170n191
   name-calling influencing, 11, 58
   normativity contrasting, 172n6
   one-drop rule and, 158n150
   as other, 70, 84, 86, 101
   in third space, 94
racial binary
   of black identity, 9
   Braidotti on, 43
   identification as, 86
   third space contrasting, 131n7
racial identification
   as binary, 86
   blackness influenced by, 161n33
   Butler on, 149n2
   of Jackson, 63–89
   by one-drop rule, 118
racial transcendence, 15
racialization
   of black body, 117
   of blackness, 25, 49, 96, 116, 175n50
   of class, 49
   whiteness excluded from, 124
racism. *See also* discrimination; policing blackness
   Angelou on, 83
   in Bible, 183n166
   biopower influenced by, 181n147
   Black Skin, White Masks on, 52
   blackness interpreted through, 116
   blackness limited by, 61
   bodiliness of, 28
   Butler on, 55, 73
   commonplace, 109–110
   Du Bois on, 143n100, 158n135
   escalation of, 187n72

   Fanon on, 52
   Fredrickson on, 183n165
   humanity withheld by, 16
   Mbembe on, 13
   of Mottola, 85
   of MPAA, 153n69
   other created by, 111
   race produced by, 54
   of Richards, 174n24
   in slavery, 181n145
   of Sterling, 174n24
   of Trump, 174n24
   Wallace on, 161n32
   West experiencing, 123, 187n74
   white flight as, 45
   Yancy on, 73
   Zack on, 55
Rankine, Claudia, 5, 117
rape, *See*. *See also* black rape fantasy; interracial rape
Reasonable Doubt, 112
Regents of the University California v. Bakke, 152n39
reverse discrimination, 152n39
Rhinelander, Alice B., 109
Rhinelander v. Rhinelander, 37
Rich, Adrienne, 46
Richards, Michael, 174n24
Riefenstahl, Leni, 177n78
Rock, Chris, 120
Roediger, David R., 20, 150n22
Rojecki, Andrew, 93

Sartre, Jean-Paul, 155n93
Scarry, Elaine, 28
Scenes of Subjection (Hartman), 42
The Second Sex (de Beauvoir), 45
self, 33
   Ahmed on, 41
   becoming, 48
   black body influenced by, 54, 117–118

Black Skin, White Masks on, 57
through blackness, 130
corporeal schema, 79
denial of, 39
Du Bois on, 119
Fanon on, 48, 57
Jackson on, 87
as other, 42–43
white gaze impacting, 41, 44
whiteness in, 94, 148n162
self-determination
of black people, 51
marginalization influencing, 32
self-fashioning, 70–86
Sexton, Jared, 19, 88
sexualization, of black people, 25–26
Shakespeare, William, 182n163
Sharpton, Al, 82, 176n60
Shilling, Chris, 165n87
Silberman, Seth Clark, 19
Da Silva, Denise, 33–34
Singleton, John, 164n69
skin bleaching
on black body, 81
passing through, 126
vitiligo causing, 83
"Slave to the Rhythm," 169n181
slavery
Fanon on, 189n100, 190n117
Freire on, 189n100
racism in, 181n145
slaves, 156n108
social concept, 7
social determinism, 1–2
The Souls of Black Folk (Du Bois), 1, 16, 29, 30, 158n135
Spillers, Hortense, 115
Spivak, Gayatri C., 13
on other, 95
on whiteness, 164n69
Stacey, Jackie, 70, 75–76
stereotypes, 49

Sterling, Donald
on Johnson, M., 147n157
racism of, 174n24
Stuever, Hank, 84

Taraborrelli, J. Randy, 173n11
Taylor, Elizabeth, 71
A Tempest (Césaire), 129–130
third space
black identity in, 18, 48
racial ambiguity in, 94
racial binary contrasting, 131n7
Till, Emmett, 46
Tillich, Paul, 163n49
To Kill a Mockingbird (Lee), 67
Touré
on black identity, 125
on postblackness, 58
transsexuality, 101, 166n122
Triumph of the Will (film), 177n78
Trump, Donald, 171n201, 174n24
Tucker, Ken, 98

underclass, 49
Undoing Gender (Butler), 17, 141n73

Vigo, Julian
on Jackson, 104
on Jefferson, M., 101–102
violence. *See also* police brutality
in black ontology, 162n38
Fanon on, 27, 68, 157n110
Foucault on, 68
Freud on, 144n114
Jackson portraying, 147n152
Mbembe on, 58
Sexton on, 88
Warren on, 87
whiteness as, 88, 132n32
vitiligo, 83, 168n154
Vogel, Joseph
on Jackson, 177n89

Vogel, Joseph *(continued)*
  on media framing, 100
  on name-calling, 174n25

Walker, David, 120
Wallace, Michele, 161n32
Warren, Calvin, 79, 87
weirdness
  Bashir exploiting, 103
  blackness with, 99
  as eccentric, 95
  of Jackson, 64, 86, 92, 99–106, 172n10, 178n99, 180n128
  name-calling of, 122
  of other, 97
West, Cornel, 77
  on homogenization, 38, 40
  on Jackson, 160n18
  racism experienced by, 123, 187n74
White, Walter, 149n3
white fear
  of black body, 47
  Black Skin, White Masks on, 47
  Fanon on, 47
white flight
  as racism, 45
  in *Why Can't We Live Together*, 153n63
white gaze
  on black body, 72
  black body impacted by, 24, 79, 111–112
  black identity influenced by, 96
  blackness policed by, 68
  as cultural norm, 147n151
  Du Bois on, 30
  Foucault on, 21
  Jackson defined by, 17
  of maleness, 86
  Oliver on, 155n93
  on other, 82
  self impacted by, 41, 44
  Yancy on, 76
White House, 82
white privilege
  double consciousness and, 164n69
  normativity benefiting, 129
white space, 49
white supremacy
  Mills on, 52–53
  whiteness studies on, 148n175
white women
  de Beauvoir on, 187n59
  black men and, 27, 46, 120–121, 147n157
  black rape fantasy of, 26–27
  in lynching, 144n113
  Till and, 46
whiteness
  Ahmed on, 48–49, 96
  assimilation into, 8
  black body oriented by, 96
  black body reduced by, 64
  black gaze of, 51
  black identity defined by, 7, 31, 39, 43, 127
  black men threatening, 113
  black people imitating, 50, 74
  blackness and, 14, 57, 110, 119, 130, 185n35
  Bourdieu on, 14
  Butler on, 69
  as censorship, 34
  double consciousness created by, 44, 127, 141n72
  Du Bois on, 140n68, 184n187
  Dwyer on, 155n102
  as dynamic, 132n28
  Foucault on, 14–15
  Frankenberg on, 14
  Frye on, 52
  Fuss on, 44

Harris on, 23–24, 53
hegemony of, 49–50, 54, 78, 123, 139n55
as honorary, 39, 60
as indoors, 65
as invisible, 148n175
of Irish people, 150n22
Jackson excluded by, 81, 83–84
Lee on, 74–75
Lorde on, 64–65
lynching minimized by, 181n146
maleness compared with, 52, 151n26
Morrison on, 43, 128
Naturalization Act determining, 73
as normative, 8, 13, 42, 53, 56, 60–61, 68–69, 102, 123–124
through plastic surgery, 165n87
as policing blackness, 177n82
as privilege, 78
as problematic, 147n151, 156n106
racialization excluding, 124
Roediger on, 150n22
in self, 94, 148n162
Sexton on, 19
Spivak on, 164n69
as violence, 88, 132n32
Walker on, 120
Wright on, 162n35, 176n53
Yancy on, 190n121

"Whiteness as Property" (Harris), 23
whiteness studies
    McKinney on, 156n105
    McMillen on, 19–20
    Roediger on, 20
    on white supremacy, 148n175
Why Can't We Live Together (documentary), 153n63
Wilderson, Fred B., III
    on black ontology, 87
    on policing blackness, 109
Winant, Howard, 38
Winfrey, Oprah, 39, 63, 85, 143n110
The Wiz, 163n54
women, 104. *See also* white women
Woolf, Virginia, 94
Wright, Richard, 155n102, 157n110, 162n35, 176n53
writing, 145n129

Yancy, George, 135n14
    on black identity, 184n1
    on passing, 149n3
    on racism, 73
    on white gaze, 76
    on whiteness, 190n121
Young, Marion, 134n5

Zack, Naomi, 55
Žižek, Slavoj, 22, 34

www.ingramcontent.com/pod-product-compliance
Lightning Source LLC
Chambersburg PA
CBHW020652230426
43665CB00008B/408